Theories of
Chinese Philosophy

Critical Inquiries in Comparative Philosophy

Series Editor: Alexus McLeod, Assistant Professor
of Philosophy, Colorado State University

This series aims to present detailed and inclusive surveys of contemporary research in multiple areas of Asian and Comparative Philosophy. Each volume outlines and engages with the current research within comparative philosophy through the lenses of traditional philosophical areas such as ethics, metaphysics, epistemology, and language/logic.

Theories of Truth in Chinese Philosophy: A Comparative Approach, by Alexus McLeod
Moral Psychology of Confucian Shame: Shame of Shamelessness, by Bongrae Seok

Theories of Truth in Chinese Philosophy

A Comparative Approach

Alexus McLeod

ROWMAN & LITTLEFIELD
INTERNATIONAL

London • New York

Published by Rowman & Littlefield International Ltd
Unit A, Whitacre Mews, 26-34 Stannary Street, London SE11 4AB
www.rowmaninternational.com

Rowman & Littlefield International Ltd.is an affiliate of Rowman & Littlefield

4501 Forbes Boulevard, Suite 200, Lanham, Maryland 20706, USA
With additional offices in Boulder, New York, Toronto (Canada), and Plymouth (UK)
www.rowman.com

British Library Cataloguing in Publication Data
A catalogue record for this book is available from the British Library

ISBN: HB 978-1-7834-8344-0
    PB 978-1-7834-8345-7

Library of Congress Cataloging-in-Publication Data
McLeod, Alexus.
Theories of truth in Chinese philosophy : a comparative approach / Alexus McLeod.
    pages cm
Includes bibliographical references and index.
ISBN 978-1-78348-344-0 (cloth : alk. paper) — ISBN 978-1-78348-345-7
(pbk. : alk. paper) — ISBN 978-1-78348-346-4 (electronic)
1. Philosophy, Chinese—221 B.C.-960 A.D. 2. Truth. I. Title.
B126.M43 2015
121.0931—dc23   2015028259

∞ ™ The paper used in this publication meets the minimum requirements of American
National Standard for Information Sciences—Permanence of Paper for Printed Library
Materials, ANSI/NISO Z39.48-1992.

Printed in the United States of America

Contents

Acknowledgments and Dedication

This book has been made possible through many courses, earlier papers, conversations, and other assistance. The number of people to whom I am indebted is enormous, and I cannot possibly mention all of them here. I'd like to name a small number of them in particular, however: Michael Lynch (in whose 2007 truth seminar at UConn I first envisioned a project like this one), Colin Caret, Aaron Cotnoir, Boram Lee, Ian Smith, and Nhat Long Vu (some of whom took that seminar with me and all of whom I discussed many of these issues with); Bo Mou and Lajos Brons (whose engagement with my work on truth in Wang Chong's *Lunheng* has been extremely helpful); my CSU Philosophy colleagues Phil Cafaro, Jeff Kasser, Matt MacKenzie, and Idris Hamid (who helped me think through an earlier version of chapter 1); organizers Michael Ing and Vincent Leung and the participants of the Empire, Ethics, and Tradition conference on Han Dynasty thought at the University of Pittsburgh in 2014, where I presented a version of part of the chapter on *Huainanzi*; the students of my Spring 2015 course on the *Huainanzi* at CSU; and my graduate students Josh Brown at the University of Dayton and Lake Davidson at CSU, who helped me think through these issues and whose energy and enthusiasm sparked my own during the times they began to flag.

A portion of chapter 6 is taken from my article "Pluralism About Truth in Early Chinese Philosophy: A Reflection on Wang Chong's Approach" in *Comparative Philosophy* 2 (1), 2011.

Finally, my wife Shubhalaxmi has had incredible patience with my unreasonable obsession with scholarship, including my work on this book, for years. This book is dedicated to her.

Introduction

THE ROLE OF TRUTH IN PHILOSOPHY

The concept of truth, according to many philosophers, is the most basic, general, and "central of all philosophical thought." It is perhaps more than any other concept definitive of the field of philosophy itself. Almost every philosopher will describe the discipline of philosophy as the pursuit of *truth*, even while disagreeing among themselves about the proper means for this pursuit. We neither agree on the issue of what truth is nor how best to go about attaining it, but we are all in agreement that the truth ought to be pursued, and perhaps that it is the primary consideration that ought to lead our investigations.

Part of the task of this book is to show that this is no less the case for early Chinese thought than it is for other traditions of philosophy, including the various Western and Indian traditions.[1] Truth is a foundational and general concept found within early Chinese philosophy as much as anywhere in the history of Western philosophy. That being said, there are often very different views (or none at all) concerning the definition of truth, the role truth plays in other areas of philosophy, and how we attain truth (if possible at all) in early Chinese thought than in much of the Western and Indian traditions. For multiple traditions to all have concepts of truth and offer theories of truth does not entail that their concepts or theories of truth look the same. Indeed, if the concept of truth at its most basic is a general and foundational one, its thin description will be one that allows for the greatest possible distribution of explanations, or "thick" accounts.[2] The concept of truth, I contend, is one the thin description of which ought to be fixed by reference to the shared content of all philosophical traditions. That is, truth in itself is a concept that requires comparative philosophy. We do not have a sufficiently general and basic shared conception of truth until we understand the way in which truth is understood across philosophical traditions. What some Western traditions take as sufficiently basic and general may turn out not to be so at all, when we look at Chinese traditions.

Why, one might ask, should we assume this about truth? Why not, that is, simply determine that some traditions may not have had a concept of truth, rather than hold truth hostage to philosophical agreement among all traditions? Part of my answer to this question (which I will get deeper into later) is that truth is such a fundamental concept that, if we wish to maintain its fundamental importance, we need to take it as a basic human construct around which philosophy is developed, rather than the other way around. There are of necessity certain foundational assumptions that intellectual historians, philosophers, scholars of religion, and other comparativists make about the nature of the intellectual project across societies, cultures, and traditions. Certain concepts we take as fundamental to human thought, and when we investigate the intellectual production of ancient cultures, we look for these concepts and indications of what people thought about these concepts rather than for whether people had these concepts. Truth, I maintain, is just such a concept. It is unclear how any intellectual project could proceed without some sense (whether well worked out or not) of truth as "how things are" that plays a central role. Everyone has a concept of truth, whether explicit or not.[3] One needs to have a concept of truth, even if one never discusses truth explicitly at all. It is a presumptive concept, of the kind demonstrated in transcendental arguments. Our very engagement in the intellectual project at all presumes that we have a concept of truth, whether or not we have any theory of truth.

A concept of truth is central to the very identity of philosophy and of intellectual activity. Thus, the role of truth in philosophy is a necessary one, and we can safely assume that any philosophical tradition utilizes some concept of truth. Of course, we may argue about what counts as a philosophical tradition (and the definition I give also turns out to be a very general one that admits much more than some contemporary academic philosophers might allow). Still, the concept of truth is broader than even this. Since any intellectual enterprise assumes a concept of truth, then regardless of what the case may be concerning whether or not early Chinese thinkers can be considered philosophers (though I will argue for the affirmative), they had a concept of truth insofar as they were engaged in intellectual production. One may object at this point—what of pursuits like art, poetry, or music? If these can be considered intellectual production, doesn't this problematize my claim for truth as fundamental? Truth is not, it may be argued, a necessary concept for music or painting, and it is unclear whether any musician or painter is operating, qua artist, based on any conception of truth, even if they may independently have such a concept. That is, the concept of truth does not come into their work, and they could operate as artists completely independently and without consideration of truth.

I grant that I am unsure of what to make of this case. It's at least not obvious to me that artists such as musicians and painters don't have an operative concept of truth as part of their work. Even if they do not, however (or if such a concept is not necessary to their project), this is only relevant here if the intellectual production of early Chinese thinkers is more akin to musicians and painters than it is to philosophers, political theorists, and essayists. I don't think even the most extreme and insistent of "philosophy-deniers" have argued this. The most dismissive claims about early Chinese thought tend to take the view that it is more akin to poetry or religious literature than philosophy.[4] Both poetry and religion fall clearly within the category of intellectual pursuits that require a concept of truth, however, even if music and painting do not. And it would be an extremely hard case to make that early Chinese authors were not making assertions, as we might say a pianist does not make assertions on her instrument. Of course, there is overwhelming reason to believe that early Chinese thinkers were not just poets and religious thinkers, but even independently of this issue, it seems clear that we should attribute to them a concept of truth.

Of course, to have a concept of truth is a different matter than having a theory of truth. There would not be all that much to say about a tradition in which most thinkers have a concept but no theory of truth. Thus it should be clear that my own position in this book is that a number of early Chinese philosophers had explicit theories of truth. Not all early Chinese philosophers had theories of truth, of course (by the same token not all Western philosophers have had theories of truth), but there are a number of explicit and interesting theories. Understanding these theories not only will give us a better understanding of the development of early Chinese philosophy, but can also help us in advancing debates surrounding truth in contemporary academic philosophy.

Although investigating early Chinese philosophy looking for theories of truth may be to some extent looking at it through the lenses of an interest that is ours rather than theirs (I grant that many early Chinese philosophers did not give center stage to theories of truth as some in the Western and Indian traditions have), it is justifiable to investigate a tradition and culture through the comparative lenses of one's own concepts and concerns, as long as one is clear that it is indeed an explicitly comparative project one is engaged in, and not the "reconstructive" project of determining how the tradition saw itself and its concerns. These are simply two different projects, and it is important to be clear about which of them one is engaged in at any given time. In this book, I engage in both to a certain extent. Although my main concern is with a concept that was only peripheral to some (but not all) early Chinese philosophers, truth was a concern in a number of early Chinese sources. While my focus is guided by contemporary concerns, what I take from the early Chinese material is not. I am not (as I will argue further below) reading a concept of truth into early Chinese thought, rather I am investigating what early Chinese thinkers had to say about the concept(s) of truth that they had and sometimes developed theories of, even if these theories were not as central to their own thought as it is to my own and that of many contemporary philosophers.

One important point to keep in mind is that even if early Chinese philosophers theorized about truth, we cannot assume that truth had the same connection to other concepts in their thought that it does in Western or contemporary traditions. Thus, though I investigate truth in this study, it will not always turn out that the early Chinese concern with truth lines up cleanly (or at all) with familiar Western and contemporary concerns. The reasons early Chinese thinkers cared about truth were often different, and the uses they made of theories of truth were likewise different. In addition, the concept clusters of which truth formed a part in many cases are unlike anything we see in most Western traditions. But all of this is to say that while early Chinese thinkers certainly thought about truth, they sometimes thought about it in very different ways than Western thinkers. I do not neglect these differences here—indeed, they are important to furthering our understanding of the concept of truth in general.

Of course, to engage in such a project of focusing on truth and neglecting sometimes more central aspects of the thought of a number of early Chinese philosophers is of necessity to miss or rather overlook much of what they were actually doing, and why. To look at truth, rather than their central concerns, runs the risk of offering an inadequate or incorrect picture of the concerns of these thinkers. I recognize this risk, and it is in part for this reason that I want to be explicit up front about my motivations and the scope of my project. Although there are theories of truth offered in much of the early Chinese material, it is not my contention in this book that theories of truth ever occupied center stage in early Chinese philosophy before the Han. In looking at pre-Qin material, I focus on theories of truth, while at the same time recognizing the limited role that these theories played in the overall thought of many pre-Qin thinkers discussed. At the same time, it is not true to say that no philosophers in early China had truth at the center of their programs. We see in the Han period, for example, a number of thinkers for whom truth was a central, perhaps the central, concern. I will attempt in this book to demonstrate that not only were there theories of truth in early China, but that some early Chinese philosophers were as concerned or even more concerned with truth than most philosophers of the Western and Indian traditions.

ON CHINESE "PHILOSOPHY"

I have thus far, and will throughout the book, made use of the term "philosophy" to refer to the forms of early Chinese thought that I engage with.
Some justification needs to be given for this, for obvious reasons. Not only
was the term "philosophy" unknown in early China, but the idea of philosophy or something like it as a unique pursuit engaged in by thinkers was not
formulated. Early Chinese thinkers, some argue, had no conception at all of
philosophy, and so cannot justifiably be said to have engaged in philosophy.[5] I respond to this challenge in somewhat the same way as I respond to
that concerning the concept of truth. While it is true that the early Chinese
thinkers had no conception of an organized area of thought called philosophy, this does not show that they did not in fact engage in philosophy. It is
not a requirement of the philosophical enterprise that one explicitly thinks
of oneself as a philosopher and one's efforts as contributing to philosophy.
Philosophy can be taken as a natural category, in just the same way as "science" or "religion." We find it relatively unproblematic to refer to certain
early Chinese thinkers as religious thinkers, simply because their thought fits
within categories we would call religious. The early Chinese had no more
conception of religion as an independent area of human pursuit, however,
than they did of philosophy. Why do we find philosophy a more problematic
category to apply to them, then?

We might make a distinction between finding philosophy in a historical text
and approaching a historical text in a philosophical manner, independently of
whether the text itself should be considered philosophy. In this book, I will
take a positive view on both concerning much of the early Chinese philosophical tradition. The thinkers and texts I examine here are philosophical in
their own right, and I am also approaching them philosophically (as myself
a philosopher, concerned with philosophy). A number of philosophers argue
for the usefulness of approaching early Chinese texts philosophically, including Bryan Van Norden, who writes:

> What I mean in saying that I am employing philosophical perspective is that
> I am equally concerned with the following: finding, interpreting, and evaluating
> arguments in the texts; clarifying the meaning of the texts by spelling out inter-
> pretive alternatives and examining whether some make better sense of the texts
> than others; and exploring whether each text is self-consistent.[6]

While Van Norden thinks that the philosophical approach to early Chinese texts can be useful and interesting even if the texts themselves should
not be considered philosophical (although he certainly appears to think they
are), some philosophers, such as myself, are committed to stronger claims

concerning early Chinese thought—namely that much of it is philosophy. My own position on this issue is somewhat close to that of Chad Hansen, who takes much of early Chinese thought to be philosophical on the basis not of similarity of particular theories, but rather on the basis of shared concerns. He writes:

> We can have a unified conception of what philosophy is and still appreciate two quite different philosophical traditions. What makes them both philosophy is not their content or shared theories. It is their shared interest in and philosophical analysis of how language, mind, and society interact.[7]

This seems plausible. What makes something philosophy rather than something else is a particular conception of method and area of concern. The case is very similar for something like history. What makes a thinker historically minded is not the focus on some particular period, people, or theory, but rather their general concern with giving an account of the past (and present) rooted in evaluating causes and outcomes of events, individuals, and groups.

Part of the problem, I think, is the assumption that while phenomena like religion, politics, or economics are universal and occur within all societies, philosophy is something limited to the West. There is a rich history of the belief that it is philosophy that makes the West unique in world history, and demonstrates its cultural superiority. This belief arose in the enlightenment period in part as a way to justify the colonial project of supplanting native structures of government with imported European colonial ones to exploit the resources of subjugated lands. Thus, the definition of philosophy given in this period itself privileged the West, as its westernness was implicitly (and often explicitly) made part of the definition of philosophy itself. On purely independent grounds not linked to geography or culture, the claims of the westernness of philosophy cannot be maintained. If philosophy is, in general, the a priori attempt to discover truths through rational methods such as argument and conceptual analysis, many cultures beyond the West, including early Chinese culture, practised this. Indeed, much of the philosophical material in the Indian tradition is almost indistinguishable from ancient Greek thought in its methods, aims, and style. So if there is not a clause added to the definition of philosophy for the disinclusion of non-Western traditions, this separation simply cannot be maintained.

I will thus assume here that we can do the same thing with philosophy that we can with religion, politics, or economics. We should not, as some are guilty of doing, reserve the term "philosophy" for the intellectual program of the ancient Greeks and those later thinkers who saw themselves as in the same intellectual lineage as the Greeks (even when they were not), or who happen to share a general region of the world with others who saw themselves as in the same intellectual lineage as the Greeks. This is to simply write "westernness" into the definition of philosophy. All of the features we often take to be hallmarks of philosophy imbued to it by the ancient Greeks—argument and method, concern with fundamental and conceptual questions, conceptual analysis, definitions, etc.—all of this can be found in other philosophical traditions elsewhere in the world as well, including those of India and China.

If we sever the implicit link between philosophy and the West (itself an ill-defined and arbitrary concept),[8] it will appear much less problematic to apply the term "philosophy" to certain aspects of the thought of early Chinese scholars and thinkers. Just as we can isolate certain aspects of their thought as political, historical, or economic, we can isolate aspects of their thought as philosophical, where they were in fact philosophical. Of course, it will turn out that not every early Chinese thinker was engaged in or concerned with philosophy. But this is to be expected. Not all early Chinese thinkers were interested in history or economics either. Sima Qian was certainly interested in both history and economics, and his magnum opus—from which most of our knowledge of the late Warring States, Qin, and early Han periods derives—the *Shiji*, was a work engaged in history if anything at all. Other early Chinese thinkers, however, such as Mengzi or Mozi, were not concerned with history (at least in any robust way), and in the case of Mengzi tended to explicitly reject any consideration of economics.[9] We should expect the same, and indeed we see the same, with philosophy. Early thinkers such as Mengzi, Mozi, Xunzi, and the Han thinkers tended to do philosophy in a fairly robust way, while it is less clear in texts such as *Daodejing, Shiji, Sunzi*, the Han histories, and other early texts. Certainly none of the early Chinese philosophers would have seen themselves as philosophers, but no early Chinese thinker would have seen himself as a historian or political thinker either. Philosophy, if we understand it correctly, shorn of a West-based definition, is both general and broad enough a concept to easily and comfortably include the early Chinese philosophers I consider in this book. Their works are examples of philosophical thought, and I contend that if you changed the names on these texts from ancient Chinese to English or German ones, there would be little resistance to accepting them as philosophers.[10]

A COMPARATIVE APPROACH

While the organizing concept of this work is that of truth, and my concern with this concept comes from the engagement with it in the contemporary "western" analytic tradition of which I am a part, I will situate early Chinese theories of truth not only with respect to contemporary analytic theories, but also with other traditions, which had an enormous amount to say about truth. To consider the early Chinese theories with respect to categories of other philosophical traditions will illuminate the early Chinese views themselves, as well as help us to better understand how truth is understood in these various traditions, and how best to approach it today.

Ultimately, the result of a comparative philosophical approach such as the one I take in this book ought to be to enrich our understanding of the concept(s) in question.[11] For this study, the concept of truth is the focus of investigation, and although the main concern is with truth in early China, the main desired end of this comparative project is also to contribute to our understanding of truth, rather than to our understanding of early Chinese philosophy (although hopefully the project has this result as well). Since this is the main aim, the comparative approach is uniquely well suited for use, as it can help us to see overarching themes in philosophical thought about the concept of truth in a number of very different cultural contexts and in often very dissimilar traditions, East and West.

The specific comparative approach I use in the book merits discussion here, because it is somewhat different than that of other comparative projects. Insofar as I use non-Chinese philosophical concepts, theories, and texts in this book, I use them mainly to frame the issues of concern in early Chinese texts. I discuss theories of truth in contemporary analytic philosophy, for example, in order to focus the investigation of early Chinese philosophy squarely on truth, as a shared general concept across traditions. This can help us to understand the role that early Chinese theories of truth might play in contemporary debates surrounding truth, as well as help us further clarify commitments, implicit positions, and arguments in the early Chinese material. This latter approach I have elsewhere referred to as the "analogical comparative" approach,[12] and although it is one that I apply less regularly here, I also consider early Chinese texts analogically to Western and Indian texts, which can yield a number of insights.

LAYOUT OF CHAPTERS

This book is organized in three distinct parts, spanning six chapters and a conclusion. In chapter 1, I tackle general issues surrounding the concept of truth, as well as outline and evaluate a number of contemporary views concerning the issue of truth in early Chinese philosophy. In chapters 2 through 6, I look to a series of early texts, and argue for particular interpretations of these texts as offering a variety of theories of truth. I aim here to demonstrate that there were a number of robust and interesting theories of truth in early Chinese philosophy, from early texts such as the Analects through to the critical texts of the Eastern Han dynasty such as Wang Chong's Lunheng. To argue this, I look to the texts themselves, as well as engage with contemporary scholars who have discussed the question of truth in the connection with these texts. Finally, in the conclusion I consider how the theories of truth that we find in early Chinese philosophy might be considered in a comparative sense alongside of other traditions, and how they can help us to achieve a better understanding of the general and foundational concept of truth.

NOTES

1. In this book in general I will use the plural "traditions" to speak of Western, Chinese, and Indian philosophy, because it is incorrect to think of these areas as single traditions. The thought and projects of Epicurus and the Stoics are as different from those of Russell and Quine, for example, than either one is from Vasubandhu and Kumarila Bhatta or Mencius and Xunzi.

2. Relying here on the distinction between "thick" and "thin" concepts coined by Bernard Williams (1985: 140–143).

3. The view that one does not have a particular concept because one does not have a single term corresponding to the concept is what Bryan Van Norden has referred to as the "lexical fallacy," which I discuss in more detail below.

4. See Zheng 2005.

5. Zhang Yunyi discusses some of these historical positions in Zhang 2007.

6. Van Norden 2007: 2.

7. Hansen 1992: 26

8. The very idea of the "West" likely has its roots in the colonial idea of the "othering" of peoples whom colonial powers desired to exploit, in racial and cultural rather than geographical terms, and which used for its justification the almost equally ill-defined earlier notion of "Christendom" in the era of Charlemagne, which understood itself mainly in light of first inter-European divisions, and later in distinction from the Islamic world. See Bonnett 2004 for a consideration of the historical development of the concept of the "West."

9. Mengzi 1A1 is a classic statement of this: 王曰：「叟不遠千里而來，亦將有以利吾國乎？」孟子對曰：「王何必曰利？亦有仁義而已矣。("The king [Hui of Liang] said: 'You have not found a thousand li too far travel to come here—do you have something to offer that will profit my state?' Mengzi replied: 'Why is it necessary for your majesty to speak of profit? I offer humanity and righteousness, and that's all.'

10. While I can of course have no hard evidence, there is at least one reason to think that if the Mengzi, for example, had been called "The Discussions of Master Mark" and had been written in English (say something equivalent to the James Legge translation), then it would have been taken seriously as a philosophical text from the moment of its discovery by the West. This reason is that Aristotle's Nicomachean Ethics has been taken seriously as a philosophical text since its "discovery" in the West in the medieval period, and this text, even though there are many differences,

offers us an ethical system in many ways identical to that of Mengzi, and certainly no more rigorous, developed, or well grounded.

11. There are of course other kinds of comparative approaches, different from the one I adopt here, that are useful in a variety of ways. Robert Smid discusses a number of different comparative approaches in Smid 2010. He captures a general account of the comparative philosophical project well, writing: "Comparative philosophers take as their subject matter traditions whose historical and cultural distance from one another is especially significant, paying particular attention to the implications of trying to traverse that distance while still remaining faithful to the traditions compared" (Smid 2010: 3).

12. "Xunzi and Mimamsa on Ritual: An Analogical Comparative Approach," and "Methodologies of Chinese-Indian Comparative Philosophy. (forthcoming)"

Chapter 1

Truth, Philosophy, and Chinese Thought

TRUTH IN CONTEMPORARY ANALYTIC PHILOSOPHY

Truth is fundamental in all philosophical traditions. The frame within which I approach truth in the Chinese tradition uses multiple traditions, as part of my comparative approach in general, discussed in the introduction. In this section, I outline the contours of thought on truth in contemporary analytic philosophy, in order to understand how early Chinese conceptions of truth fit into contemporary categories.

One may ask at this point: "Why begin with contemporary analytic theories?" There are a few reasons for this. First and foremost, perhaps, is the fact that I come from a background shaped by contemporary analytic philosophy, and I assume most of my readers have similar backgrounds. It is truth and its consideration within this tradition from which we begin in our own thinking about truth and its relevance in early Chinese philosophy. Second, since we as contemporary Western academics (or Western-influenced academics, at least) speak the *language* of contemporary English-language philosophy (in the sense of having the technical background, not in the sense of natural language), Even if we do not consider ourselves part of the "analytic tradition," we are inevitably saddled with certain conceptions of truth as part of the background against which we think about the concept. Since this is so, we might as well use rather than resist these categories and ways of thinking about truth, using them to our advantage. We certainly *can* understand early Chinese theories of truth in the light of the categories, concepts, and theories of contemporary analytic philosophy. Third, understanding early Chinese theories of truth against the background of contemporary categories (even while these categories do not perfectly fit Chinese theories) will allow us to

1

more easily integrate insights and arguments from early Chinese thinkers into contemporary debates on the topic.

The account I offer in this section is a very rough overview of major developments and theories in contemporary analytic philosophy on the issue of truth, and much of what I say here is filled out in more detail in later chapters, in which I consider particular early Chinese theories of truth and their connection to contemporary theories.

Philosophical reflection on the concept of truth in analytic thought really has its beginnings in the early stages of the "analytic" movement with philosophers such as Bertrand Russell, G.E. Moore, and Gottlob Frege in the early twentieth century. These philosophers focused on analysis of language, and looked for the concept of truth as a *linguistic* concept, having to do with evaluations of linguistic entities with assertoric content. Philosophical thought about the concept of truth in the West certainly did not begin with the analytic movement and these philosophers—indeed truth has been a central focus of Western philosophy since its beginnings in ancient Greece—but the consideration of truth as primarily an issue in linguistic and conceptual analysis has its beginnings here. This is significant for us because it is by and large still in this way that most contemporary academic philosophers think about the concept of truth. As we will see in the Chinese tradition (as well as the Indian tradition), there are a number of no less important ways of thinking about the concept of truth as independent of evaluating linguistic entities with assertoric content, and it may turn out that getting things right concerning this *linguistic* sense of truth requires getting things right about truth in other contexts and in the concept's fullness. However, the way in which the early analytic tradition and most contemporary analytic philosophers envision the issue of truth, and by and large the way in which I approach and discuss it in this book, is as a property or function associated with assertoric linguistic entities. When we ask "what is truth?" in *this* sense we are asking "what does it mean to say that *x* is true, where *x* is a statement, proposition, or assertion?"

The question of just *what* kinds of linguistic entities take truth values is an important one, but the one that we will see is more disputed in the contemporary analytic tradition than in the early Chinese tradition. Still, it is useful for us to look at the issue of the proper bearer of truth values, as this issue comes up again when we consider various issues in Chinese theories of truth.

To call something a linguistic entity with assertoric content is relatively vague. What kinds of entity have such content, and are each of these able to have truth values? One view holds that it is *sentences* that have such content, where sentences are concrete linguistic constructions, such as "the sky is blue" or "I woke up at 6am today." What *makes* these sentences true is a matter of theory independent of this issue, which I get into in depth below, but the sententialist view takes them to be the primary truth value-bearers.

In the early development of the analytic tradition, philosophers such as Bertrand Russell recognized that there might be a problem with taking sentences to be truth-bearers. One issue is whether we take sentence types or tokens to be the bearers of truth value. It seems clear that sentence types will not work. The reason for this is that a sentence type may mean very different things in different tokens, or utterances, of it. How do we make sense of the truth of the sentence "I woke up at 6am today" as a type, given that two different utterances of the sentence, one of which is made on a Tuesday on which I did wake up at 6, the other on a Wednesday on which I didn't wake up at 6, will have different truth values? Because of the *indexicality* involved in the sentence (both "I" and "today" refer differently depending on the individual who utters the sentence and the time of its utterance—or writing), we have to say that the two sentence tokens, which have different truth value, also have different *meaning*, that they say different things. And thus not only can it not be a sentence type that bears truth value, but it also looks like we have a problem making sense of how two tokens of the same type can have (possibly *very*) different meaning.[1]

Another problem with sentences, as Russell pointed out, is that there are certain sentences for which the truth value seems undetermined. Sentences referring to nonexistent or fictional individuals, for example, seem to fall into this category. Russell's famous example of such a sentence was "The current King of France is bald." We cannot seemingly accord this sentence token *any* truth value, not because of any failure of the predicate, but because there is no current King of France, and thus the first part of the sentence fails to refer. But if this can be the case, that we have sentences that cannot take a truth value, how do we make sense of sentences as the primary truth-bearers? There must be some way to analyze this sentence, Russell and others thought, that could make sense of it as *false*, rather than simply as meaningless or without truth value.

The answer for Russell was to move to an alternative view of assertoric linguistic content, one that held *propositions* to determine the content of sentences and to be the primary bearers of truth value. Propositions, according to Russell, are *expressed* by sentences but not identical to sentences. One way we might think of them is as the content of sentences, what the sentences *say* or *convey*. Thus, if we return to an above example, the sentence "I woke up at 6am today" uttered by me this day expresses the proposition that [Alexus McLeod woke up at 6am on September 11, 2014]—a proposition that just turns out to be true. The move to propositions allows us to analyze the problematic sentences that Russell considers, because propositional content is in some sense *hidden* in some sentences. That is, the straightforward reading of a sentence does not always suggest the proposition expressed by the sentence. Russell analyzes "the present King of France is bald" as expressing the propositional content [there is some x such that x is the present King of France, and x is bald]. This proposition is clearly false, because the first clause of the first conjunct is false. There is no x such that x is the present King of France. Since this is the case, the entire proposition takes the value of false. The propositional view here transforms this sentence into an existential statement and a predicative one.

Propositions, however, have their own difficulties. One of the biggest is specifying just what kinds of thing propositions are. They seem unacceptably mysterious. Propositions are the content expressed by sentences, but are not themselves sentences. How do we make sense of a linguistic content that is *expressible* in sentence form, but analyzable independently of sentences? How do we approach the existence and identity of such things? It seems like we can only really work with sentences and get at propositions through them—but then how do we make sense of what propositions are in the first place, beyond the claim that whatever they are, they are what make sentences (derivatively) true? This lack of clarity led some to reject the idea of propositions.

The right position concerning truth-bearers should be largely independent from theory of truth, although we will see that there tend to be connections between these views. Indeed, one of the major points of contention in the debate on truth in early Chinese thought is whether there are any linguistic entities discussed by early Chinese philosophers that are capable of being truth-bearers. When we discuss *theories of truth* proper, we generally have in mind the kinds of views concerning how we understand the predicate <is true> in "x is true" for any proper truth-bearer x. What property, if any, is expressed by this predicate? Or is there something else going on? Is what seems to be a predicate merely a semantic tool for generalizations? Or does the predicate express *different* properties in different contexts of discourse? There are a number of different theories in contemporary philosophy surrounding the truth surrounding these issues.[2]

Part of the difficulty here is that, in general, when we seek an account of truth we are looking for that which all statements that are true have. We want to discover what it is that truths (in plural) share in common that makes them true. We say that it is true that "the sky is blue," that "$2 + 2 = 4$," that "harming others is wrong," and that "slavery was an important issue underlying the American Civil War." If there is a predicate of truth that expresses a robust property, then there must be some property held by all true statements, and the task of the philosopher is to discover and give an account of just what that property is and how a statement comes to have such a property.

Of course we will see that, in the early Chinese tradition no less than in the analytic tradition, there are those who disagree that there is a property of truth at all. In contemporary philosophy, this is most often held by those who deny that <is true> represents a legitimate predicate. In English, it *looks* like it signals a predicate because of its grammar, but the actual role of the truth operator is not predicative—it does not attribute any robust property (though it may attribute *some* property). These kinds of views are versions of what we can call "deflationism."[3] The issue of what truth operators look like *in classical Chinese* will be a major concern for us here, although we should not, and early Chinese philosophers did not, allow grammatical constraints to guide their philosophical concerns in the way contemporary philosophers of language do—and this is probably a good thing. In general, early Chinese philosophers saw linguistic difficulties surrounding truth as having to do primarily with *concepts* rather than grammar. This, I think, is a strength of their program, because concepts may be universal (at least some of them, thinly specified), while grammar is limited to a linguistic tradition. How can we make overarching claims about the concept of truth if we're constrained by the grammatical considerations of a single language?

Realist theories of truth come in a variety of forms.[4] In general, realists hold that there is a genuine and robust property (whether more or less robust) expressed by the predicate <is true>, that belongs to the assertoric linguistic entity in question (I will call them "statements" so as not to beg any questions concerning the debate mentioned above about truth-bearers). While the realist view is often seen as the "traditional" view in the Western traditions, this is not the case in early Chinese philosophy. This is important because part of the argument of realists can sometimes be that the presumption is in favor of realist views because they are the most "common sense" or "intuitive" views of truth.[5] Again, as with looking only at the English language in considering grammatical constraints on theory, this is an unfortunate position, as it fails to consider whether realist views are the default common sense position in other traditions. Why is this important? one might ask. Well, if we are genuinely interested in *truth* as a universal and robust concept that transcends traditions, and not simply a provincial relic that only has force within analytic philosophy in Western languages, we have to consider intuitions globally, not just within the narrow confines of English-speaking philosophy. Maybe there are interesting things to say about a concept only of use to Western analytic philosophers, and maybe such a concept would be worth studying and trying to understand. But this is hardly ever the reason we give for *why* we should care about truth in the first place. Why does truth matter? Presumably the reason we take truth as so crucial to the philosophical project is that we take it as a general and foundational concept with wide scope, and hold it to have a certain key value.[6] Any concept limited to certain wings of Western analytic philosophy, however, certainly does not meet this description.

I identify here four major categories of the realist truth theory. First, there are what might be called *correspondence theories*. In this type of theory, truth is taken to be a relation between statements (propositions or sentences) and facts or states-of-affairs. Many of the proponents of correspondence theory claim for it the status of most consistent with common sense. There is a strong intuition underlying our notion of truth, one we might call the "correspondence intuition," that a statement is true when the world is as it claims the world is, when reality lines up with a statement. While this is probably the case, even across traditions, it turns out that there is no privileged connection between the correspondence *intuition* and the correspondence *theory*. It may not be the case that the best way to flesh out the intuition, or explain why we have such an intuition, involves correspondence theory. Perhaps, as some claim, the correspondence intuition can best be explained on a *deflationist* account of truth!

In general, correspondence theories take states-of-affairs to make statements true (generally thought of as propositions here, but there can be alternatives as well), in virtue of standing in the relation of correspondence. There are a few problems here, however, that the correspondence theorist will have to deal with. First, what does it mean for a state-of-affairs to *correspond to* a statement? It is not that the statement describes or otherwise expresses the state-of-affairs (it may do this as well, but this is not what its truth consists in). It is unclear how we ought to understand this relation, and what explanation of it we could possibly give beyond the basic claim of correspondence. The relation seems hard to define. In addition, we have the problem of specifying states-of-affairs. What is the scope of a state-of-affairs? Does a statement correspond to the entire "way the world is"? Or instead to some part of it? But how do we make sense of correspondence with some narrowly specified state-of-affairs unless we already have a concept of truth prior to correspondence, to specify the proper contours of the state-of-affairs? That is, it cannot be something within our statement itself that determines the states-of-affairs—these have to be independent of our statements. But then is it plausible to think that states-of-affairs are distinguished in the world in discrete ways that can be captured by statements? That my act of pouring coffee this morning is ontologically distinct from other acts, including that of lifting the mug to avoid spilling while pouring my coffee? As we will see, while something like a correspondence intuition may have been widespread in early Chinese philosophy (although certainly nowhere near universal), the correspondence *theory* as understood in contemporary Western philosophy was less influential (although we may take some early Chinese views as radically different versions of a kind of correspondence theory, such as what we find in *Zhuangzi* and *Huainanzi*, discussed in chapter 5 below).

A second category of realist theory of truth is *coherence* theory. These theories are ones that hold truth for a statement to consist roughly of whether the statement coheres or fits consistently with other statements that form one's world-view. The classical coherence theories in the West were linked to idealist metaphysics, and we will see in traditions such as Chinese and Indian philosophy this tends to be the case as well. There are wider antirealist concerns that can motivate such a position, however, that go beyond idealism. Kantian "idealist" concerns could generate such a view, given that we cannot know anything about the world beyond the phenomenal, even though it is there. Indeed we need not even accept something as idealist as Kantianism.

A third category is *pragmatism*, with which we will become very familiar due to its strong influence among scholars of early Chinese philosophy, if not early Chinese philosophers themselves (in my opinion). While, as mentioned above, pragmatist theories of truth tend to get short shrift in contemporary analytic philosophy, they are taken seriously in some corners of academic philosophy, as well as within the continental tradition, with which they are most associated in contemporary thought. The development of pragmatist theories of truth came from considerations of the notion of empirical respectability and truth as a concept useful for the empirical sciences. How do we determine whether the truth of a statement in empirical science is a matter of checking the effects expected from a statement against our experience—the scientific method. This is the heart of *experiment*, the testing of claims against the hard standard of reality. The truth of a statement is determined in part by its having predicted effects in reality. But how do we determine this? In the scientific method, part of what makes a hypothesis a law is its repeated observation consistent with reality, and importantly the fact of agreement between experts about its truth. This *actual* agreement, however, can be thought of distinctly from *hypothetical* agreement at the limit of understanding. So one measure or determinant of truth on one kind of pragmatist theory is that a statement is true when at the limit of understanding people would agree on its representing reality. This is roughly the view of Charles Peirce, who offers a concise statement of this view:

> Different minds may set out with the most antagonistic views, but the progress of investigation carries them by a force outside of themselves to one and the same conclusion. This activity of thought by which we are carried, not where we wish, but to a foreordained goal, is like the operation of destiny. No modification of the point of view taken, no selection of other facts for study, no natural bent of mind even, can enable a man to escape the predestinate opinion.[7]

Thus while it is the case that truth is determined by (or rather is *identical* to) agreement at the limit of understanding by those looking for the truth,[8] what occasions that agreement is not human decision or anything dependent on us at all, but a "force" outside of the mind. We are *compelled* to agree at the limit. This might occasion the question "what is it that compels us, and why isn't *this* the determinant of truth, rather than agreement?" That is, if reality is ultimately mind-independent, why shouldn't we simply be some variant of correspondence theorist? One response to this might be that reality, although it exists mind-independently, can only be grasped by us through human experience, and thus only what is experientially relevant can have truth value for us. The concept of truth is thus, we see here, a concept inextricably related to and dependent on human experience, rather than language alone. For the correspondence theorist (and the deflationist, as we will see below), the truth of statements has to do with facts about the statements and the world, independently of human minds. Perhaps statements cannot exist without humans and language, but their truth is completely independent of us. The pragmatist theory fundamentally disagrees about the *kind* of concept truth is. Truth is a scientific and investigatory concept that has first and foremost to do with human understanding. There is no truth, we might say, absent minds to know the truth—there is only *reality*. If this is the case, then a statement can only be true when it is linked sufficiently to human understanding—and it is not enough to just have certain observable effects, but also to command assent at the limit of understanding.

An alternative kind of realist theory of truth with more recent influence is that of *pluralism*, which also we will see has representatives in early China.[9] The pluralist position is roughly that there may be *different* properties associated with the predicate <is true> in different domains of discourse. So what makes a statement true in the domain of ethics, for example, may be different than what makes a statement true in the domain of physics. Of course, there is one obvious problem with this proposal (although we will see other more difficult ones in later chapters): if there are different properties expressed by truth in different domains of discourse, how can we make sense of truth as a single and univocal concept across domains? That is, truth should *mean* the same thing across domains, but it will be hard to explain how this can be if the truth predicate picks out different properties in each domain. Why does not the meaning of truth change as well? Possible answers to this objection include making truth a second-order property, a functional property,[10] or a property defined by a set of "platitudes" about truth that pick out certain specific properties in a given domain.[11]

RECENT VIEWS CONCERNING TRUTH IN EARLY CHINESE THOUGHT

Hansen on Truth

The issue of truth in early Chinese philosophy is a contentious one, and the debate surrounding it can be strange at times. Not only are there disagreements concerning what kinds of theories of truth are represented in early Chinese philosophy, there is a larger and overarching debate concerning whether there is a concept of truth in early Chinese philosophy at all. In this section, I attempt to untangle the strands in this sometimes convoluted and always difficult debate, including making explicit a number of assumptions that guide each of the positions discussed here, before moving on to offer an argument for the presence of a concept of and theories of truth in early Chinese philosophy.

Perhaps the most well-known argument for the view that there is no concern with truth in early Chinese thought is that of Chad Hansen.[12] Hansen places his focus on "pre-Han" philosophy,[13] and contends that while there is a pragmatic concern in early texts, there is no semantic concern, and thus no concern with truth. According to Hansen, early Chinese thinkers were concerned exclusively with the connection between language, primarily words rather than sentences, and behavior, moral action, and roles. He calls this concern pragmatic, which he distinguishes from the semantic concern, represented in much of Western thought (he mentions Plato as the key representative), in which there is concern about statements (or linguistic entities with assertoric content) and their connection with the world. Thus, issues such as truth and meaning, and related issues surrounding belief and knowledge, take center stage in a tradition grounded in semantic concerns, while role, behavior, and virtue take center stage in a tradition grounded in pragmatic concerns.

One problem I see with Hansen's approach is its scope problem. That is, Hansen compares pre-Han Chinese philosophy with the entirety of "Western" thought. There are problems with this comparison. First, it is unclear that we are warranted in making any general claims about broader traditions when we look at a small piece of one tradition as compared to the entire history of another. If we focused our attention only on medieval philosophy on the Western side, we would certainly miss many of the concerns developed at different periods, both before and after, in Western thought. In addition, and perhaps an even greater difficulty, as scholars such as Alasdair MacIntyre argue, there is good reason to see the "Western tradition" as not legitimately a single tradition at all.[14] The concerns, concepts, assumptions, and arguments of the ancient Greek philosophers were very different from those of the medieval western Europeans, which in turn are very different from those of contemporary analytic philosophers, for example. Even in traditions existing side-by-side in the same time and place, there can often be unbridgeable differences. Some argue that there are fundamental differences between the analytic and continental traditions, for example. What should we say of this? How can we lump not only the two of these, but also every other philosophical "school of thought" of the West, into a single tradition, and compare it to one tiny sliver of Chinese thought in the three hundred or so years between the fifth and second centuries BCE? Given such a comparison, we should be

unsurprised to find the Chinese "tradition" lacking a whole number of concepts, assumptions, and arguments found on the Western side. We have the
entirety of Western thought from which to draw on one end of the comparison. A more even comparison, perhaps, would be between "pre-Han" Chinese philosophy and "pre-Hellenistic" Greek philosophy. But when we make
such a comparison, we do not see such glaring absences on the Chinese side.

While it may be true (but not obviously so) that early Chinese philosophers
for the most part placed a greater emphasis on practical and ethical issues
than ancient Greek philosophers, they were not without concerns that are
"semantic" on Hansen's definition.[15] Hansen argues that because the focus
in early Chinese texts tends to be on words and strings of words rather than
sentences, this precludes semantic concerns, but this seems to me wrong.
First, although it is certainly true that names (*ming* 名) get much more attention in early Chinese texts than perhaps any other linguistic construct, there
are certainly semantic issues concerning names throughout early Chinese
thought—whether names are acceptable, and also whether they correspond
to reality, actuality, or the world (often discussed in terms of *shi* 實). The
Chinese focus on names *is* semantic (though not *only* semantic).[16] Part of the
problem is that Hansen seems to accept that only sentences can properly take
truth value, because only such constructions make claims about the world or
count as a statement with assertoric content, in ways that names (*ming* 名) do
not.[17] While this may be true in English and other languages, it is not clearly
the case in classical Chinese, at least in the way early Chinese philosophers
thought about their language. There were multiple questions about names the
early Chinese philosophers asked. Certainly they were concerned with the
question of whether a given name was properly used—this is the basis of the
"rectification of names" (*zhengming* 正名) that was such a concern for Xunzi.
But they tended also to be concerned with the issue of whether a name corre-
sponded to an "actuality." Numerous early philosophers were concerned with
the issue of the connection between *ming* 名 and *shi* 實(name and actuality).
"Actuality" in pre-Han texts does not *obviously* refer to a mind-independent
world, states-of-affairs, or other such notions. But there is a plausible reading
of *shi* as having such a sense, and the fact that this is clearly the case in Han
philosophical texts suggests (as I argue further below) that it can be read this
way in pre-Han texts as well.

Hansen argues that since the focus in early Chinese texts is on names or
terms rather than sentences, there could not be reflection on truth. There are
of course sentences in classical Chinese, but Hansen's argument is that the
early philosophers never took sentences as objects of reflection (part of his
argument for this turns on the early Chinese lacking a term for "sentence"—
a problematic argument I address below), and thus while they may have *de
re* had a concept of truth, they did not *de dicto* have such a concept. Even if

it were true that there is no focus on sentences or similar linguistic entities (I address this below as well), certain single-term constructions in classical Chinese can be seen as involving implicit predication—this is something Hansen himself discusses but seems to miss the significance of. The term *ming* 明 ("bright") can be read as "it is bright" used by itself, which is clearly a statement predicating brightness of an implicit subject. Almost any term can be used this way, and terms often are. One can use a term like *zuo* 作 (create, make) in a number of ways—it can stand for the noun "creation," the verb "to create," or it can be used alone to express the statement "he/she/it creates," or the command "create!" Single terms can simply do a whole lot more in classical Chinese (and modern Chinese, for that matter) than they can in English. When we take these possibilities into consideration, a focus on terms or names then certainly cannot rule out concern with the truth value of statements, as terms can themselves *be* statements, can themselves have assertoric content.

Hansen writes:

> When Chinese philosophers did raise semantic issues, they did not formulate them in ways that used the notion of the compositional sentence (the unit to which "truth" applies) as semantically significant, as distinct, that is, from mere strings of "names." Thus, although there were both pragmatic and semantic theories of names, any issues about language above the level of names were primarily analyzed pragmatically rather than semantically.[18]

I think Hansen is wrong here in at least two ways. First—the claim that the "compositional sentence" is the only entity to which truth applies assumes a particular conception of language based in English, and English theorization about language, as discussed above. It is also unclear to me why names in themselves *cannot* be considered in terms of truth value in a different way. The concept of *satisfaction* is certainly a semantic notion closely related to that of truth,[19] and names are at the core of this concern. There is plenty of reason to believe that at least part of what early Chinese philosophers were concerned about when they worried about names was whether a particular thing or person (or anything at all) satisfied the description suggested by some name. *Ming*, in the ways early Chinese philosophers theorized about it, even though we translate it as "name," did not generally refer to proper names such as "Kongzi",[20] and general names/terms could be taken as descriptions. A concern with satisfaction in which *ming* play the role of descriptions is one of the only ways to make sense of passages such as *Analects* 12.11, in which, responding to a question about proper government from Duke Jing of Qi, Confucius responds:

君君，臣臣，父父，子子

Jun jun, chen chen, fu fu, zi zi.

I leave this here untranslated because there is disagreement as to the proper way to understand what is going on here, and I want to consider two ways of understanding this, one of which I think is far more plausible than the other. One way this is sometimes understood is as an example of *zhengming* (rectification of names). On this reading, Confucius is advocating that we "apply the name ruler (*jun*) to the ruler, apply the name servant (*chen*), to the servant, apply the name father (*fu*) to the father, and apply the name son (*zi*) to the son." On this reading, then, the first instance of each term is in verbal sense, such that it refers to the act of considering something as or naming it "ruler," "servant," etc. Indeed, this seems to be the way Hansen is inclined to think about such passages (though he doesn't mention this one specifically or cases like this). While this reading is linguistically possible, I don't think it makes much *philosophical* sense here, and there is another linguistically possible reading that makes better sense of it. Actually, whether or not the reading I will suggest is ultimately the correct one doesn't really matter for purposes of the point I am trying to make about names functioning as description—it only needs to be a possible way of making sense of the Chinese. Instead of reading the first term in each of the four statements in the verbal sense, we can read the *second* in the verbal sense. The first term then refers to the subject, the ruler, servant, etc., and the second serves as a predicate concerning action. Thus we can read it as "the ruler rules, the servant serves, the father acts as father, the son acts as son." The suggestion here is also that normativity is implied, given that it is a response about how best to create proper government, so the translation should be "the ruler should rule, servants should serve, fathers should act as fathers, and sons should act as sons." I think this is the more likely reading because not only does it fit the language, it also makes better sense as a guide to harmonious society, given other Confucian views on the importance of adherence to roles based on ritual (*li* 禮). And if this reading is right, it shows that not only can names (*ming*) be understood as descriptions in such a way that a consideration of the acceptability of names can be seen as consideration about whether particular things satisfy certain descriptions, but it also shows us that Confucians, at least, would have perfectly good reasons for thinking about names in just such a way—adhering to ritual and enacting proper government is in part a matter of individuals performing their proper roles, so in a consideration of particular descriptions/names, we have reason to be concerned with whether individuals (and which individuals) satisfy them.

The issue of whether names should be understood in a descriptivist or non-descriptivist way may be seen to map fairly well onto contemporary debates in the philosophy of language concerning the same issue. The descriptivist view of reference in the Western tradition was initially developed by philosophers like Gottlob Frege and Bertrand Russell. The view holds that a name has reference with respect to a description connected to the name, constituting its meaning. Thus, names contain descriptions inherently—similar to the position on *ming* that I outline here. This theory can be extended to various kinds of names—both proper names, such as "Kongzi" or "Chad Hansen," or kind names, such as "water" or "wood." "Water" is connected with the descriptions (for example): "The stuff that fills Earth's oceans, makes up a significant part of the human body, falls from the sky as rain, etc."[21] On a descriptivist view of names such as this, whether a particular name fits a given thing depends on whether that thing satisfies the description connected with the name. This issue of satisfaction is certainly a semantic issue, and even beyond this, if the early Chinese position on *ming* involved not only the *coining* but the *application* of names and issues of proper application, then insofar as there were descriptivist theories of *ming*, we should conclude that the concern with *ming* was also the concern with statements, and truth is a crucial issue here. To say *"x is water"* is not to say that "the term 'water' is applied to *x*," but to make a statement about *x*, such that "*x* is of the class of stuff that fills the Earth's oceans, etc." This is clearly a truth-evaluable statement.

If this is how many (or any) of the early Chinese philosophers thought about *ming* and reference,[22] then the early Chinese focus on names rather than sentences does not entail lack of a concept of truth or concern about truth, and Hansen is simply wrong when he claims:

> The concept of truth is both unnecessary and discordant with [early Chinese philosophers'] linguistic focus on *ming* ("names") rather than on sentences. No truth theorizing occurred because no theorizing about things to which "truth" applies occurred.[23]

Robert Neville offers an additional argument in support of Hansen's view and against the above consideration of the rectification of names as having to do with satisfaction of descriptions.

> The Confucian theme of the rectification of names should not be understood as an attempt to get the right icon or description but as the attempt to get the right index. The right index causes the interpreter to be properly comported toward the object, treating it according to its true nature and worth. A description might be involved in a rectified name, but then again the descriptive or iconic elements of the "right name" might be quite fanciful, plainly false if interpreted literally. Chad Hansen's "Daoist" interpretation of language can be seen as rightly emphasizing the indexical, as opposed to iconic, character of reference, according to Peirce's categories.[24]

The problem with this is that Neville's consideration of the possibility of "fanciful" names (which can certainly be resisted as the case in the literature) does not demonstrate a lack of concern with truth. It may show, if indeed the case, simply that proper (or true) descriptions might simply be ones with different properties depending on the domain or purpose. It does not any more show that early Chinese thinkers (of the kinds who thought like this anyway) were not concerned about truth than that they were *pluralists* about truth. Are there *any* times in which descriptions are accepted as properly involved in a rectified name *because* they match certain features of the world in a "correspondentist" way that most of us would recognize as truth? If so, this suggests that truth was a concern (if we clearly have to take this as truth concern), and when there are descriptions that don't seem to have this property taken as acceptable in the rectification of names, why not simply think that truth may have been thought about in a pluralist way, rather than that sometimes they cared about truth and sometimes it was something else they cared about, all under the heading of *zhengming*?

There is an additional problem with Hansen's account of truth given another feature of classical Chinese that he takes note of:

> Virtually any term [in classical Chinese], since it may conceivably be in such a propositional context [S Fs x can be understood as S believes x is F], can function syntactically as a two-place verb.[25]

It is especially curious that Hansen mentions this, given that one of his later arguments in the paper is that one of the reasons Chinese philosophers did not think about a concept of truth is that they had no conception of belief as possibly contrasting with reality. Early Chinese philosophers, according to him, understood belief expressions as "action expressions" based on the reasoning above. Hansen comes close to committing (or maybe outright commits) what we might call the "lexical fallacy,"[26] arguing that there is no term or string of terms in classical Chinese that correspond to the terms "belief," "believe," or the phrase "believes that." We should *expect* as much, however, if Hansen is right about the ability of terms to function in the way described in the above quote. If "S Fs x" can be translated as "S believes that x is F," then the lack of a specific term marking belief does not entail the lack of a concept of belief in which there is an issue about the accordance of belief with reality. The terminology of belief is simply not *necessary* since the concept is built into other aspects of the language. And Hansen has not made the case that a belief context in which *action* is considered should be understood as less clearly about reality or the world than belief in any other context.

Discussing what he takes as an example of the relevant differences in Chinese language, Hansen writes:

The belief structure of ancient Chinese language signals a different philosophy of mind as well as a different epistemology. It does not generate a picture of some "mental states" with a sentential, propositional, or representational content. Corresponding to King Wen's "belief" [in the statement "King Wen beautifuls Chang An"] is a disposition to discriminate among cities. He discriminates among cities in such a way that Chang An falls on the beautiful side.[27]

Presumably, however, there is still an open question as to whether the King's discrimination is *proper*, especially when we move from aesthetic evaluations to ones more obviously based on mind-independent facts. Discriminations may be based on individuals, but the *authenticity* or the matching-of-reality of those discriminations is presumably not—this is a matter of the world. If "Zhuang Zhou capitals Chang An," is to mean that he discriminates between cities such that Chang An falls on the side of being a capital, the actual state-of-affairs in the world is certainly relevant to the question of whether this discrimination is proper, or dare we say, *true*. So, perhaps we can say to Hansen that even if it is not *sentences* that are considered and taken as the primary bearers of truth value in early Chinese philosophy (though I think we should not concede this), certainly *discriminations* (*bian* 辨) are considered in terms of truth. No early Chinese philosopher would have thought that it is *not* an issue of "the way things are" or "reality" to discriminate in certain ways rather than others, and to make sense of the justification of discriminations.

Hansen is fixated on sentences and the apparent absence of consideration of sentences in early Chinese philosophy, so he misses the above point, as well as a fairly clear representation of an entity in much of early Chinese philosophy that can take truth value, namely *yan* 言 (saying, statement, what is said). Indeed, Wang Chong in the Eastern Han dynasty explicitly makes *yan* the focus of his analysis, investigating various *yan* for truth value. *Yan* ("statements") did not all-of-a-sudden become possible truth-bearers with Wang Chong in the first century CE. While he was certainly innovative, no one is *that* innovative. *Yan* had this sense long before Wang's time. Hansen overlooks this concept. He writes:

Classical writers did not use the modern term *ju* (sentence) in their theories of language. The next larger unit of language they spoke of was a *shuo* (explanation), and then a *dao* (guiding discourse).[28]

By neglecting *yan*, which clearly has assertoric content, and using *shuo* 說 (which was actually less often discussed even the pre-Han Chinese texts), Hansen creates a presumption in favor of pragmatism. It is less clear that explanations can be truth-bearers (although maybe they can) than it is that statements or teachings can be (which must be the case, as making assertions).

Secondly, Hansen's claim about the lack of theoretical concern with sentences is simply false. Early Chinese texts *do* talk about sentences and their acceptability or applicability, in both Han and pre-Han contexts. There is discussion of *yan* 言, which is certainly more than just a group of names, but has the connotation of "what is said" (as discussed above). While *yan* are not the subject of prominent named theories like *zhengming* 正名, and so there is not, in pre-Han texts at least, as much discussion about them as a pivotal part of theories of language, there certainly are, even in pre-Han texts, discussions of *yan* and their acceptability, which as often as not have to do with connection with reality (*shi* 實), just as in the case of individual terms/names. In the Han period, which Hansen neglects,[29] consideration of *yan* and their connection with reality becomes much more prominent, and theories we would have a hard time rejecting as about truth come to the fore. In order to maintain the view of early Chinese philosophy as lacking a concept of truth, one has to ignore the Han. And even with this oversight, it will turn out difficult to justify such a position in the light of the available evidence.

It is also strange that Hansen takes "pragmatic" concern to be in itself antagonistic to concern with truth (another aspect of his argument for the lack of a truth concept in early Chinese philosophy). Although he uses Peirce's categorization distinguishing the semantic, syntactic, and pragmatic, he neglects the fact that Peirce and his pragmatist heirs develop *theories of truth* that are pragmatic at the core. A fundamental pragmatic bent does not necessitate a lack of a concern with truth, and certainly not a lack of a concept of truth. Pragmatists about truth such as Peirce and James do not, even though they offer definitions of truth that take it to be based on the connection between language and features of *persons* rather than language and the world (and so not semantic in the sense discussed here), do not reject the correspondence *intuition*,[30] and it would be strange to say that Peirce and James weren't actually talking about *truth* when they offered their pragmatist theories of truth. This would be to beg a major question against the pragmatist. Why can this not also be the case for the early Chinese philosophers, if they were indeed committed to pragmatism as Hansen claims?[31] Peirce himself defined *meaning* in a pragmatist way that lent itself to pragmatic consideration of truth. He wrote:

> The essence of belief is the establishment of a habit, and different beliefs are distinguished by the different modes of action to which they give rise.[32]

So far this looks consistent with Hansen's interpretation of early Chinese thought. But if we take belief to be linked with habits in this way, facts about meaning and truth will also be so linked, and this is indeed what Peirce says.

The second link in the pragmatist chain ending in his theory of truth is his view of meaning, on which he says:

> The whole function of thought is to produce habits of action. . . . If there be a unity among our sensations which has no reference to how we shall act on a given occasion, as when we listen to a piece of music, we do not call that thinking. To develop its meaning, we have, therefore, simply to determine what habits it produces, *for what a thing means is simply what habits it involves.*[33]

So far we are still very close to Hansen's understanding of the early Chinese philosophers. One of the key differences he claims for them from "Western thought" is that they see the key connection of language to ways of action. So does Peirce. The next step Peirce makes seems the most obvious one, and it is unclear why Hansen should deny it for the Chinese tradition, given that he seems to see a nearly perfect mirror of Peirce in their philosophy. If meaning boils down to habits of actions, then this suggests, rather than elimination of truth, that truth should instead be understood in the same way as semantic and epistemic concepts like meaning and belief are understood— that is, pragmatically. Peirce writes:

> The opinion which is fated to be ultimately agreed to by all who investigate, is what we mean by the truth, and the object represented in this opinion is the real.[34]

Now, one might be less than satisfied with this, for a number of reasons, including that it seems that Peirce may be walking back his pragmatism here when we focus on the "fated" agreement, suggesting that there is some independent ground guiding our belief that should *itself* be deemed reality. Independently of this, however, it is certainly clear that one with clearly and solely pragmatist leanings can have a concept and a clear theory of truth, even without so-called "semantic" theoretical concerns of the connection between sentences and the world. Note that on Peirce's theory, there need not be anything special about the status of sentences as opposed to names or terms.

So why should Hansen think that the early Chinese philosophers have no concept of truth on the basis of their supposed pragmatism? He writes:

> A concept is a role in a theory. If the theories of language were pragmatic, and the metaphysics, epistemology, and theory of heart-mind motivated by that attitude toward language, then there would be no role for a concept of truth.[35]

This seems to me extreme. It is not enough to rule out a concept of truth for Hansen to show that they were primarily (or even *solely*) concerned with pragmatism—for this would also entail that Peirce and James had no concept of truth, which is absurd given that they explicitly spoke about it and constructed pragmatist theories that they took to be theories of truth.

Perhaps Hansen might respond that philosophers such as Peirce and James, though they offer pragmatic theories of language and understandings of meaning, truth, and other concepts that we generally take to be "semantic," as well as metaphysical concepts, were writing in a background in which so-called "semantic" understandings of language were commonplace, and so their theories must be understood as responding to or somehow containing these. But it is hard to make sense of this—even if Peirce, for example, wrote in a "truth-soaked" climate, the theory *he* offers, on Hansen's grounds, could not have contained a concept of truth. But certainly there is a role for truth in Peirce's theory—and he explicitly discusses its role.

Perhaps one might respond that even though Peirce, James, and other pragmatists and antirealists *call* their theories theories of truth, they are not actually talking about truth at all. This seems to me not only implausible but also question begging against the pragmatist. We would already have to have a worked-out conception of what truth is to determine that pragmatist truth is not *really* truth. The only ground on which one could make that claim is the assumption that pragmatic concerns cannot be truth concerns, thus there can be no pragmatic theory of truth. And this seems to be close to one of the ways Hansen argues concerning the early Chinese philosophers. Not only is this a question-begging view that assumes without arguments that truth must be nonpragmatic, but it neglects ways in which we can make better sense of some of the arguments of early Chinese texts by attributing to them a pragmatist conception of *truth*. The Mohist arguments using the "three standards" from the *On Ghosts* chapter, for example,[36] may be weak arguments for truth if we take truth to be construed in a realist sense, but on a pragmatist or other antirealist construal of truth, these arguments may be far more reasonable. Thus, charity does not necessarily lead us to reject the idea that there was a concept of truth in Mohist thought, but only to reject that there was a robustly *realist* conception of truth in Mohist thought. And this is just *Mohist* thought—to say nothing of the views of the other schools and philosophers in the pre-Han periods.

I reject the idea, however, that early Chinese philosophy as a whole was primarily pragmatic in nature. Many early Chinese philosophers were indeed concerned with "semantics," with the connection between language and the world, or reality, and explicitly theorized concerning this. While the main concern of most of the pre-Qin philosophers was with ethical issues such as social harmony (*he* 和), how to cultivate virtue (*de* 德), and determining and following (in some sense) the *dao* 道, a nonnegligible number of philosophers thought that it was important to this process to "get things right" in the sense of language corresponding somehow to reality, where reality was considered not as determined by practical effect, but in the "correspondentist" (if you will) sense of how things objectively are, independently of human minds.

Hansen cannot be completely blamed for what I think is a misreading of the tradition, however. I think he is on to *something*, and the problem is a matter of scope. I think part of the reason he oversteps and reads early Chinese philosophers in general as thoroughgoing pragmatists (although as I point out above that the pragmatist still generally has a concept of truth) is because he focuses overly much on the Mohists,[37] their concepts, and their terminology. It is certainly strange to draw general conclusions about early Chinese philosophy from the highly idiosyncratic Mohists, and many of the Mohist concepts that Hansen considers, such as *zhen* 真, *ke* 可, *dang* 當, and the Mohist use of *ran* 然 are not the best concepts to investigate if one is concerned with truth. *Ran* as understood in other early texts, along with *shi* 實, need to be taken into consideration. In addition, Hansen's consideration of the "three tests" of the Mohists is a red herring. Hansen's argument to show that the "three tests" do not concern truth cannot have any wider implications concerning whether the Mohists or any other early Chinese philosophers did or did not have a concept of truth, even if it is conclusive (which I think it is not). However, there are *many* counterexamples in early Chinese texts that undermine Hansen's position (chapters 2 through 6 offer a number of them). In addition, since demonstrating that the Mohists' "three tests" are not about truth ultimately says nothing at all about whether the Mohists or any other early Chinese philosophers had a concept of truth (any more than showing that Einstein's equation $E=mc^2$ has nothing to do with the concept of time demonstrates that Einstein had no concept of time), I will not respond to this aspect of Hansen's argument here (though I return to consider the Mohist "three tests" in chapter 3).

Another reason one might be led to read the early Chinese tradition in the way Hansen does is that the focus of early Chinese philosophers was clearly on questions of ethics and politics. This was doubtlessly the main concern of most of the pre-Qin thinkers at least (things change considerably in the Han).[38] Having a primarily ethical and practical focus does not, however, entail that a philosopher has no metaphysical, epistemological, or "semantic" concern, let alone no concept of truth.[39] It is true, of course, that early Chinese philosophers (at least before the Han) did not discuss issues of metaphysics and epistemology to the extent Plato did, for example, but this was not because they had no concern for these issues, but rather because they didn't see them as central to the ethical project as Plato did. Many pre-Han philosophers were content to simply bracket these questions and put them to the side. But in the Han period (206 BCE–220 CE) things drastically change, beginning with texts such as *Huainanzi* and *Chunqiu Fanlu* in the early (Western)

Han, and continuing through Wang Chong's *Lunheng* and Xu Gan's *Zhon-glun* in the late (Eastern) Han period.

One major weakness of Hansen's argument is that he does not consider philosophical thought in the Han and thus is unable to explain *why* we see such a shift in the Han. Why is there suddenly a concern with truth, if concern with such a concept was absent in earlier Chinese thought due to the structure of the language? Did the language suddenly change? Such a recognition of problems surrounding a concept of truth would be truly unheard of in the history of phil-osophical thought if there had not been a concept of truth "in the philosophical air" prior to the Han. It would be almost as amazing as developing Newtonian mechanics in a culture lacking the concept of a distinction between appearance and reality. So many things would need to happen philosophically to make Newton possible that it would strain plausibility beyond anything acceptable to hold that his mechanics appeared spontaneously out of such a cultural milieu. The same is the case for truth in the Han dynasty. Given the sophisticated ways in which Han philosophers think about truth and their debates surrounding this concept, it is almost inconceivable that no concept of truth whatsoever existed in Chinese thought just before their time. As brilliant as the Han philosophers were, they could not have single-handedly developed a concept of truth where there was none before, and advanced an understanding of this concept within the few dozen years after the rise of the Han Empire. There must have been a concept of truth in play before the Han. In later chapters (especially 5 and 6), I look carefully at Han philosophy, to show the extent and sophistication of their thinking about truth, and also to find the *roots* of this thinking in pre-Han philosophy. The theories of truth developed in the Han all rely on concepts and theories that were discussed in the pre-Qin period.

For example, the Eastern Han philosopher Wang Chong explicitly claimed that his project was one of uncovering *shi* 實, as specifically a feature of *yan* 言 (saying, teaching, statement, what is said), and rejecting *yan* that have the property of *xu* 虛 (emptiness). Wang's is clearly a truth concern, and not one that popped up overnight. We cannot explain this concern by Buddhist influ-ence, because during the first century CE when Wang Chong wrote, there *was no* Buddhist influence in China. This did not begin until the twilight years of the Han and more so in the Wei-Jin period in the third century CE. And a similar discussion of the truth value of *yan* can be found in even earlier work. The *Huainanzi*, from the second century BCE, also evaluates *yan* 言 in terms of *shi* 實 and *xu* 虛.[40] This concern with *yan* and evaluation of it in terms of concepts that clearly look like truth values could not have suddenly arisen with the Han dynasty. Liu An's authors in compiling the *Huainanzi* drew on earlier sources, and aimed to create a philosophical system that the intended audience, namely Emperor Wu, would have understood. It is hard to imagine that innovation of a novel concept of truth where none had existed before would have lent itself to being understood by anyone, let alone the emperor. Thus, in evaluating the concept of truth in early Chinese thought, it is essential to examine the concepts of *shi* 實 and *xu* 虛 as they apply to *yan* 言. Yet Hansen neglects these issues.

Hall and Ames on Truth

David Hall and Roger Ames also famously reject that early Chinese thinkers were concerned with truth in anything like the way Western philosophers conceive of it. In a chapter considering truth in early China in their book *Thinking From the Han*, they consider what they think would be necessary for there to be a "Western-style" conception of truth at play in early Chinese texts.[41] The way they begin their considerations seems to me to already poison the well, as they take certain conceptions of truth to be uniquely Western notions, and they claim to look to Chinese texts to see if they can find a "Western-style notion of truth." Why, I wonder, should they be doing this? If one fails to find a concept sufficiently Western, or an understanding sufficiently close to the variety of understandings of truth found in the Western traditions, why does this mean that Chinese thinkers did not have a concept of truth? This seems to unfairly make Western traditions the measure and arbiters of the concept of truth and what counts as truth. This is a dubious practice, if truth is truly general and foundational. To make the claim that it is also "Western-based" is to thereby deny its generality and basicness.

In a number of ways, Hall and Ames' considerations overlap with those of Hansen. They appear to take pragmatic concern as undermining the possibility of "semantic" concern or truth concern, similarly to Hansen, though, unlike Hansen, they admit the possibility of pragmatic theories of truth in Chinese thought. They do not reject the idea that early Chinese philosophers had a concept of truth, but they understand this concept as defined and constrained by pragmatic concerns. They seem, however, like Hansen, to have a view of the concept of truth that takes it to be necessarily linked to a not only correspondence theory, but also particular types of correspondence theory. They seem uncomfortable referring to the kind of "pragmatist truth" that they think exists in early Chinese thought as "truth" at all. Thus they seem to have an unsettled or ambivalent position concerning truth in early Chinese thought. They're committed to it, while at the same time resist it.[42] This can be seen when they write:

> The historical rejection of the Mohists and Logicians as contributors to cultural orthodoxy of classical China, along with the gradual submergence of Buddhist speculations in the Confucian synthesis of the post-Han period, are instances of the general rejection of the cultural requisites for a concept of theory of truth.[43]

This is strange for a few reasons. First, they seem to claim that the Mohists and the School of Names thinkers *did* work with a concept of truth, or at least offered the "cultural requisites" necessary for such a theory. Rejection by the "orthodoxy" notwithstanding, if this is so why does it not count as "Chinese"? This seems to suggest a very strange view in which an entire culture and philosophical traditions of this culture are painted with the broad brush defined by whatever is determined (for unknown reasons) as orthodoxy. If we adopt such a view, this would mean that the concerns of the Buddhists were nonexistent in "Indian thought" before the conquests of Ashoka, and then again became nonexistent with the Hindu revival. Were not the Mohists and School of Names part of "Chinese thought"? These are just some of the problems we get into when we attempt to give single-focused accounts of an entire complex of philosophical traditions. Imagine trying to characterize how *philosophers* have thought worldwide through history. The situation for trying to singly characterize Chinese thought is not much easier.

Also, the above quote shows that Hall and Ames read the Mohists as concerned with at least some of the foundational issues that might lead to the adoption of a theory of truth (they think), unlike Hansen who understands the Mohist concerns very differently, as pragmatic in the same way that Hall and Ames think the rest of Chinese thought is. Reading early Chinese philosophers *in general* as pragmatists (or any other particular kind of theorist) seems to me highly problematic. Certainly *some* were,[44] but there is little evidence that all of them were, even in the pre-Han period (any more than there is evidence that all early Greek philosophers were metaphysical dualists about worlds *a la* Plato). And there is a great deal of evidence that different philosophers held sometimes very different theories of truth, just as we find in the Western traditions. Early China was no more an intellectual monolith than any particular period in Western intellectual history.

Hall and Ames begin with consideration of a number of theories of truth adopted in Western philosophy, and investigate the early Chinese texts to see if there are parallels. Hall and Ames claim that early Chinese philosophers did not think of the world as a "bounded whole" with which statements can cohere or to which statements can correspond, and which is completely determined. They write:

> Since the classical Chinese have no important regard for systematically complete contexts such as referenced by the "Cosmos," the "Mind of God," the "Laws of Nature," or the "Repository of Eternal Ideas," all contexts, both textual and social, must be immanent and, in a special sense, open-ended.[45]

This is a curious statement for a few reasons. If this is true, then much of the criticism of schools such as the Confucians and Mohists in the *Zhuangzi* cannot be made sense of. If we switch out "classical Chinese" for "Daoist/ Zhuangist" in the above quote, Hall and Ames *may* be right (though I offer a very different interpretation of Zhuangists in chapter 5). But given that this position was advanced *in opposition* to some perceived opponent who did not hold such a view, how do we make sense of this? Were the Zhuangists' opponents simply fictional, imagined possibilities of what one *might* hold? And even if so, this would suggest that they were aware of the possibilities of seeing the world as a discrete and "closed" whole, even if they disagreed with this position.

Hall and Ames argue for a kind of coherence view in early Chinese philosophy, but one that is based not on coherence between propositions accepted or believed, but instead between rituals that enjoin certain action.[46] Coherence is a matter of having or adopting a coherent set of rituals such that one can act in a consistent manner. But this cannot be all there is to a ritual coherence view, because there are many different ways to make actions or rituals consistent, but early philosophers such as Confucians insist on a particular collection of rituals as necessary for self-cultivation and social harmony. A vicious set of rituals can be as coherent as any other, yet presumably the Confucian would reject these.

Hall and Ames argue (similarly to Hansen) that early Chinese philosophers did not have a concept of "logical truth," on the grounds that they made no distinction between appearance and reality (at least in terms of belief). This is similar to a view that we also find in Hansen's work. It seems to me shocking to hold that any culture does not recognize an appearance-reality distinction. How could one make sense of misinterpretation of perception (as the early Chinese did)? And how could we make sense at all of the famous "story of the butterfly" from chapter 2 of the *Zhuangzi*? If no one holds a distinction between appearance and reality, Zhuangzi's criticism is completely empty. He is arguing against no one. And not only this, even if we completely ignore the intended point of the passage, the distinction he draws should make no sense at all if there is no appearance-reality distinction in early Chinese philosophy. He formulates (discovers, in fact!) a distinction that no one holds. The butterfly passage runs thus:

昔者莊周夢為胡蝶，栩栩然胡蝶也，自喻適志與！不知周也。俄然覺，則蘧蘧然周也。不知周之夢為胡蝶與，胡蝶之夢為周與？周與胡蝶，則必有分矣。此之謂物化。

Previously I dreamed that I was a butterfly, flying around like a butterfly, just like I was following my own intentions. I did not know I was Zhuang Zhou. When I woke, I realized I was Zhuang Zhou. Now I don't know whether I'm Zhuang Zhou who dreamed of being a butterfly, or a butterfly dreaming I'm Zhuang

*Zhou. Between Zhuang Zhou and a butterfly, there must be a difference. This is
called the transformation of things.*[47]

One might argue that there is no distinction drawn or implied here between
appearance and reality, but rather between two things, Zhou and a butterfly.
But this reading cannot be sustained, for a couple of reasons. If the distinction
(*fen* 分) being discussed here is simply between Zhou and the butterfly, there
should be no problem in making it. The distinction can be easily drawn, and
in fact *is* drawn when Zhuang Zhou claims to have been a butterfly and had
not known that he was Zhou and then Zhou and not knowing he dreamed of
being a butterfly. There is no danger of mixing up the two entities here, Zhou
and the butterfly. So it does not make sense that the passage would refer to
the distinction between them as problematic or important if it is only between
these two entities.

What *would* be problematic and create an issue needing to be discussed?
If it is an issue of *identity* (which one is he?), it makes sense to consider the
distinction between Zhou and the butterfly, as the suggestion generally is that
one cannot both be human and a butterfly. This also would make sense of the
"transformation of things" claim at the end of the passage. But the claim here
is that Zhou did not know whether Zhou dreamed of the butterfly or the butterfly dreamed of Zhou—he speaks of making a distinction in terms of *this*.
There has to be a distinction between the two, in which one is the "real" and
one is the "merely dreamed." That is, making the distinction will take one
of the states (Zhou or the butterfly) to cohere with reality or the way things
"really are," while the other is somehow imaginary or illusory. Whether
we read this, as I think we should, as a rhetorical statement suggesting that
we *should not* and need not make a distinction between the two states as to
which is "real," it really does not matter how we read this last section. Even
if we take Zhuangzi completely seriously as claiming that there indeed needs
to be a distinction made between the two, this shows the understanding of
a distinction between appearance and reality. If my own reading is correct,
Zhuangzi is attributing this perception of the appearance/reality distinction
to his (likely Confucian) opponents, or alternatively he himself accepts the
distinction. Either way, the passage does seem to show that such a distinction was known in early Chinese philosophy, and accepted as legitimate by
someone, either Zhuangzi or his perceived opponents. After all, Zhuangzi had
no reason to argue against views no one would hold.

Hall and Ames offer a view of "Chinese thought" in general that seems to
render completely inexplicable much of what is in the *Zhuangzi*. Not because
it misses the thought of the *Zhuangzi*—indeed, Hall and Ames' position is
more in line with the spirit of this text than many others in early China—but
because if they are right about Chinese thought as a whole, the *Zhuangzi*'s

criticisms of other philosophers and schools who *do not* hold similar views do not make sense at all. If the entire Chinese tradition thought like Zhuangzi, then *who* exactly was Zhuangzi criticizing?

This puts in relief the problematic tendency in some interpreters to argue for blanket claims about "Chinese thought" as a whole. This is in part what gets us into the problems outlined in the work of Hansen, Hall and Ames, and others. If "Chinese thought" is monolithic, then we need only find one representative, through which we can understand the entirety of the tradition. Both Hansen and Hall and Ames seem to get things right concerning *one* thinker, but reading the rest of the traditions as mirroring these thinkers is where they get into trouble. Hansen, for example, gives a plausible reading of the Mohists (although it's not true to say they had *no* concept of truth), but his analysis breaks down when he attempts to read "pre-Han" Chinese philosophy in general in this Mohist way. He calls his view a "Daoist" theory (in Hansen 1992), but it appears to me much closer to Mohism than Daoism. As regards Hall and Ames, on the other hand, if we extract their claims about the "Chinese tradition" in general and replace that with "Daoism/Zhuangism," we seem to get things right. Zhuangzi *is* making many of the claims that they suggest are inherent in the Chinese tradition. The problem is that many other philosophers in schools in early Chinese philosophy are not.

We should, I think, resist the urge to make overarching claims about a so-called "Chinese thought," in just the way we would never think about making such claims about "Western thought." Scholars of ancient Greek philosophy would not dream of discussing the "ancient Greek" way of thinking about the world—they generally would break it into the Platonic and Aristotelian ways of thinking, which are very different. And this is not to mention the very different still Hellenistic thinkers of later years. Early Chinese thought, like Western thought, is diverse and complex. There is little to be gained from a consideration of the features of "Chinese thought" in general, because there are so many strands, traditions, and differences within it. Chinese philosophers disagreed and had different concepts, assumptions, and worldviews as much as Western, Indian, Native American, or any other kinds of philosophers.

Let's take a further look at Hall and Ames' reasoning here. They write:

> Correspondence theories of truth require that a proposition must be independent from the state of affairs it characterizes. On the one hand, this argues for the transcendence of principles and, on the other hand, for the dualistic relations of propositions and states of affairs. Without such independence, both in the sense of dualism and transcendence, nothing like logical truth may be formulated.[48]

There are some clear problems with this. It turns out that there are a host of theories of truth that do not rely at all on any notion of "states-of-affairs."

Hall and Ames here seem to identify correspondence theories of truth with "logical truth," holding that if there cannot be correspondence theories of truth, there cannot be "logical truth," perhaps taken as truth *simpliciter*. This is an assumption that we sometimes see among correspondence theorists, but it's wrong. This view arises from a failure to recognize the distinction between correspondence *theories* of truth and the correspondence *intuition*— the latter of which all kinds of noncorrespondence theorists can (and do) accept. Regardless of what one thinks about the correspondence intuition (some want to do away with it as well), accepting it does not entail accepting a correspondence theory, and lack of correspondence theory does not entail lack of acceptance of the correspondence intuition. Indeed even the deflationist about truth, who does away with a truth "property" altogether, can accommodate the correspondence intuition (or so they claim).[49]

Hall and Ames also claim that *literal* language has precedence over *figurative* language in Western texts, and that such a situation is a prerequisite for truth. They write:

> Both correspondence and coherence theories of truth require some means of characterizing propositional forms as univocal or unambiguous. This would be possible only if there were an unambiguous way of indicating the literalness of a proposition. For this to be so, literal language must have precedence over figurative or metaphorical language. This means that, in addition to richly vague sorts of language associated with images and metaphors, there must be concepts as candidates for univocal meaning.[50]

While they may be right about this, the problem is that they associate this primacy of literal language with Western languages like Greek,[51] and deny it of classical Chinese. This seems to me odd. Whether one's language is literal or figurative has mainly to do not with the syntax or semantics of the language itself, but with authorial intention. Ancient Greek, German, English, and Portuguese can be used figuratively as much as classical Chinese, and there is no preference or precedence for one use *built in* to the language. If there were, this would be to say that the poetic imagery of Homer, Sappho, or Pindar was secondary usage of the language and the more precise usage of Aristotle was primary. But even this has a problem. Aristotle's language is far from the precision of formal logic, and there are to this day ongoing interpretive debates about issues in his works because of the ambiguity of even basic predicatory terms like *esti* ("is"). This certainly doesn't speak well for the precision of this language, and no other language is in a better position. As for images and metaphors—what devices does *any* language have for marking when one is using such figurative language, other than just baldly claiming "I am using figurative language now." Absent this, we only understand whether something is literal or figurative by understanding the intentions of the author, understanding the basic plausibility of the claims being made (if we read a passage telling us pigs are flying through the air on blue magic, this generally gives us an indication—as we try to read charitably—that it is not meant literally), or other such nonlinguistic means. Indeed, this is just the way that religious believers and scholars of religious literature determine what, in their texts, to take as literal and what as figurative. There is nothing in the Hebrew or Greek languages to tell a reader of the Bible, for example, whether something is to be meant as an image and a metaphor or as literally the case. This presumably is why there are such major disagreements over the issue of just how we should read certain controversial passages. The book of Genesis recounts God's creation of the world in seven days. Is that figurative or literal language? Part of the reason why many read this as figurative is the basic plausibility problem one has if reading it literally. That is, before the creation of the world, how does it make sense to talk of a *day*, which is defined by the earth's rotation? Are there "God-days," and are these God-days roughly equivalent to earth-days? Do they mean it took what would have been the length of time of seven days had days existed then? And why would it take a supreme being this amount of time (or any amount of time at all) to construct the world? These are the difficulties that lead many to conclude that the passage should be read figuratively rather than literally. There is nothing in the original Hebrew language, or the language of the Greek or English translations, that necessitates such a reading.

On the other side of the coin, there is nothing about the classical Chinese language that is necessarily figurative or that privileges a figurative over a literal reading. When Xunzi says something like 人之性惡，其善者偽也 ("human nature is evil, and its becoming good is a matter of deliberate effort"),[52] it is certainly meant literally, and this literal meaning is neither secondary, parasitic on figurative meanings, nor is there anything in the language itself that tips us off to this literal meaning. If the language were primarily figurative, we would need some linguistic sign that this is to be read literally, or some other suggestion from Xunzi. We read this literally simply because it seems within the realm of plausibility, seems like something someone may be committed to, is not outlandish or clearly fictional, and it seems to fit with the intentions of someone who we already know is a Confucian moralist. On the other hand, when we read the *Daodejing's* claim 天地不仁，以萬物為芻狗 ("heaven and earth are not benevolent—they take the myriad things as ritual straw dogs"),[53] there is nothing in the language itself to mark this as figurative. The reason we generally do so is that it makes little sense on a literal reading—the world cannot literally take bits of itself, trees, humans, other animals, houses, etc., dress them up in ceremonial garb, put them on an altar, perform a ritual, then throw them away or burn them after the ritual is over. This impossibility, just like in the case of the seven days of creation in the book of Genesis, is what marks this as figurative or nonliteral, not any feature of the language. One might, if one was in the grips of a powerful delusion, put forward such a claim in exactly this wording and mean it literally. But given the principle of charity that we all generally operate with in daily life (that is, we generally try to make sense as best we can of the claims of another on the assumption that they are normal persons sufficiently like ourselves), we will read *Daodejing* 5 as figurative, unless we had independent reason to believe that the author meant this literally. What might such reasons consist of? It certainly would not be any feature of the language itself. That is, we could not determine whether this was meant figuratively or literally by looking more closely at the language. The only way we could determine it would be the same way we would determine it if it had been written in Greek, Sanskrit, Russian, or Amharic. Maybe we discover that the author was a well-known madman in the community, or that he was a fiction writer. This might lead us to read the passage literally. Knowing that the author of the passage was attempting to do philosophy or make a broader point about behavior and thriving, however, tells us that this ought to be read figuratively. And all of us, when we approach the *Daodejing*, approach it with the understanding that this is an ancient philosophical/religious text.

How would a person who knew classical Chinese but was completely ignorant of ancient Chinese thought approach this text? What would they think about it? This situation is almost impossible in today's world, as anyone with knowledge of classical Chinese must have gained it *through* a study of such texts, and there is a rich historical background already in place that can't be avoided. But we can *imagine* such a case, and what might be plausible in it. We have no reason to think that such a person would not *first* try to read the *Daodejing*'s claims as literal, until they could no longer make sense of them as such. This is part of the inherent principle of charity. In order to successfully communicate with one another, we have to assume that the person we communicate with understands things roughly as we do and is being straightforward when they tell us something. This is no less the case with texts than it is with face-to-face conversation. We might imagine that after reading a few passages of the *Daodejing*, the reader would begin to realize that much of the language was figurative. But again, it is not plausible to think that this conceptually innocent reader would make this determination based on any features of the Chinese language, but rather would make it because of the inability to make sense of the text in a literal way. And this is exactly the way we distinguish literal from figurative statements in *any* language.

Hall and Ames consider the extent to which there could be something like a *coherence* theory of truth at work in early Chinese thought. Although they think that something like coherence is at play, they deny that there is anything like a theory of *truth* based in this coherence. For such a theory of truth, they argue, an objective world representing a "closed" (and perhaps unchanging) system is necessary.[54] There is no conception of such a world in early Chinese thought, they claim. Instead, what is taken as sufficiently basic are a set of *traditions* and rituals, and coherence should be thought of in terms of the coherence of novel ways of practice with these traditions.[55] The problem with this is that if this is the case (which I do not think it is), it seems not so much like a coherence theory of truth is being rejected, but that "reality" here is simply construed as the base tradition, which itself is unchanging, objective, and certainly in that sense represents a complete and "closed" system—just the kind of thing Hall and Ames claim the early Chinese had no conception of. Why wouldn't such a tradition, accepted as basic and foundational, count as "reality" for these thinkers? And if it can, then it looks like we have no reason to deny the possibility of a coherence theory of truth in early China with the tradition, rather than "the world" (whatever that is) as the base with which statements, rituals, or whatever is evaluated as true, must cohere.

It is perhaps for this and other reasons that Hall and Ames seem to recognize that they are on shaky ground. They tentatively endorse the idea that there was a conception (not *conceptions*, mind you, but *a* conception) of truth in early China, roughly a pragmatist conception. But they are ambivalent about calling this "truth." They write:

> It is doubtful that we should call this an understanding of truth in the more classical senses of the term. For the pragmatist surely shares with the Chinese thinker a disinterest in the cultural requisites that underlie classical theories of truth.[56]

What do they mean here by "classical theories of truth"? If by this they mean correspondence theory, then to deny this of pragmatist thinkers would be true, but also trivial. But it seems question begging to say that any conception of truth other than that of correspondence theory is *not* truth "in the classical sense." There are lots of different ways of thinking about truth. What makes correspondence theory "classical" in ways that other theories are not? It's not altogether clear that anyone before Bertrand Russell ever accepted correspondence theory (rather than the correspondence intuition) anyway. We have to keep distinct correspondence theory and the correspondence intuition. The intuition does not entail a particular theory, and is not part of a theory—it's part of our basic understanding of the *concept* of truth. Insofar as there are pragmatist thinkers in China, as in the West, they have particular theories of truth that of course differ from correspondence theories and lots of other kinds. But it is not clear at all that they mean anything different by "truth" and have a different *concept* of truth than any other philosopher.

Hall and Ames, then, are in a somewhat tentative position when it comes to truth. They seem to have some commitment to a version of truth that they nonetheless identify uniquely with Chinese thought, and so are hesitant to call it "truth" due to associations with a so-called Western concept.

One feature that all of the arguments rejecting truth in China have in common, especially those of Hansen, Hall and Ames, and Munro (as well as perhaps Graham) is that they deny the kind of intellectual diversity in early China that we see in every other culture and intellectual tradition. For these scholars, "the Chinese" have *a* way of thinking about (or not thinking about) truth. This seems to me implausible, given the massive disagreements and very different systems and even radically different ways of looking at the world that we see in early Chinese philosophy. Any overarching theory of "Chinese thought" that purports to make sense of the shared views of, say, Xunzi and Zhuangzi, must be thin indeed. If one were to write a book on the features genuinely shared between them (of philosophical interest, not trivial facts like "humans breathe"), that would have to be a very short book. And since this is the case, even if we *can* determine some overarching features of "Chinese thought" (which I doubt that we can), how illuminating could that possibly be, given the diversity within early Chinese philosophy?

Proponents of Truth

While the positions of Hansen and Hall and Ames are the best-known "anti-truth" positions in English-language scholarship in Chinese philosophy, there are an increasing number of scholars, in more recent literature, who take a different view. We might call these scholars representatives of the "pro-truth" camp, and the number of such scholars is growing. While these scholars all have different positions concerning what the theory or theories of truth in early Chinese philosophy *are*, they are all in agreement that early Chinese thinkers did in fact have a concept of truth and did theorize about this concept.

A number of philosophers disagree with the views of the scholars discussed above concerning both truth and argumentation in early Chinese philosophy. While these views all more or less echo my own, in this section I spend some time looking at the details and differences between these responses, in order to give an account of different views concerning truth in early Chinese philosophy among contemporary scholars.

Bryan Van Norden argues that a truth concern in a basic sense, in terms of "getting things right," is necessary for any intellectual project like that of the early Chinese philosophers.[57] They could not have gone on in even a pragmatist fashion without a concept of what makes an assertion (however understood linguistically) correct, and this is just what we mean by truth. I think that part of what Van Norden is gesturing to here, but does not fully flesh out, is the fact that truth is a basic, foundational, and general concept, necessary at the very beginnings of the intellectual project to be able to formulate it at all. We have to have a way of distinguishing what is right from wrong, acceptable from unacceptable, or there are no grounds for rejecting anything whatsoever, including completely meaningless strings of language.

A number of philosophers see the Chinese "truth" concern as surrounding the concept of *dao* in general, and offer interpretations of truth theory in early Chinese thought as connected to considerations of *dao* found in the early material. While certain aspects of the concept of *dao* in *some* early Chinese thinkers involves aspects of a more general truth concept, and theories of philosophical method are even more often connected to the attempt to attain *dao* (*de yi* in the *Huainanzi*, for example), I do not agree with these scholars that the *dao* concern in early Chinese thought in general can be taken as parallel to the truth concern in Western philosophical thought. Here I briefly outline and appraise some of the arguments offered by the philosophers in question.

A. C. Graham gives voice to the idea that concern with *dao* in early Chinese philosophy plays a fundamental grounding role akin to that of truth in the Western tradition, writing:

> [Early Chinese philosophers'] whole thinking is a response to the breakdown of the moral and political order which had claimed the authority of Heaven; and the crucial question for all of them is not the Western philosopher's "what is the truth?" but "where is the Way?" the way to order the state and conduct personal life.[58]

While Graham is certainly right that most early (pre-Han) Chinese philosophers were concerned primarily with political and personal conduct, this concern did not preclude a concern with truth (indeed this is one of the core claims I defend in this book) any more than the Stoic central concern with *ataraxia* (peace of mind) ruled out their concern with truth, or than Aristotle's central concern with attainment of *eudaimonia* (thriving) through political art ruled out his concern with truth. Nonetheless, a number of philosophers have cited (and others have doubtlessly been influenced by) Graham's position, seeing the *dao* concern as trumping any truth concern (insofar as there is one in the work of the early Chinese philosophers at all, which we have seen that some deny).

Cheng Chung-ying identifies *dao* with reality or a ground of reality, on which we can determine semantic notions.[59] At the same time, as a number of other philosophers and interpreters do, Cheng denies that there is a concern in early Chinese thought with a distinction between appearance and reality, a consideration that he attributes to ancient Greek thought.[60] Cheng develops a conception of *dao* on the basis of what he claims can be found in *Daodejing* that can serve as basis for an overall "Chinese" understanding of *dao* as the foundation of truth, or the *reality* determinative of true statements. One clear difficulty here is that, even if Cheng is correct about the *Daodejing*, he does not offer any evidence for the claim that we should take this to be a general "Chinese" outlook rather than a particular early Daoist one. There was deep disagreement concerning key concepts in early China, and *dao*, along with other key notions such as *xing*, *tian*, and *de* (among others), was one of the most contentious. Indeed, the more fundamental, abstract, and difficult a concept was, the more likely there was to be widespread and fundamental disagreement about it. This is no different in the Western tradition or any other traditions.

Part of the problem with attributing "*dao* concern" to early Chinese philosophers in general is that it requires essentialization of the early Chinese tradition. It is no coincidence that we find in authors who endorse the "*dao* approach" claims about "Chinese ways of thinking." To claim that the *dao* concern characterizes early Chinese philosophy and that early Chinese philosophers envision *dao* as the ground of reality is to assume that all early Chinese thinkers understood *dao* in the same way, and saw it as playing the same role in their overall theories. This is a highly problematic claim. Not only did early Chinese thinkers disagree among one another on *dao*, but they used it in ways that suggest that they did not always even *mean* the same thing as one another when they wrote about "*dao*." Even if we concentrate only on those philosophers who can be plausibly interpreted as understanding *dao* as metaphysical or at least linked to ontology in some way (whether deter-minative, grounding, etc.), it is unclear whether we can construct a shared conception of how to understand *dao* and how it connects to justification of assertoric language.

Bo Mou's investigation of the "*dao* concern" as parallel with truth is more careful here. He specifically focuses on early Daoist views of *dao*, rather than essentializing Chinese thought and presenting the entire tradition as having a shared coherent position.[61] Mou argues that the Daoist concern with *dao* and that with truth in Western thought are in essence the same concern. The way this concern is expressed and understood, however, differs. One major difference is the possibility of the human agent being the bearer of truth on the Daoist position, unlike the "Western" position that takes statements or other linguistic entities to be truth-bearers. The reason this can be the case, according to Mou, is that the Daoist views the agent as the source of belief, action, etc. which can be in whatever relevant sense in line with (correspond-ing to?) *dao*.[62]

WHAT IT MEANS TO HAVE A CONCEPT OF TRUTH

As pointed out above, truth is a basic, foundational, and general concept in human thought, and as such it must be at the ground of not only our philosophical traditions, but also thought in general. All languages have some way of marking a statement as *being the case* or *not being the case*, and likewise all languages have ways of making statements. This is all that is needed for truth, and this necessitates truth.

If we think about truth in a very narrow sense, such that it corresponds (no pun intended) with a particular theory of truth, we are not only begging the question against other truth theories, but we are also neglecting the sense in which truth is general and fundamental. Regardless of what the correct theory of truth is, the account that fills out the theory, it is still the case that everyone holds a general, perhaps unreflective, or perhaps just pre-theoretical, concept of truth—and it is *this* that we have to mean when we are discussing the concept of truth in itself—that is, if we take truth to be truly foundational, general, and informative. If we hold the ideal of the ancient Greeks, in which philosophy is the search for truth, which is taken as good in its own right, and even if we have any other view that truth is *normative,* that is, that truth has built-in value, then we cannot see truth as merely a linguistic tool of use only in Western languages. Any such concept with the features that we attribute to truth, especially generality and normativity, would have to go beyond this, and be something that is understood (even if implicitly) by every human culture and tradition. Thus, a consideration of the very features of the concept of truth that make us so eager to pursue truth or truths in the first place also privileges a view in which the *assumption* must be that all philosophical traditions have a concept of truth, and our job as comparative philosophers becomes to uncover what those concepts are and how they are differently understood in different philosophical traditions.

To say that all philosophical traditions have a concept of truth is not to say that they all think about truth in the same way, any more than sharing a concept of truth would commit any given philosophers to the same *theory* of truth. We need not here even make a distinction between *thick* and *thin* concepts[63] to explain how traditions can have the same concept yet very different understandings of them. We need not do so in part because the concept of truth, as we have already stipulated, is sufficiently general, basic, and foundational. It is *already* a thin concept wherever it is held, and can be no more than this. What may differ between accounts of truth are *theories* of truth—explanations of what makes a linguistic entity true, possession of what property makes something true, or performing what function makes something true. Part of the issue here is that the *meaning* of "true"—whether we think of it in English or any other equivalent concept in other languages and traditions, should be of a general, basic, and thinly described concept. Our theories of truth will offer a robust account of the concept, but will not change the basic meaning of "true," and will not add complexity to the concept itself. An analogy is the concept of *time*. Every culture on earth has a concept of time, as we all live in time, and understand what it is to move through time. The concept itself is basic and general. Different *theories* of time, however, will offer very different views of related issues, including what causes time, how to understand how it passes or moves, how it relates to other concepts, etc. We may all share the concept of time without sharing theories of time. And to claim that any culture has no concept of time based on their lack of theories that look very much, or anything at all, like theories of time we are more familiar with or that are held in Western traditions, is to completely miss the boat concerning the generality and basicness of the concept of time. We should much sooner abandon the notion that theories of time are constrained by the options available in Western thought than the notion that all human cultures and traditions have a concept of time. How could one live in the world without a concept of time? Things are much the same for truth. We ought to *begin* with the assumption that there is a concept of truth in Chinese philosophy as well as every other tradition, and move from there to the consideration of perhaps the very different ways these traditions think about truth. When we can find no understanding of truth similar to those we are familiar with in our investigation of a thinker or tradition, it is far more likely that this thinker or tradition simply thinks about truth very differently from the ways we are used to than that they don't have a concept of truth. We should always begin with the most likely explanation for something and only move to more exotic ones when these explanations have been ruled out.[64] Surely it is more likely that one thinks about truth very differently than you than that they do not have a concept of truth. Hansen, Hall and Ames, and others have failed to rule out the most likely explanation.

The claim that early Chinese philosophers did not have a conception of a Russellian correspondence theory of truth is unproblematic and unsurprising (and maybe even uninteresting). But most early Chinese philosophers (I cannot claim to speak for all of them) had both a *concept* of truth and a variety of *theories* of truth. Some of these theories looked somewhat like the Russellian correspondence theory, though none of them I think came very close to this. All of them accepted the correspondence *intuition*, as does generally everyone who takes seriously a concept of truth. In the chapters to follow, I investigate how early Chinese philosophers conceived of truth, both in outlining a cluster of concepts related to truth, and considering the variety of theories of truth on offer in early Chinese philosophy, some consistent with, and some very different from, theories of truth found in the West or in India.

OTHER SENSES OF TRUTH

Part of what is at issue here is just *what kind* of truth theory we are talking about. While when we discuss "truth" in contemporary analytic philosophical circles, it is generally understood that we mean narrowly the concept of the value of an assertoric linguistic entity, captured by attachment of the predicate <is true>; even in English this is but one of the numerous ways that we use the term "true." Perhaps we might say that these are simply different terms said in the same way, simply homophonous terms that are nonetheless distinct. But this is not the case. The different senses of truth relate to a single concept, and users of the English language would generally recognize the truth discussed in all of these contexts as being the *same* concept, rather than distinct ones. Perhaps we are confused about this. Maybe they are distinct concepts but we run them together for some reason. But it is more likely, especially given how foundational and basic truth is, that philosophers are the ones "getting it wrong," that our concerns with truth are only a concern with *one aspect* of truth. And it may be just this that leads to our confusion concerning the concept. This is certainly something some of the early Chinese philosophers covered here would endorse.

Of course, as we have already seen, there has been a years' long controversy concerning whether there is a concept of truth or theories of truth in early, pre-Buddhist Chinese philosophy. Arguably, there is no term in classical Chinese that corresponds closely to the English term "truth" as used in much of contemporary philosophy of language, as an evaluative term somehow attached to assertoric linguistic entities—whether propositions or sentences. Generally, when we discuss truth as a philosophical concept, we have some sense of this meaning in mind. It has of course not always been this way. While we perhaps associate this narrowly linguistic notion of truth with the Western tradition, it is actually a relatively recent development of philosophy. The Western tradition stretching from Plato through modern existentialist thinkers has included a sense of "truth" as more than just this linguistic evaluative concept, even though we tend to limit it to this now.

Denying a concern with truth in a tradition on the basis that there was no robust concern with evaluative predicates for assertoric linguistic entities, then, is to deny that there was a concern with truth for most of the history of Western philosophy. Or at least to say that much of the discussion of truth was not about truth at all, but something else.

It is noncontroversial that the concept of truth outside of philosophical circles in the West has been understood very differently, and perhaps more in line with earlier Western philosophical conceptions of truth. The from Shakespeare's *Hamlet*, "doubt truth to be a liar," has been used in philosophical discussions of the concept, even lending itself to the title of Graham

Priest's 2005 book on the topic. But even though the Bard does often use "truth" as an evaluative term for statements, often ignored are the evocative nonlinguistic ways in which truth is used in the work of this most foundational of English writers. Truth can mean the genuine, authentic, or meaningful, in human life or reality in general, independently from language. Truth is not only something one can *speak*, but something one can *have*, or *represent*. The Duke of Exeter in *Henry V* praises his lord on parting:

> Farewell, kind lord; fight valiantly to-day; And yet I do thee wrong to mind thee of it, for thou are framed of the firm truth of valour.

Or in *Macbeth*, Malcolm's address to Macduff:

> Child of integrity, hath from my soul
> Wiped the black scruples, reconciled my thoughts
> To thy good truth and honour.[65]

These uses of truth reveal an aspect of the concept in the English language and in the West in general that has generally been neglected or completely ignored in contemporary analytic work on the concept of truth. And this neglect is not due to any inability to access the concept in a rigorous way. This sense of truth is no less tangible and definable than other analytically evaluable concepts like "virtue," "good," or the notorious "being," which contemporary analytic thought has also moved away from. I think it is a mistake for analytic philosophy to give up on these central concepts of truth and being, and argue below that in the early Chinese tradition these multiple senses of truth are linked. Indeed, these senses of truth are linked in the concept itself, and to neglect all but one sense in our investigations will make it impossible for us to understand the nature of truth. I don't want to simply give lip service to this sense of truth and quickly then move on to understanding it as a property of assertoric linguistic entities, as we see in some contemporary work. We should *take this sense seriously*. Even though I spend most of the space in this book dealing with the linguistic sense, then, it is important to understand how early Chinese thinkers understood other senses of truth, and to what extent they saw these other senses as connected to the sense that contemporary analytic philosophers are generally concerned with. This itself can tell us useful things about the concept, and even about whether the way we tend to think about it today is ultimately advisable.[66]

Independently of the issue of the scope of truth, however, we can consider the question of whether traditions like the Chinese tradition have theories of truth where truth is considered as an evaluative linguistic concept. That is, does the Chinese tradition worry about truth in this contemporary linguistic

sense at all? If not, then perhaps while it is not correct to say that the tradition has *no* concept of truth, it may still be accurate to say that they have no
conception of truth as it is understood in contemporary analytic philosophy.
This is still not correct. While there is indeed a much greater emphasis in the
Chinese tradition on the sense of truth discussed by Shakespeare's Duke of
Exeter and Malcolm, there is also some concern with truth as we understand
it in contemporary philosophy. This can be overlooked in analysis of Chinese
philosophy as much as other senses of truth can be overlooked in Western
thought. It is largely with this sense of truth as connected to assertoric
linguistic entities that I am concerned in the following chapters.

NOTES

1. This is not an issue for this book, but the question of the meaning and proper
analysis of indexicals is a major area of contemporary philosophy of language.

2. There are some important issues associated with truth in contemporary analytic
philosophy that I will mainly ignore in this book, simply because the early Chinese
philosophical tradition has nothing (or very little) to say about them. One of these is
the issue of paradox surrounding truth in the philosophy of language, which is a major
area of focus in contemporary philosophy concerning truth.

3. One quick note on conventions in the philosophy of language as practiced in
English-language philosophy departments (for the most part)—we can often treat
English as if it is the privileged language, or is all there is. Intuitions are taken from
English grammar and tested against it, and positions are asserted as plausible or not
based on how well a particular insight fits with the grammar of English. This seems
to me wrong. Even if the *truth* we are looking for is construed narrowly as *truth in
English*, as opposed to *truth in Chinese*, which it is unclear to me that we should want
(and certainly not if we're realists about truth), why take grammatical conventions as
a reliable guide to how operators can work in a language, especially given that grammar changes quite radically over fairly short periods of time, while presumably the
operation of key concepts like truth do not?

4. It is important to note here that "realism" means different things to different people. I take realist theories of truth to be those that hold that there is a robust
metaphysical property associated with the concept of truth. On this understanding,
pragmatism will also turn out to be a realist theory.

5. See Alston 1996. Michael Devitt rejects the idea that certain theories of truth
are connected with (scientific) realism, while he takes himself to defend realism in
general. (Devitt 1984: 5). Notably, Alston had a different conception of "realism"
than the one I use here. He associated realism with something like a correspondence
theory, and would likely be unwilling to extend the category to include pragmatist
theories, for example. My own view is closer to Devitt's.

6. Michael Lynch expresses a position most realists about truth would agree with,
arguing "that truth is objective; that it is good to believe what is true; that truth is

a worthy goal of inquiry; and that truth is worth caring about for its own sake" (Lynch 2005: 4). It is not clear this would be the case for a provincial concept confined to analytic philosophy, especially for those outside the fold. Why would anyone except those few of us in academic philosophy have reason to care about such a concept?

7. Houser and Kloesel 1992: 138.

8. "The opinion which is fated to be ultimately agreed to by all who investigate, is what we mean by the truth" (*Ibid*: 139)

9. I discuss pluralism in more depth in chapter 6, in considering Wang Chong's theory of truth.

10. Both of these approaches are developed by Michael Lynch, in Lynch 2004 and Lynch 2009.

11. This approach is advanced primarily by Crispin Wright in Wright 1992.

12. Hansen's 1985 article "Chinese Language, Chinese Philosophy, and 'Truth'" (Hansen 1985) is still the key representation of his view and the pivotal work in this area around which many of the debates I discuss have formed. He also elaborates on this view in his *A Daoist Theory of Chinese Thought* (Hansen 1992). These works (especially his 1985 article) form the basis of my account of Hansen's position here.

13. Perhaps in part, though he does not mention this, because his thesis would be hard to justify in the light of the Han texts in which truth concerns become more explicit. However, the increasing concern with truth in Han causes overwhelming difficulties for Hansen's analysis anyway, I argue below.

14. MacIntrye first suggests this in *After Virtue* (MacIntyre 1981), but works this out most completely in MacIntyre 1988, in which he distinguishes different traditions within Western thought. There is of course also the issue here of just what it means for something to be a tradition, which I get into in more detail in chapter 7.

15. Hansen uses Peirce's definition of semantic, as opposed to syntactic and pragmatic concerns (Hansen 1985: 495). Saunders (2014) argues that the Later Mohists, for example, clearly had a concern with semantic adequacy.

16. Hansen admits later in his article that there was *some* semantic concern in early Chinese philosophy, but since it was primarily with terms rather than sentences, this precludes a concept of truth.

17. "Truth is the semantic value of sentences and therefore of beliefs" (Hansen 1992: 17).

18. Hansen 1985: 495–496.

19. Indeed, Tarksi takes satisfaction as even more basic than truth, defining truth in terms of satisfaction.

20. Although *ming* did have this sense in classical Chinese as much as in contemporary Chinese languages, this sense of *ming* was not at issue in *zhengming* and *ming-shi* considerations.

21. A number of philosophers later challenged descriptivist theories, on the grounds of problems concerning modality and other issues. Hilary Putnam famously envisioned the possibility of a "twin earth" on which the chemical XYZ plays the exact functional role that water, H20, plays on earth (Putnam 1973, 1975, "Meaning and Reference," "The Meaning of 'Meaning'"). It thus fits the description connected to the term "water," but, Putnam concluded, XYZ is *not* water, because water is H20.

Such criticisms occasioned a move toward non-descriptivist theories such as Saul Kripke's causal theory (Kripke 1980).

22. Interestingly, studies suggest that this is exactly how *contemporary* Chinese people intuitively understand naming and reference. Machery et. al 2004 describes an experiment that suggested the intuitions of East Asians tend more toward descriptivism about reference, while the intuitions of westerners skewed toward causal-historical theories. Dan Robins claims that the Mohists, at least, did *not* think about *ming* in a descriptivist way, at least concerning proper names. He argues that the Mohists saw proper names as differing in their reference. Robins 2012: 369–370.

23. Hansen 1985: 502.

24. Neville, *Ritual and Deference* (Xunzi volume, 67–68).

25. Hansen 1985: 500.

26. A term Bryan Van Norden uses in his discussion of such positions. The lexical fallacy in general is the idea that since there is no "term for" a particular concept in a language, in the sense of a term that can be directly translated as an English equivalent, then there is no corresponding concept. Van Norden offers a humorous example to demonstrate the inadequacy of this reasoning. Hardly any of us know the term "aglet," which refers to the plastic or metal tips at the end of shoelaces. Still, all of us who wear shoes have the concept of such things (Van Norden 2007: 22).

27. Hansen 1985: 501.

28. Hansen 1992: 45.

29. His view that the Han represents a "philosophical dark age" may have something to do with this, but presumably this position could only be founded on the basis of investigating and finding the Han lacking in terms of philosophical development, which Hansen has not done (Hansen 1992).

30. Michael Lynch writes, in the introduction to the section on pragmatism in his collection *The Nature of Truth; Classic and Contemporary Perspectives*: "[William] James also insists that the pragmatist can concur with the correspondence intuition that true ideas agree with reality. The pragmatist, according to James, is not denying this platitude; rather, he is trying to explain the nature of this 'agreement'" (Lynch 2001: 186).

31. Though I argue below, we have reason to reject this as well. Though *some* early Chinese philosophers primarily focus on pragmatics, by no means can we claim that this was the main focus of the early philosophers.

32. Peirce, *How to Make Our Ideas Clear*, Lynch 2001: 199.

33. Peirce, in Lynch 2001: 201, emphasis added.

34. *Ibid*: 206.

35. Hansen 1985: 493.

36. Roughly, any statement can be accepted that passes three tests: proof of acceptance by the sage kings, consistency with the beliefs of the people in general, and effectiveness at bringing about social value—in terms of benefit (*li* 利) if accepted.

37. Almost *exclusively* on the Mohists in his 1985 article.

38. One of my main contentions here, and against Hansen, is that we simply *cannot* ignore the Han in any consideration of the concept of truth in early Chinese philosophy. It is akin to ignoring Hellenistic philosophy in an investigation of the

concept of mental equanimity (*ataraxia*) in ancient Greek and Roman thought, and then determining that the ancient Greeks had no such concept. The parallel here is very close, because although *ataraxia* becomes the major concern only in the Hellenistic period, earlier Greek philosophers did have a conception of it, even if less well developed and less central in their thought.

39. Kwong-loi Shun points out something along these lines: "Individuals moved primarily by practical concerns can still have a reflective view of the relevant subjects that they seek to convey in their discourse, and although their practical concerns might lead to unsystematic presentation of their ideas, this does not preclude the possibility of interesting connections among such ideas" (Shun 1997: 6). Bryan Van Norden also points out similar problems with the view that pragmatic concerns somehow undermine a conception of truth (or argumentation) (Van Norden 2007: 10–15).

40. For example in the following passage from *Jingshenxun*: 眾人以為虛言，吾將舉類而實之。

41. Hall and Ames 1997: chapter 6, "Cultural Requisites for a Theory of Truth in China."

42. Robert Smid notes Hall and Ames' peculiar conception of truth in early Chinese thought in the following way: "For their own part, Hall and Ames have been explicit about their refusal to give up on the notion of truth altogether, but the notion of truth they espouse is distinctly Chinese in character. [. . .] Part of the difficulty in assessing Hall and Ames' work in this respect is that it is not entirely clear what account of truth they espouse in their own philosophic work. At first glance, in the context of their commendation of classical Chinese philosophy as a promising alternative to the shortcomings of contemporary Western philosophy, it would seem that they adopt that alternative in their own work. Yet . . . this does not seem to adequately account for their strong concern to represent Chinese traditions of philosophy (to use their parlance) if not to get those traditions right?" (Smid 2010: 126–127).

43. Hall and Ames 1997: 134.

44. Mohists seem to have somewhat of a pragmatic bent. Confucians are less so than often claimed by Hall and Ames. Although there are many passages in the *Analects* that speak of the primacy of practice, there is very little to justify pragmatist readings in terms of Peirce, James, or Dewey in either the *Analects* or the *Mengzi* and *Xunzi*. Of the three texts, the *Analects* is easiest to read as pragmatic, but the reason for this is likely that the *Analects* is much less explicit about its positions than the *Mengzi* or *Xunzi*. The *Analects* is suggestive where *Mengzi* and *Xunzi* are clear and make arguments. Zhuangists are hard to interpret, but I doubt whether they can be classed as pragmatists in any real sense. Legalist thinkers may be pragmatists to some extent. Hardly any of the Han philosophers is pragmatists.

45. Hall and Ames 1997: 125.

46. *Ibid*: 125.

47. *Zhuangzi "2:29 (Ziporyn), ZZJJ, p. 112–113. For citations from the Zhuangzi, I use the numbering from Brook Ziporyn's translation, as well as the page number from the 3 volume Zhuangzi Jijie (ZZJJ), 2004."* Translations from the Chinese are my own unless otherwise noted.

48. Hall and Ames 1997: 127.

49. Paul Horwich, who endorses a kind of deflationism he calls "minimalism," argues that even his position is consistent with the correspondence intuition—it can be seen as what he calls a "weak correspondence theory." He writes: "[The minimalist view] agrees with Tarski that a full theory of truth should do nothing more than in some way *generalize* that trivial biconditional [<snow is white> is true *iff* snow is white]. It agrees that such an account will implicitly capture the idea that 'truth is correspondence with reality', but with the advantage of not having to resort to the obscure notions of 'correspondence' or 'reality': thus it will qualify, in Jan Wolenski's terms, as a 'weak correspondence theory'." Horwich 2010.

50. Hall and Ames 1997: 136.

51. "In the west literal language has been privileged over figurative language." *Ibid:* 140.

52. First sentence of the *Xing e* chapter of *Xunzi*.

53. *Daodejing* 5.

54. Hall and Ames 1997: 125. See note 41 and accompanying quote above.

55. *Ibid*, p. 125–126.

56. Hall and Ames 1997: 145.

57. Van Norden 2007.

58. Graham 1989: 3.

59. He also associates the concepts of *tian* and *taiji* with this reality (Cheng 2008: 299).

60. Cheng 2008: 299: "This point shows the difference between the Greek way of thinking or the modern European way of thinking which separates reality from appearance, the subjective from the objective, the human from the natural, and the Chinese way of thinking which does not make such a dichotomy." I do not think there is a general "Chinese" way of thinking any more than there is a "Greek" or "European" way of thinking. To accept that there is amounts to denial of the diversity and deep disagreements concerning foundational concepts within each tradition.

61. Mou 2006: 331–332. See also Hansen, "The Metaphysics of Dao", David Hall, "The way and the truth" in *A Companion to World Philosophies,* and "The Import of Analysis in Classical China—A Pragmatic Appraisal" in *Two Roads to Wisdom.*

62. Mou 2006.

63. A distinction coined by Bernard Williams (Williams 1985: 140–143), also used recently by philosophers and sinologists such as Bryan Van Norden (Van Norden 2007) and Aaron Stalnaker (Stalnaker 2007).

64. This reasoning is related to, but not identical to, the famous "Occam's Razor."

65. *Macbeth* IV.3.

66. Correct? True? We see here it becomes extremely difficult when one wades into the issue of truth. Such considerations are what led some to endorse a *primitivist* theory of truth. See Asay 2013.

Chapter 2

Lunyu and Mengzi

In this section of the book (chapters 2 through 6), I investigate a number of texts from the Spring and Autumn Period through the Eastern Han and outline the theories of truth on offer in these texts. As I argued in chapter 1 above, we can profitably take the early Chinese texts to offer different ways of thinking about truth. Although there is a *concept* of truth at work in all early Chinese philosophical texts, not all of them construct theories of truth, and some of them that do only peripherally do so, or construct theories of truth as an inessential part of wider theories of proper action, government, or thought. The texts and thinkers discussed in this chapter, then, are the ones in which I think we can find relatively developed theories of truth, some of which are related to one another, especially within "schools" such as "Confucianism," early Daoism, and later Mohism, which I will treat separately. There may be some who question here why I stick to the "standard" texts for the most part in the pre-Han literature that I discuss. Part of the reason for this is that I hope for this consideration of theories of truth to contribute to debates in scholarship on early Chinese philosophy as well as contemporary theories of truth, and these texts and philosophers are the ones with most philosophical "cache" in contemporary scholarship. These are the texts that philosophers are looking at, working with, and engaging in comparative projects with. Thus it is primarily the theories of truth in these texts that I am concerned with. I want to be clear at the outset that the theories of truth I offer here are not the *only* ones on offer in early Chinese thought. Rather, independent considerations such as the ones I mention above guide my selection of these theories, and space considerations disallow my offering accounts of *all* the available theories of truth in pre-Buddhist Chinese thought.

EARLY CONFUCIANISM AND THE
FOCUS ON NAMES (名 MING)

There is controversy surrounding the question of the identity of the earliest philosophical texts of the Confucian tradition.[1] Traditionally, the *Lunyu*
(Analects) is given this distinction, but this may actually turn out to be a later
text than commonly believed, and it could be texts such as *Mozi* or even
Mengzi. Fortunately for us, the question of temporal priority is not of high-
est importance here. I treat the texts in the traditional ordering, not because
I am committed to this temporal (or other) ordering, but simply as a useful
tool given their traditional ordering. The question of the historical development and relationships between the theories of truth offered in these texts
is an interesting one, and would require much more to be said concerning
their dates of construction in relation to one another. That task, however, is
for another work—here I am concerned mainly with bringing to light and
explaining the theories of truth to be found in each of these texts.

LUNYU (ANALECTS)

The *Lunyu* is famously a difficult work to interpret, as it consists of aphoristic and suggestive statements attributed to Confucius and his students,
which are not always clear or straightforward as we see in texts such as
Mengzi and *Xunzi*. The short passages and sometimes cryptic language of
the *Lunyu* are often consistent with numerous wildly differing interpretations, and this can be seen in both scholarship on the *Lunyu* as well as
the numerous and very different translations of the text.[2] The *Lunyu* lacks
chapters organized around specific topics or argumentative essays as we
see in *Mozi, Xunzi,* and even *Mengzi*. Given the challenge of interpreting
even single passages of the text, let alone any cluster of passages, drawing
a theory of *anything* from the text is a daunting task. Many scholars have
attempted such a task, but in the case of the *Lunyu* this sometimes is reduced
ultimately to the "cherry-picking" of passages open to some particular interpretation to build a theory that may have more (or often less) to actually do
with early Confucian thought.

Part of the difficulty here, in addition to the fragmented and aphoristic
nature of the text, is that the *Lunyu* is almost certainly a *composite* text, constructed from a number of different authors and sources. The brief stories,
quotes, and teachings that make up the *Lunyu* are gathered "rememberings"
of the teachings of Kong Qiu (better known as Kongzi—"Master Kong,"
Latinized as "Confucius") by students, students of students, and other various and sundry people with something to say about "the Master." The text

likely developed over hundreds of years, with a core of passages collected by early generations of students of Confucius, and through later years and additions grew to the text we know today. This likely happened by the late years of the Warring States period or the early Han.[3] While the *Lunyu* is not the only composite text in early Chinese thought (many of the texts of early China were), it is perhaps the most problematic, because what are collected are short passages rather than essays including extended arguments and theories.[4]

Fortunately, in order to uncover how the authors of the *Lunyu* thought about the concept of truth, it is not necessary to have sustained argument in cohesive essays. The *Lunyu* is one of the early Chinese texts in which we do not find a worked-out theory of truth, but in which we can find a number of important clues as to how early Confucians used and thought about the concept of truth. It turns out that, if the *Lunyu* is a preamble to philosophical thought in China, it can also be seen as a preamble to thinking about truth.

There are not a great many passages in the *Lunyu* that one can point to as being unproblematically *about* truth, and if one were to look at the *Lunyu* alone, one would be most justified in agreeing with Hansen about the lack of concern with truth as a concept to be explicitly theorized about in early Chinese philosophy. Nonetheless, we can find that there are some passages in which Confucius or his students say things that suggest certain understandings of truth. That is, while perhaps we don't find any worked-out theories of truth in the *Lunyu*, we *can* find hints and assumptions about truth that can show us how particular intellectual schools in early China thought about (in a general way) truth concepts, in such a way that can help us to understand the more explicit and developed theories of truth that we see in later Confucian (and other) texts. While one could simply list and explain a variety of passages from the *Lunyu*, I think a better way to approach truth in this unique text is through *terms* and their related concepts, discussed in various passages that look like they offer concepts of truth.

One perhaps obvious term that comes to mind is *ran* 然 ("being the case"; "being so"). *Ran* is often used in the *Lunyu* as an affirmation of some statement or a reiteration of some situation. Despite Hansen's claims, it can clearly apply to *yan* 言 ("statements"), as in the following passage:

仲弓問子桑伯子，子曰：「可也簡。」仲弓曰：「居敬而行簡，以臨其民，不亦可乎？居簡而行簡，無乃大簡乎？」子曰：「雍之言然。」

Zhonggong (Ran Yong) asked about Zisang Bozi. The master [Confucius] said, "He is able, he can be concise." Zhonggong said, "Remaining in respectfulness and in practice concise, one draws near to the people. Is this not also acceptable? Remaining concise and in practice concise, does it not reach the great concision?" The master said, "Your statement is true" (yong zhi yan ran).[5]

Here Confucius' final statement is an endorsement of what Ran Yong has just said, in a way that clearly expresses not just that Confucius likes or can accept Yong's statement as something that ought be followed or something consistent with ritual, but as an accurate account of *how things are*. How do we know whether *ran* is intended to be used in this way? The other sense of *ran* mentioned above, reiterating events that have taken place, suggests just this meaning. In *Lunyu* 11.16, in a conversation with his student Zigong, Confucius passes judgment on two other students. He says:

師也過，商也不及。

Shi errs in going too far, while Shang errs in not doing enough.

Zigong's response to this uses the sense of *ran* described above, as he then asks Confucius:

然則師愈與？

Given this is so, is Shi superior?

Ran here is meant to refer to the previous statement made by Confucius, and to treat it as though it were *true*. Assuming the truth of Confucius' statement, Zigong suggests that Shi is superior. Consider here the role that *ran* would play if it were merely an indicator of the acceptability of Confucius' statement in terms of ritual practice. Confucius has made a descriptive claim about what Shi and Shang do—we would have to reread this as a normative claim that "Shi goes too far and this is not proper, Shang does not do enough and this is not proper." Then *ran* used by Zigong would have to be a statement not on the descriptive aspects of Confucius' statement (that Shi goes too far and Shang does not do enough), but instead on the normative claim about the propriety of these acts. It seems implausible here then to read *ran* as something like "acceptability" independent from consideration of truth. And even if we could read *ran* as referring to propriety rather than the way the world is, isn't it still most plausibly read as concerning *truth*? It is simply *moral* truth that would be at issue. There is an important connection between the statements "it is true that Mars is the fourth planet from the Sun" and "it is right that one care for one's parents when they get old." Both *true* and *right* are evaluative terms here. But if Confucius' statement includes this normativity, then Zigong's comment using *ran* is doing something *more* than simply repeating Confucius' statement—it is *confirming* (or here provisionally confirming) Confucius' statement, whether this is a descriptive statement about the world or a normative statement about proper practice. If this is the case, then *ran* here signals an evaluative concept that works much more like the concept of *truth* than that of *rightness*.

Notice that, for example, semantic ascent is possible using "is true" in ways that it is not using "is right." If it is true that Mars is the fourth planet from the sun, then it is also true that it is true that Mars is the fourth planet from the sun. This way of speaking may be awkward, but the concept can work in this way. If it is right to care for parents when they get old, however, it is not the case that it is also right that it is right to care for parents when they get old. Why is this? Partly because "is right" evaluates *acts*, not statements. And so when we ascend from discussion of an act to discussion of statements about acts, we can no longer apply "is right."

Another problem in the *Analects*, or perhaps rather complication, is that *yan* 言 does not always refer to a statement of linguistic entity with assertoric content that can be or fail to be *ran*, but is also sometimes identified with attitudes, ideals, and other norms. In *Lunyu* 15.6, for example, Confucius responds to a question by Zizhang on conducting oneself (*xing* 行) in the following way:

言忠信，行篤敬，雖蠻貊之邦行矣；言不忠信，行不篤敬，雖州里行乎哉？

If your yan *are full of effort and sincere, and your conduct is genuine and respectful, then even if you travel to the land of barbarians, your conduct will hold up. If your* yan *are not full of effort and sincere, and your conduct is not genuine and respectful, then even if you are in your own state, how can your conduct hold up?*

Here, *yan* seems more akin to *xing* 行 (conduct). It is evaluated not in terms of *ran* or any other semantic concept having to do with "being the case," but rather in terms of active and emotive categories. One's *yan* ought to be consistent with efforts suggested by them—such that, for example, when one's *yan* express desire to learn and practice widely, something Confucius talks a great deal about, one's efforts are consistent with this. There is no issue of truth here, at least explicitly. In addition, one's *yan* ought to be sincere, in the sense that they are meant as an accurate portrayal of one's desires, and one is also consistent in their action with these stated desires. Again, there is no clear and explicit focus on truth here, even though one may need a concept of truth in the background to make sense of such a position on *yan*. We cannot conceive of a *sincere yan* if there is not some fact about the individual's actual intentions and whether the *yan* reflect these actual intentions, motivations, desires, etc. And we need the concept of truth to make sense of this connection. Or at least a truth-like concept. About this, however, no one would disagree. Even Hansen's position is that the early Chinese philosophers (like any human thinker) have a folk concept of truth that they use *de re*, but that they simply do not theorize, they have nothing to say *de dicto* about truth. *Lunyu* 15.6 is perfectly consistent with this, as is much else in the *Lunyu*.

What we *do* find in the *Lunyu*, however, is a consideration of *yan* in terms of truth values such as *ran*. It is not only the use of 15.6 that we see in the *Lunyu*, but also that which becomes a much greater focus in later works, especially in the Han period, and which is a major component of a number of theories of truth in early Chinese philosophy.

But there is more to be found in the *Lunyu* concerning truth, and which can show us how, in general, early Chinese philosophers thought about the concept in a general way before clear theories began to be developed.[6]

Probably the most promising, and most controversial, concept in the *Analects* that might offer us some implicit conception of truth is that of the *rectification of names* (*zhengming* 正名). While the theory of rectification of names does not get anywhere near the coverage in the *Analects* that it does in the *Xunzi* (which I discuss below), there are a few passages that may refer to it, either explicitly or in suggestion. The only use of the phrase *zhengming* itself occurs in *Lunyu* 13.3, and all of the references to it are in the context of governing (mainly in Books 12 and 13). It will be useful to look at two passages in particular.

The possibility cannot be ignored here, however, that the passages about governing in the *Lunyu* have nothing to do with *zhengming* at all, and that 13.3 itself was a late interpolation from Xunzi-inspired Confucian scholars.[7] I personally think that we (philosophers) spend too much time and effort worrying about *Lunyu* 13.3, given that it is the only instance of *zhengming* that occurs in the entire text of the *Lunyu*. This obviously does not bode well for its being an important concept in early (pre-Xunzi) Confucianism. The amount of philosophical attention that 13.3 has received is far out of proportion with its position in the text or even with understandings of the Confucian path found in the *Lunyu* itself and other early literature. Confucius' students, associates, and other related thinkers never mention *zhengming* as an essential (or even existent) aspect of the Master's way. It is curious that contemporary philosophers should become so wrapped up with this side concern. My suspicion is that the passage and others like it draw so much philosophical attention because they seem to offer us considerations about language and semantics that we don't find elsewhere in the *Lunyu*. These concerns are of central importance to Western and contemporary philosophers, and we tend to get excited when we find the issues *we* care about in the texts of other traditions. Still, since we are considering here positions on *truth* in early Chinese philosophy, it is essential to look at this *zhengming* position found in the *Lunyu* (both explicit and implicit), as this is the only possibly semantic concept in the *Lunyu* explicitly discussed, rather than simply employed. It is only with *zhengming* that we can hope to find a voiced position concerning something like truth—without this, we are left to piece together the uses of seemingly truth-like terms to flesh out general theories.

The issue of just how we ought to understand the *zhengming* theory, in either the *Lunyu* or *Xunzi*, is controversial (as also discussed in chapter 4). It not even agreed upon that the theory has anything to do with language in particular, rather than regulation of behavior.[8] While I do not wade into this debate here (though I do get into it a bit later in a discussion of *Xunzi* where it is inevitable), there are a few things that we can say about *zhengming* in the context of the *Lunyu* and its link to a concern with truth, independently of debates concerning the purpose of *zhengming* and its larger role in the political and ethical theory or theories of the *Lunyu*.

In 13.3, Confucius responds to a question by Zilu asking what Confucius himself would do if the ruler of Wei were to hand over responsibility of governing to him. Confucius responds:

必也正名乎！

It would be necessary to rectify names!

Asked further about what this entails, Confucius explains (after first chiding Zilu):

名不正，則言不順；言不順，則事不成；事不成，則禮樂不與；禮樂不與，則刑罰不中; 刑罰不中，則民無所錯手足。

When names are not rectified, then statements are not followed, when statements are not followed, then affairs are not completed. When affairs are not completed, then ritual and music are not established. When ritual and music are not established, then punishments do not hit the mark. When punishments do not hit the mark, then the people are without the ability to use their hands and feet.

While 13.3 is the only passage in the *Lunyu* that explicitly mentions *zhengming*, 12.11 is almost always associated with 13.3 in being about *zhengming*, even though here Confucius only uses the term *zheng* 政 (proper governing) to describe the process. The passage reads:

齊景公問政於孔子。孔子對曰：「君君，臣臣，父父，子子。」公曰：「善哉！信如君不君，臣不臣，父不父，子不子，雖有粟，吾得而食諸？」

Duke Jing of Qi asked Confucius about proper governing. Confucius answered: "Ruler rules (jun jun), ministers minister (chen chen), fathers father (fu fu), sons son (zi zi)."⁹ The duke said: "This is good! Honestly, if the ruler does not rule, the minister does not minister, the father does not father, and the son does not son, then even if there is grain, could I attain and eat it?"

Loy Hui-Chieh argues convincingly¹⁰ that 13.3 at least commits the author to the position that application of the correct name, a function of language, has a particular effect on sociopolitical events or features of the world.¹¹ It seems clear that in this passage, at least, *zhengming* must at least be taken as having some semantic component, in which an act of language of some kind is connected to reality, however construed.¹² In addition, the *effect* of this act of language is described by Confucius as a kind of sociopolitical order. There is some connection between the ruler's language act and this order that is left unclear in 13.3. What is this language act of the ruler, and how does this lead to the order that Confucius discusses? More specifically for our purposes here, does the *zhengming* doctrine reveal early Confucian thinking about truth concepts?

Yan here is thought of more in terms of a *command* than an assertion, and we know that a command, without assertoric content, cannot have truth value. The sentence "bring me a sacrificial ox" cannot take a truth value, because it makes no assertion about "how things are." So we do not (here, at least) see *yan* in the sense of assertion. But notice that the same thing can be said of the English word "sentence." The above-mentioned command is a sentence no less than assertoric sentences like "the sky is blue" is a sentence. There are different kinds of sentences, not all of which can have truth values (if sentences are the bearers of truth value at all, and not propositions, statements, utterances, or something else). So the identification of *yan* here with command does not entail that *yan*, every time it is used, refers to a command or some other entity without assertoric content. Indeed, it is just where *yan* has assertoric content that *ran* is used to endorse it (where it is accepted *as* true), as in *Lunyu* 6.1.

Still, what can we say about *ming* in connection with truth, given the statements of 13.3? Confucius does not here give an explicit *definition* of *zhengming* (of course he rarely does this for anything), but instead illustrates what follows from a failure of the ruler to properly rectify names. Most immediately, failure of *zhengming* leads to *yan bu shun* (statements/commands not being followed). If we take this in the sense of command, then we see that failure to rectify names leads to the situation in which the people do not follow the orders of the ruler. Why should this be? One simple interpretive resolution is that if names are not properly fixed to objects, people will lack the ability to follow the ruler's orders. I cannot possibly follow the order "bring me a sacrificial ox" if I don't know which things in the world count as sacrificial oxen. This is the reading that I think is the right one, and it follows from taking rectification of names as a matching of objects with descriptions, where names play the role of descriptions, and rectification is a matter of determining which objects in the world satisfy these descriptions, and codifying this somehow.

This interpretation of *zhengming* is controversial, however. Some scholars, such as Chad Hansen, see the *zhengming* in the *Lunyu* not as definitional, but rather as the application of names or titles to particular individuals in society who properly model the roles that the ruler wishes to associate with the name.[13] This gives us an easy connection to sociopolitical order, as it becomes possible to rectify the actions of the people when there are clear models of the kind of action required of a given role. One problem I see with this, however, is that it is not in practice different than an interpretation Hansen rejects, which is that the ruler's *zhengming* is basically a construction of definitions of terms. Hansen argues that the early Confucian concern is with the ability of people to understand the norms indicated by language. Thus, he claims, a simple list of definitions would not be of any help, as presumably this confusion about language would multiply.[14] If I don't know what my role of father requires, and I'm told that "a father cares for his children, educates them, etc.," this may not be of much help, as it is left up to me to determine what is meant by care and education. Thus, the suggestion is that fixing *models* of good fatherhood would be more effective. But I am not at all sure that this is the case. There is as much reason, even given early Confucian claims, to think that Confucius and others would misconstrue the proper actions of an exemplar. And this is not just a matter of the specificity of practice versus the generality of descriptions. If we're told that some set of persons P are exemplars of fatherhood, we're left to our own devices to figure out what makes them good fathers. Presumably it's not *all* of their features, or even all of the features that they share in common. They all breathe, they're all ministers, perhaps. And also presumably they will not all exemplify fatherhood in the same way, so one person's caring for his children will look different than another person's caring for his children. The most we could generate from studying this set of exemplars is that the good father *cares for his children*, but this assumes two things already: (1) we know what it is to be caring, in order to recognize what these fathers do as care, and (2) we can distinguish the *caring* acts, from the acts that have nothing to do with fatherhood (good hygiene, insistence on military competence, etc.) as those at the core of fatherhood in these exemplars.[15] The exemplar method, seems both more complicated than the definitional method, and also to rely on it. So it can't be offered as a way to avoid purported difficulties with a definitional model. Perhaps in the case of young children, who truly are unaware of what caring or other important concepts mean, modeling exemplars is all we have, but in the case of adults, definitions surely play a larger role.

Additional complications are added to the *zhengming* picture if we take Confucius to be suggesting that the rectification goes beyond just matching names to objects properly. Kurtis Hagen argues that *zhengming* in the *Lunyu* plays a *constructive* role—the ruler creates descriptions through naming, playing a more active role in bringing about the associations of a name.[16] According to Hagen's position, then, *zhengming* is ultimately a conventional process, and as such may have little to do with "getting things right," "mirroring reality," or any other plausible truth-focused project. Hagen's reading of the *Lunyu* passages, however, are mainly based on his understanding of Xunzi's position on *zhengming*, which is both more developed and more explicitly conventionalist than anything we find in the *Lunyu* (although a conventionalist reading of Xunzi can be resisted to some extent as well, as I demonstrate below in chapter 4).

What we can find in the *Lunyu* is some indication of the implicit attitude concerning truth of early Confucians, and some hints concerning conceptions of truth in these schools. The concept of truth itself, as general and basic, we clearly see is at work here, in the *de re* sense that Hansen mentions, and which none of us presumably can avoid. Regardless of whether the "definitional" interpretation that I offer or the others mentioned here are ultimately correct, there must be some conception of a proper connection between language and reality that presents itself as semantic and truth-like. Even the most ontologically sparse theories of truth make room for the general idea that truth is based on a connection between language and reality. Deflationary theorists in contemporary philosophy generally take their positions to be compatible with such "correspondence" in some sense.[17] Various passages of the *Lunyu* also seem to recognize at least something like a correspondence intuition (which may be a necessary feature of the general concept of truth as robust property), a notion that proper (assertoric) speech is that which is grounded in reality or fits "the way things are." It is just in the case of *zhengming* that this comes out most clearly. In later material, the concept of *shi* 實 (actuality) is understood as the reality in which any acceptable ming must be grounded. There must be correspondence between names as descriptions and individuals in the world that satisfy these names for names to be proper. But if this is so, it also needs to be the case that there are *filled out* descriptions that are proper. That is, it makes no sense that a thinker would have the semantic concept of *satisfaction* without that of *truth*. Indeed, the two are fundamentally related, as I explain further in chapter 4 below in discussion of the relationship between names (*ming*) and actualities (*shi*) in the *Xunzi* and later texts.

MENGZI (MENCIUS)

There is much more concern with the issue of truth as explicit theoretical concern in the *Xunzi* than in any other early Confucian text. The *Mengzi* contains relatively little on truth or on language in general, as in the case of the *Lunyu*. Yet the issues of truth and language in *Mengzi* have received little scholarly attention, unlike the issue of *zhengming* in the *Lunyu*, even though as little is explicitly said about the topic in the *Lunyu* as the *Mengzi*. There are some passages in the *Mengzi* suggestive of both a considered conception of truth and a particular theory of truth that ought to be mentioned here. Specifically, we see the term *shi* 實 used in the text to refer to a truth concept, as we will see it throughout the texts dealt with in this book. This term is a complex one, and is not always used with the sense of "truth," but its wider sense makes it a useful term for referring to truth.

Shi is probably best translated as "fullness," "fruit," or "substantiality."[18] This wider definition can be applied in specific cases, however, as a truth predicate. This is part of the difficulty with *shi* in early texts. It is a broad term, and the predicate <is fruitful> as applied to either linguistic entities such as *yan* 言 (statements), or anything else (as *shi* can be universally applied) is much broader than truth. Truth can be *one of* the ways in which a thing is fruitful, complete, useful, or substantial, but it is certainly not the only way. And it is for this reason that we find the usage of *shi* in texts like *Mengzi* that has nothing to do with truth, alongside usages that seem explicable only in terms of truth. Being fruitful, as I explain in greater detail in the section on pluralism below, is amenable to a pluralistic reading. Depending on the context and domain of discourse, and depending on what kind of entity possesses the property and its relational context to us and our concerns (people for whom the entity is fruitful), either real or ideal, the property picked out by <is fruitful> will be different.[19]

In *Mengzi* 4A27,[20] we see an example of *shi* used in connection to non-linguistic entities, as well as implicitly as property of entities that assumes predication, even though it is not stated directly here. The passage reads:

仁之實，事親是也；義之實，從兄是也。智之實，知斯二者弗去是也；
禮之實，節文斯二者是也；樂之實，樂斯二者，樂則生矣

The fruitfulness of humanity is looking after one's ancestors. The fruitfulness of appropriateness is following one's elder brother. The fruitfulness of wisdom is not abandoning these two things. The fruitfulness of ritual is tying together these two things in culture. The fruitfulness of music is the enjoyment of these two things. If there is such enjoyment, then [virtue] grows."

The passage goes on to discuss further the fruitfulness of all these things. Looking at the first part here, however, we see that *shi* is attributed to a number of "virtues," and then a comment is made on what the fruitfulness of each of these virtues is. Here we see a miniature statement of pluralism about *shi* in the case of the virtues. While *ren* 仁 and *yi* 義 both have their fruitfulness (*shi*), what makes them fruitful is different. The fruitfulness of *ren*, according to this passage, is care for relatives, and the fruitfulness of *yi* is following of elder brothers. We might also understand *shi* here as representing "fullness."

In other passages of *Mengzi*, *shi* is used as a value of *yan* (statements), as in 4B45:

言無實不祥。不祥之實，蔽賢者當之。

Words that are without *shi* are not auspicious. The fruit (*shi*) of not being auspicious is obscuration of the fittingness of the sages' activity.

Notice that here *shi* is used in two senses within the same passage. We can read them both as "fruit," but clearly here "fruit" is something different in the case of *yan* and in that of inauspiciousness. Already here, we see a "pluralist" conception of *shi* at play (I will argue later in the chapter that a particular pluralist conception of *truth* using *shi* as central concept is developed in the Eastern Han). What is the *shi* of a statement? It *might* be truth, but, one may argue, it might equally be "appropriateness," "acceptability," or something *less* than truth. What is clear, however, is that *shi* offers us a property of a statement (*yan* 言) that has some kind of positive value. While we cannot show that this property is a *truth* property (yet), this certainly shows that early Chinese thought, by the time of Mengzi, has the ability to express a truth property as belonging to assertoric linguistic entities, and also then presumably to theorize about such properties.

Other terms that have been associated with a truth concept appear in the *Mengzi* in various ways. *Ran* 然 is used to evaluate statements positively, for example. And it cannot be the case that *ran* is used merely to endorse a claim as acceptable in some way that does not entail its matching reality or "the way things are," as what is endorsed as *ran* is often a factual or descriptive claim rather than a normative one. For example, in *Mengzi* 1A7, after hearing of King Xuan's compassionate response to the ox being taken to slaughter, Mengzi tells him:

是心足以王矣。百姓皆以王為愛也，臣固知王之不忍也

This heart-mind is sufficient to be a true king. The people will all take the king to have compassionate concern, and the ministers will be solidified in their knowledge that the king is unable to endure (the people's suffering).

To which the king responds: *ran*. This is clearly an endorsement of a factual statement about the king's actions and a claim about what will follow from the extension of those actions. It cannot be that the king is stating moral acceptability of some normative claim attributed to him, or making a normative claim himself, along the lines of "that's how things should be." Mengzi describes the king's actions and intentions, along with the results of those actions and intentions, and the king agrees with Mengzi that this is an accurate description of how things went and how things *will* go in the future if he follows the course of extending this heart-mind (*xin* 心) of compassion to the people in general (and not just sacrificial oxen).

We can compare this concept of *ran*, which gives us some idea of what is necessary for truth theory, and is almost certainly a matter of "getting things right," to that of *ke* 可, which has, in the *Mengzi* at least (and in a number of other sources), a far more normative character. Often *ke* seems to suggest that something either is or isn't (*bu ke* 不可) the way things should be, independently of the way they *are*. One example of this comes in *Mengzi* 1A3. Mengzi offers a story illustrating a point to King Hui of Liang about proper governance. The larger point of the story is not a major concern here, but the crucial bit reads:

填然鼓之，兵刃既接，棄甲曳兵而走。或百步而後止，或五十步而後止。以五十步笑百步，則何如？

Some run one hundred paces and then stop, and others run 50 paces and then stop. Is it proper for those who ran 50 paces to laugh at those who ran 100 paces?

To which the king responds:

不可，直不百步耳，是亦走也。

It is not ke. *They did not run 100 paces, but they fled all the same.*

Here it is most plausible that *ke* should be read normatively, as "they should not," rather than "they did not" or "it is not the case" or as any evaluation of a description. While truth certainly can be understood as attaching to normative statements as well as descriptive ones (that is, we can make perfectly good sense of the claim that it is *true* that one ought to be charitable, independent of any particular normative or metaethical theory), in the case of *ke* we have an additional difficulty. Even in the case of normative claims, truth claims have to do with *the way things are*. In calling a normative claim true, one endorses this normative claim as accurately representing the way things are. Things are such that one ought to be charitable.[21] *Ke* cannot play this role, given the way it is used. In response to Mengzi's question *ze he ru* 則何如 (literally, "How is this like?"), King Hui responds, "It is not *ke*." For this to be a truth value appraisal of a normative claim, there would have to be a hidden normativity in the claim made (or rather the story told) by Mengzi. But what could this be? That it is *proper* for the people who ran only 50 paces to laugh at those who ran 100? Presumably when Mengzi is asking the king *he ru* 何如, he is asking the king what he thinks of the *situation* described, not what he thinks about an implied normative claim of the rightness of the act of the people who ran 50 paces. *Ke*, then, is more plausibly read as itself a normative evaluation, along the lines of "right" or "morally acceptable." And it appraises *acts* rather than linguistic entities such as *yan* 言.

Ke also has a sense that it retains in modern Chinese, of "fittingness," "ability," or "possibility." The word *keyi* 可以 (able to) expresses this. This construct is used in the *Mengzi*. In 1A5, Mengzi says:

地方百里而可以王

> *Within one hundred* li *it is possible (*ke yi*) to become a true king.*

This construction is used in a number of other passages, including 1A7 and 1B11. In addition, there is discussion of "ability to do" (*ke wei* 可為),[22] "ability to establish" (*ke li* 可立), and a host of other such uses. There is not much in *Mengzi* (or, I think, other early Chinese sources with the exception of "School of Names" thinkers and Later Mohists) to suggest that *ke* should be read as anything like a term signifying a truth concept.

Dang 當 is also not used in the *Mengzi* in a "truth-like" manner, and it is not until the Mohist texts that we see it used in any way suggesting something like a truth concept.

We certainly do not yet have any *theory* of truth in the *Mengzi*, but it appears that we do have the necessary concepts and constructions for such theories to develop. The evaluative terms in *Mengzi* and other texts most likely to offer us concepts of truth are *ran* 然, *shi* 實, and *shi* 是, rather than *dang* 當 or *ke* 可. This perhaps explains the development of these concepts in later texts. *Dang* and *ke* play larger roles in Mohist texts than Confucian or Daoist texts, and the use of these terms in later work, such as that of the Han dynasty, can suggest certain chains of influence.

The fact that there is no explicit theorizing about truth in the *Mengzi*, then, is not because there is no concept of truth at work, but simply because the concerns of the *Mengzi* are not with truth. To reject the notion that there was a concept of truth in early Confucianism on the basis of this would be like reading J.S. Mill's *On Liberty*, failing to find within it a theory of truth, and therefore concluding that Mill had no concept of truth. Not all philosophers are concerned with or theorize about truth. Even today, only a small subset of professional philosophers worry in any robust way about truth, at least from a theoretical perspective. In most philosophical work, the concept of truth is in the background, a "folk" conception in the same way as we see it in the *Mengzi*.

NOTES

1. Michael Hunter argues for a Han origin of the *Analects*. See Hunter 2012.

2. A dubious honor that the *Lunyu* shares with probably the most often translated text of early Chinese thought (or any period of Chinese thought for that matter), the *Daodejing*.

3. Bruce and Taeko Brooks are well known for their development of what they call the "accretion hypothesis" concerning the *Lunyu* (Brooks and Brooks 1997).

4. The *Zhuangzi*, for example, is also likely a composite text (see Liu 1994), but it is composed of longer essays, each of which can be read integrally and as developing a particular view, argument, or theory.

5. *Lunyu* 6.1.

6. As I have pointed out above, the dating of the *Lunyu* is problematic, and it should not be assumed that, as traditionally maintained, it is the earliest of the Confucian texts and the "first" philosophical text in early China.

7. Arthur Waley suggests this (1938: 22); Brooks and Brooks (1997: 190) and Bryan Van Norden (2007: 86–90) agree with this as well. I myself find something suspicious about 13.3 given that this issue is mentioned nowhere else in the *Lunyu*, but I suspend judgment about the issue here.

8. A number of readings of *Xunzi* on rectification of names take the latter view, including that of Kurtis Hagen, which we look at in chapter 4.

9. There is no way to translate this passage into English without begging interpretive questions, simply because the lack of connective terms in English would make nonsense of the passage in English: "father father, minister minister," etc. I've attempted here to translate it as closely as possible to the Chinese, with the qualification that the English commitments required in the translation are not meant to be interpretive decisions.

10. Loy 2003.

11. Loy writes: "Some correct mode of speaking and naming on the part of the political elite is a necessary condition for socio-political and ritual order" (Loy 2003: 35).

12. And this appears to be the case whether *ming* is construed visually, as marking a graphic character, or aurally, as Jane Geaney argues it should be understood (Geaney 2010).

13. Hansen 1992: 68.

14. *Ibid:* 67.

15. These are problems that arise with exemplarism in general. Linda Zagzebski's influential "exemplarist virtue ethics" is at the core of Amy Olberding's account of

what she sees as exemplarism in the *Lunyu* (Olberding 2012), which can help us to understand what underlies Hansen's account of *zhengming* (though Olberding does not specifically discuss *zhengming* in her book). She writes: "One way to understand the exemplars proposed in the *Analects* is as illustrations of the text's more abstract moral claims. On such a reading, exemplars function to enliven and illuminate antecedently developed moral reasoning that, because it is abstract and general, may prove elusive to understand or difficult to apply. Such is to acknowledge that an important struggle in moral philosophy is making the move from abstract moral claims to the application of those claims in practice" (Olberding 2012: 20). The problem with this as applied to the *zhengming* case as it appears in *Lunyu* 12.11 is twofold: (1) the passage seems to already assume a familiarity with the application of terms such as ruler 君 or father 父, as they are used without comment; (2) a full definition of the duties of fatherhood, especially if it is filled out with injunctions such as "a good father cares for his children," should not be any more elusive or difficult than determining the relevant practices of an exemplar.

16. Hagen 2002: 35–36.

17. Paul Horwich (2010: 79), See chapter 1, note 49.

19. There is no basis for the argument Hansen seems to make that classical Chinese does not have the standard subject-predicate structure and that this undermines a concern with truth, as I explore in the first chapter. *Shi* (fruitfulness) is clearly predicated of entities in the early texts, even if in a different fashion than often seen in English. Rather than a topic-comment structure, we will often see a claim of property, such as in *Mengzi* 4A27.

20. For citations from the *Mengzi* I use the traditional book/section division that most editions and translations follow. I have here used Lau 2006 for the source text.

21. Of course this will only be the case on theories of truth in which there is a property expressed by the predicate <is true>, a complication I will get into in greater detail below in further discussion of minimalism, deflationism, and theories like these.

22. *Mengzi* 1B20.

Chapter 3

Mozi

While I disagree with Chad Hansen that we should take the Mohists as "setting the philosophical [and linguistic] agenda" in early Chinese thought,[1] the Mohists certainly do have an important role to play in theorizing about the concept of truth in early China. Part of the reason for this is their unique ways of understanding language, as well as the fact that it is with the Mohists that we see the first consideration of language itself as a philosophical area to be addressed directly. The Mohists are concerned with the philosophical issues behind the use of language, not just with using it, as are the earlier Confucians. This concern with language remains part of Chinese philosophy from this point on, and the Mohists certainly deserve some credit for instigating much of the concern with language that we see in later Chinese thought. A. C. Graham understands the Mohist position as in some sense bridging the gap between completely pragmatically minded early Confucians and Legalists, on the one hand, who were concerned almost solely with ethics and politics, and the 名家 *mingjia* (School of Names) thinkers, who were concerned exclusively with puzzles about language and its use. Graham writes:

> [Mohists] commit themselves fully to disputation [*bian*], not because they have forgotten about serious problems but because (like their contemporaries in Greece, of whom they know nothing) they think that only logic can solve these problems.[2]

There is perhaps a deeper problem in trying to offer an account of the "Mohist view" of truth than there is in offering one of the early Confucian or even Daoist views. This is because there appears to be deep disagreement concerning key features of language and metaphysics within the Mohist school, including whether we should take seriously the *tian zhi* 天志 (will

59

of Heaven) as justificatory either for belief of statements or as a guide for behavior,[3] as well as whether the views and practices of the sage kings of the past should have any normative force on us.[4] There are a number of theories as to why we see such discrepancies in the *Mozi*, ranging from accretion theories of the text to the position that the text represents the thought of three distinct Mohist schools.[5] Still, we can piece together coherent positions concerning pragmatic and semantic features of language, including on the concept of truth. I am more concerned here with outlining and investigating the various theories of truth in early Chinese thought than I am with identifying *whose* theories these were—whether they represented Mohist, Confucian, Daoist, or other positions.[6] Whether or not we can make sense of a "Mohist" theory of truth given the disparity between positions in different Mohist texts is not a problem that I'm attempting to solve here. What I show is that there *are* theories of truth to be found in Mohist texts, and I thus refer to these under the heading of "Mohist" theories of truth simply to fix them to the texts in which we find them developed. It is best seen as an expedient categorization, rather than a substantive one.

The most substantial discussion of issues of language is found in the later Mohist *Canons* (經 *jing*) and *Explanations* (說 *shuo*). The *Canons* and *Explanations* have a difficult history in Chinese thought, mainly because of the disorder into which the passages and fragments fell in the years after their construction. Little sense could be made of the material, even while it continued to be copied. The work of Chinese scholars such as Liang Qichao, Luan Tiaofu, Tan Jiefu in the early twentieth century, and A. C. Graham's work in English in the 1970s were of immense value in helping to piece back together this work.[7] Due to this work, we have a much better understanding today of this later Mohist material than was possible for much of the history of thought since the later Mohists wrote in the early centuries BCE, and it is possible to investigate this material here in a consideration of theories of truth.

While the *Canons* and *Explanations* contain the most explicit and in-depth consideration of linguistic issues, the "core chapters" of the *Mozi* also deal with these issues in different ways. Concerning truth in particular, I think there is actually *more* we can get from the core chapters than from the later Mohist material (although as I explain below, we can add to the picture of truth for the Mohists by looking to the later Mohist work). Probably the most well-known Mohist theory of language, truth, and belief appears in the chapter *Fei ming* 非命 (Against Fate), and is applied as well in chapters such as *Ming gui* 明鬼 (On Ghosts). The Mohist theory of the *san biao* 三表 or *san fa* 三法 (three standards) is outlined in the *Fei ming* chapter in three different ways, suggesting differences between different Mohist camps on the theory.[8] This is also suggested by the fact that the term *biao* 表 (guide), referring to a gnomon, is used in the first description of the theory in the first part of

Fei ming, while *fa* 法 (standard, law) is used in the other descriptions of the theory in the second and third sections of *Fei ming*.

What is clear is that the "three standards" theory concerns language and its application, either in a semantic or epistemic sense, or both. Whether the Mohists propose a theory of *truth* here is very much in question, and is the source of dispute among scholars. We can look to *Fei ming* itself for a statement of the Mohist position. At the opening of the chapter, Mozi presents a rough overview of a position he rejects—the idea that fate or destiny (命 *ming*) determines all of the outcomes of one's life. The suggestion here is that it is an unsatisfactory doctrine because it leads to a moral and social torpidity. This is one of the most well-known problems of determinism in general. If things are determined, what reason do I have to put forth effort to try to make certain things the case?[9] Following this, Mozi explains that in order to properly evaluate the "fatalist" doctrine, we need some standard of evaluation. The key passage reads:

然則明辨此之說將奈何哉？子墨子言曰：「必立儀，言而毋儀，譬猶運鈞之上而立朝夕者也，是非利害之辨，不可得而明知也。故言必有三表。」何謂三表？子墨子言曰：「有本之者，有原之者，有用之者。於何本之？上本之於古者聖王之事。於何原之？下原察百姓耳目之實。於何用之？廢以為刑政，觀其中國家百姓人民之利。此所謂言有三表也。

Being that this is the case, how do we distinguish between doctrines to be evaluated? Mozi said, "A standard must be established. Evaluating a statement without a standard is like relying on a potter's wheel to determine day and night. One will be unable to distinguish between or understand right and wrong, beneficial and harmful. Therefore to evaluate statements there must be three tests [biao] applied." What are these three tests? Mozi said, "that from the root/base, that from the source, and that from use. How do we determine basis? The original root is the affairs of the ancient sage kings. How do we determine source? The source is in the examination of the reality of what the people have heard and seen. How do we determine use? Abandoning governing by punishments, observe how [the statement affects] the benefit of the people. This is called applying three tests to statements."[10]

From this statement, it is unclear exactly what role the Mohist understands these three standards as playing. Clearly, the standards allow us to appraise whether a statement should be accepted, connecting this back to the point made in the first passage from *Fei ming*. Whether or not a statement is acceptable (in some sense) has to do with whether it "passes" the three tests. But in *what* sense is a statement (*yan*) acceptable when it passes these tests?[11] Whether the Mohists are discussing *truth* here or something else will have much to do with what they think these tests tell us about the statement(s) in question—in which ways statements become acceptable. We know that acceptable statements will be ones that enable us to distinguish between right and wrong, benefit and harm, and that will lead to the establishment of the first of each of these pairs, but with respect to *what* property does a *yan* have such an effect?

The following passages in *Fei ming* give us some hint of what may be going on here. Mozi applies the first standard to belief in fate (以命為有 *yi ming wei you*).[12] He points out that the sagely government of the ancient kings Tang and Wu took place in the same times (respectively) as the corrupt government of Jie and Zhou. In addition, the sage kings did not themselves accept a role for fate in their writings on the subject of government. In response to the doctrine of fate's failure of this test, Mozi asks 豈何謂有命 哉 *qi he wei you ming zai* ("how can it be said that there is fate?"). This could be taken to be about the acceptability of the belief or the assertion, though there seems to be no justification here for reading this in an epistemic manner. It begins to look problematic to hold the three tests as standards to determine the *truth value* of a statement, however, when we look at other applications of the tests, and what they tell us.

In the "On Ghosts" chapter, Mozi applies the three tests to the position that ghosts exist. What he claims to be evaluating is the *shuo* 說 (statement, saying) that ghosts exist, so as to determine whether this *shuo* is acceptable or permissible (可 *ke*). However, his evaluation of this *shuo* in a number of places seems ambiguous. Clearly, he views acceptability of the *shuo* that ghosts exist to mean that we should accept or believe the claim, and also that we should accept the claim because it passes the "three tests," but it is unclear just what properties a *shuo's* passing the three tests demonstrate that it has. Are the three tests meant merely to show epistemic value like warranted assertability, where warrant is based only on the tests themselves (thus rendering the claims "metaphysically innocent")? Or is there additionally a semantic claim being made—that what makes the *shuo* that ghosts exist permissible is that it is *true*, that it either represents the way things are, coheres with an overall worldview, or otherwise possesses some truth-making property? Part of the difficulty here is that if we are not already beginning with a decided-upon notion of what qualifies as a concept of truth, it will be difficult if not impossible to tell whether the Mohists in the *Ming gui* chapter are discussing truth or some other concept. From the broadest and most general possible understanding of truth, it seems relatively unproblematic to describe the Mohist arguments in the chapter as arguments for the *truth* of the *shuo* that ghosts exist.

According to Chad Hansen's interpretation (which we have seen briefly in chapter 1), the standards are meant to be guides as to the proper use of language in a particular social context, which does not have to do with the semantic value of statements or sentences, but rather with the sociopolitical effect(s) of making or endorsing the statement.[13] The standards, then, are pragmatic tests. As I argued in chapter 1, there seems no good reason to reject the possibility of a pragmatic *theory of truth*, and if this is indeed what the Mohists are doing, then we simply ought to hold that their conception of truth is a pragmatic one, rather than holding that they do not have or concentrate on a conception of truth.[14] What the three standards reveal in a statement that makes it acceptable (*ke*) is that the statement has the effect of bringing about *li* 利 (profit, benefit). The third standard then is the most important. Some later Mohists do seem to adopt such a stance, consolidating the three standards into a single standard relying on the usefulness of a statement (*yan* or *shuo*) in creating profit/benefit.[15]

We have as much reason to read the Mohist discussion of the three standards as offering a way to evaluate the truth of statements, however, whether this is seen as pragmatic or otherwise. It is not altogether clear, however, that the conception of truth under discussion here *is* a pragmatic one. It has become a tenet of faith that the Mohists had a primarily pragmatic conception of the acceptability of statements, even among those who accept that the Mohists had a conception of truth.[16] There has been discussion of whether the Mohists distinguished between pragmatic claims and semantic ones, and much of this has surrounded the three standards.[17] There is little evidence, however, that the Mohists held that there *was* an important distinction between these two. That is, even if they did recognize a distinction (which is by no means obvious), they may have simply accepted that this distinction is ultimately an artificial one, and that it *ought* to be collapsed. This would not be altogether different from the tactic taken by pragmatists about truth in the Western tradition. The distinction that numerous interpreters draw between pragmatic and semantic concerns in Mohism (then associating truth concern with the latter) seems to me to unnecessarily rule out the possibility that the Mohists simply conceived of truth in a pragmatist way, just as did Western theorists like Peirce, James, or Rorty. The descriptive and normative need not be seen as distinct, and indeed one of the unique features of early Chinese theories of truth is the combination of the two (we will see in consideration of Han philosophers how this kind of theory is ultimately developed into a sophisticated pluralism).

Hui-Chieh Loy, in explaining possible difficulties in accounting for this seeming movement in Mohist texts between normative and descriptive, writes:

> By itself, this is not a problem since nothing said so far implies that the Mohists are not interested in description of facts. If anything, the presence of [the standard of human testimony] suggests that the Mohists do not conceive of the

nature and function of language in purely pragmatic terms totally detached from concerns of truth. The problem is that they do not explicitly distinguish descriptions from prescriptions and commands. Furthermore, they sometimes move seamlessly between arguing for what looks to be a factual claim ("providential spirits exist," "fate does not exist") and a more straightforwardly action guiding *yan* ("people should speak and behave as if the spirits exist" and "as if fate does not exist," i.e., because doing so serves a pragmatic purpose).[18]

This so-called problem that Loy discusses is only a problem if they *ought* to make the distinction between normative and descriptive or if something they assume in their theory commits them to acceptance of this distinction. It is unclear to me that either one of these is the case. Loy and others frame the discussion in terms of whether the Mohists *recognized* that there could (must) be such a distinction, but this seems to me the wrong way to approach the question. Yes, a distinction *can* be made between two different kinds of statement, but on this basic level *should* there be? Is such a distinction ultimately a well-grounded one? The features of reality, language, etc. make all kinds of distinctions *possible*, but only certain ones are *useful*. We should consider the possibility that the Mohists, and other early Chinese thinkers, considered the normative-pragmatic distinction as artificial when it came to discerning *truth*, though potentially useful in other areas.

One shared feature of the discussions of a number of scholars on the Mohist position is a very narrow conception of truth. Fraser, Loy, and Hansen seem to identify truth *not* with the general and basic property of statements grounding both *the way things are* and *what we ought to do*, but rather with specific correspondence property holding between descriptive and assertoric subject-predicate sentences and something like states-of-affairs. This seems to miss the possibility of the Mohists or other early Chinese thinkers having conceptions of truth different from Russellian correspondence theory, and also seems to suggest that many contemporary Western theories of truth are also not theories of truth.

Part of the problem here is that "truth" as scholars of early Chinese thought are using it is not clearly defined, and often not defined at all. Thus, we may be relying on correspondentist intuitions concerning truth picked up during our training as philosophers (early twentieth-century analytic philosophy, in which correspondence theory of truth dominated, is almost universally taught in graduate institutions, whereas contemporary theories of truth are studied only by those with particular interest in the topic). It is curious we should think of truth in this narrow Russelian sense, however, given that most contemporary theories of truth are very far from this. Those steeped in contemporary truth debates may find it curious how scholars of Chinese philosophy think about truth, and thus how they determine what kinds of truth concern can be found in early Chinese texts.

This assumption goes so deeply that Loy reads the Mohist argument for the acceptance of ghosts as requiring the unstated implicit (descriptive) premise that "ghosts exist," to get to the desired (pragmatic) conclusion "we ought to believe that ghosts exist."[19] Loy, however, holds that though the Mohists had some conception of "descriptive truth," this conception was nothing more than the acceptance of something like the equivalence schema of Tarski and the deflationists about truth who draw inspiration from it.

Even those scholars who accept that the Mohists are concerned with truth and that the "three standards" are meant to appraise statements for truth value[20] appear to be operating with a specifically Western and correspondentist account of truth, in which truth is a property only of descriptive assertoric statements.[21] If this is the concern of the Mohists, however, and the aim of the standards is to evaluate statements in this way, then there are both missing steps in the Mohist arguments in the *Ming gui* and *Fei ming* chapters, and illegitimate moves back and forth between descriptive and normative claims. It is no coincidence that those who accept that the Mohists were after something like descriptive correspondence truth dismiss the Mohist arguments as weak. As indeed they are if this was the Mohist aim.[22] The alternative is often taken to be Hansen's route—denial that the Mohists were interested in anything like "truth," but instead with pragmatic features of statements. This move, however, makes the opposite mistake, of taking pragmatic considerations as ruling out descriptive ones. Why is it so difficult for us to make sense of the goal of early Mohist argument concerning the "three standards"? I think it is primarily due to the fact that we are insisting on a distinction that does not *need* to be made, and that the Mohists in fact did not make—that between the descriptive and normative as concerning a concept of truth. If indeed acceptability (*ke*) in Mohist thought had a primarily pragmatic connotation, this need not, pace Hansen, rule out the concept as either a concept of truth or as one compatible with some kind of descriptive content alongside the pragmatic. Truth can be, and sometimes *is*, taken as both descriptive and normative. And this is just how we should treat it in the Mohist case.

Chris Fraser describes a general and basic concept that he says grounds Mohist thinking on the acceptability of statements, but he does not associate this concept with truth, because he seems to think that truth is only one version or application of this concept. He writes:

> We might say that the Mohists are applying a very basic, primitive conception of correctness, of which truth, obligation, permissibility, and other notions are species. The crucial point is probably that their main theoretical focus is not descriptive truth, but the proper *dao* (way) by which to guide social and personal life. This focus on *dao* leads them to run together the empirical question of whether ghosts exist with the normative question of whether we should act on and promulgate the teaching that they do.[23]

Why not think that *truth*, rather than Fraser's notion of "correctness," is the more basic concept here? Indeed, how can we even make sense of obligation, permissibility, correctness, etc. without some prior and more basic conception of truth? If we read Fraser's use of "truth" in the narrow correspondentist sense, then perhaps this is right. But what reasons do we have to read truth in this way, especially when it comes to the Mohists? Is this an implicit expression of the conviction that the correspondence property is what truth *actually is*? But if we are not willing or able to go to bat for a particular theory of truth (and we should never be in interpretive work), we should operate with as broad and uncontroversial a conception of truth as we can, that requires fewest possible commitments. Otherwise, we run the real risk of begging the question. And that appears to me as just what is happening here concerning the Mohists.

The right way of reading the Mohist theory of truth, and one that connects it to later developments in Han philosophy as well, is that they collapsed the distinction between the normative and descriptive on the most basic and general level on which truth operates. A closer look at the Mohist texts can show how this is. And this position is further bolstered when I investigate later Chinese theories of truth that share this position concerning truth. The Eastern Han philosophers Wang Chong and Wang Fu, as I show in later chapters, have a similar conception of truth. It is not one that arose unprecedented onto the scene in the Eastern Han, but rather it goes back at least as far as the early Mohists.

In the *Ming gui* chapter,[24] we see the application of the three standards applied to the question of the existence of ghosts. The first determinate *yan* (statement) considered in the chapter, and to which the standards will be applied, is a statement said to be made by those who reject the existence of ghosts (今執無鬼者 *jin zhi wu gui zhe*), that "ghosts and spirits certainly do not exist" (鬼神者，固無有 *gui shen zhe gu wu you*).[25] The problem is that this leads the people to doubt the existence of ghosts, which then leads to disorder in society. Clearly, the major concern here is with the effect of this *yan* (or rather *shuo*) on society in terms of *li* 利 (benefit/profit). The standards are then applied with this in mind. When Mozi goes on to discuss the standard of using what the people know through their senses concerning ghosts, he says that this will allow us to determine whether we should accept or believe that ghosts exist. If the people have heard and seen them, then we should accept that ghosts exist (*bi yi wei you* 必以為有), while we should reject that they exist if the people have not seen and heard them. What we are to *believe* or *take as the case* (*yi wei* 以為) is at issue here. The assumption on which Loy, Fraser, and others are working is that there is necessarily a distinction between two separate statements concerning ghosts, a descriptive and normative one. They can be distinguished into the following:

(1) *Ghosts exist—*鬼有。
(2) *We should (or must) believe that ghosts exist—*必以為鬼有

The argument one might expect here is that using the standard of what the people have seen and heard is sufficient evidence to demonstrate (1), and that (2) follows from this, with the addition of the general principle (P):

(P) We should believe things that are the case/are true.

Since (1) expresses the truth of the statement that "ghosts exist" (assuming the equivalence schema here that should hold for any conception of truth, that ["x" is true iff x]), we can generate (1a):

(1a) It is true that ghosts exist

And we have the conclusion (2). This, however, is not how the Mohists seem to argue the case for (2) at all. If they recognized the distinction between (1) and (2) or saw it as important, should we expect the above argument structure?

The text gives us plenty of reason to believe that the Mohists accepted something like (P) above. The crucial issue here becomes not whether they accepted (P), but whether "being the case" uniquely picked out either (1) or (2), or instead (as I argue) some hybrid of both. The descriptive and normative, for the Mohists and some other early Chinese thinkers, can be distinguished, but they believed that the two should *not* be distinguished in consideration of *truth* concerns. Any distinction that we make between the two is ultimately artificial, and for the purpose of focusing on distinct *aspects* of truth.

We can see the various arguments given in the *Ming gui* chapter as in support of *both* (1) and (2), and also that, as Loy points out, the focus seems to shift back and forth between them, simply because most plausibly the Mohists do not see (1) and (2) as distinct in the consideration of the acceptability of a *shuo* or *yan*.

Looking at the first application of the standard of the people in *Ming gui*, we see an argument that can most plausibly be reconstructed as one for a conclusion combining (1) and (2), which are never clearly distinguished in the way acceptance of ghosts is discussed in the chapter—discussed in terms of *xin* 信—"trusting"—that ghosts reward and punish, and distinguishing between whether there are (*you* 有) or are not (*wu* 無) ghosts. Given that we do seem to see an easy motion back and forth between the normative (*we should believe that ghosts exist*) and the descriptive (*ghosts exist*), consider that the Mohists may have been arguing for the following:

(1b) It is the case that ghosts exist, where "being the case" entails normative value of a statement *and* its descriptive accuracy.

What reasons do we have to think the Mohists were arguing for (1b)? First, this makes sense of their easy and unmentioned movement between the normative and descriptive in their argument. They can do this without the need for invoking missing or implicit steps in the argument. For the early Mohists, there is another important aspect—the role of *tian* 天 (Heaven). Indeed, one of the reasons that the Mohist position on truth may be so controversial and difficult to cull out is the major shift between the early and later Mohists concerning *tian* and its role in Mohist epistemology and philosophy of language.

In the third part of *Tian zhi*, the Mohists discuss the use of the intention of *tian* as a standard (*fa* 法). While much of what is discussed in the chapter seems to suggest that it should be a standard for our action and belief, rather than one demonstrating descriptive truth, this is based on a distinction that *we* bring to the text. It is not one that the Mohists themselves make. Neither in this chapter nor any of the others do the Mohists distinguish between *fa* that determine the acceptability of a *yan* or *shuo* as guide to action and *fa* determining acceptability of a *yan* or *shuo* as accurate description of the world. This of course led scholars like Hansen to reject that the Mohists were concerned with the latter, since they were uncontroversially concerned with the former. But, again, to make this claim is to impose a distinction on Mohist thought that it did not accept, simply because we think it's one they should have accepted. The fact that the Mohists were primarily concerned with language as a guide to action does *not* show that they were not also concerned with language as a description of the world. Why not? Because Hansen and others have failed to show that they took the descriptive and normative to be separable in this way.

Even if we investigate the history of Western philosophy, we will see that there is a rich and problematic history concerning these two aspects of language. In contemporary philosophical thought, it tends to be taken as a writ of faith that the descriptive and normative are necessarily separable.[26] Before the seventeenth and eighteenth centuries, however, especially in medieval and ancient Western philosophy, the separability of the descriptive and normative spheres was not so obviously desirable. Akeel Bilgrami argues that the "new science" of the Royal Society in England represented by figures such as Isaac Newton played a large role in the rise of this cleft between the normative and descriptive[27], one that had not existed in much previous philosophical and scientific thought. Indeed, the fact that David Hume's insistence on the distinction between the normative and descriptive is the best-known formulation shows that the insistence on this comes relatively late in the history of Western philosophy, and emerges during the heyday of Empiricism, which not only insists on the fundamental distinction between the normative and descriptive, but insists on the latter as primarily representing the nature of reality, and not the former. It is not until there is such a cleft made between the normative and descriptive that we get such problems as metaethical problems and ones concerning the metaphysical foundation of normativity. It is much the same as structurally similar problems in philosophy of mind and epistemology. There is no mind-body problem until we insist on the separability of the two in a kind of Cartesian dualism, and there is no problem of skepticism until we insist on the distinction between appearance and reality. Perhaps these distinctions are ones that we should make. But often there is no argument for this—they are just distinctions that we *do* make. And once we make them, the attendant problems they engender come along for the ride. This may have been part of the point of the *Qiwulun* chapter of *Zhuangzi* and similar writings.

It looks as if the argument that a distinction between the normative and descriptive in consideration of the acceptability or truth of statements relies on assumptions derived from features of the history of modern Western thought. It is by no means a universal component of thinking about truth that we distinguish the two—either in Western or any other philosophical tradition. Instead of taking the ambiguity between descriptive and normative as a failure to distinguish the two and concentration on the normative as showing that the Mohists were unconcerned with the descriptive, perhaps we should take this as showing that the Mohists saw them as connected. That is, for the Mohists, arguments for the position that we ought to *accept* or *believe* that ghosts exist were also at the same time arguments for the position that ghosts exist. We should consider the possibility that for the early Mohists, the descriptive statement *ghosts exist* is not distinct from the statement *we ought to accept the existence of ghosts*. Of course, we may think that commitment to such a view would render it impossible for the Mohists to make sense of things like *useful falsehoods*. If we consider some other features of the Mohist view, however, we can show that this is not the case.[28] There are two ways we might understand this connection between the normative and descriptive concerning ghosts:

(3) ghosts exist = we ought to accept the existence of ghosts
(4) ghosts exist *iff* we ought to accept the existence of ghosts[29]

It seems implausible to think that the Mohists accepted the first, as this would suggest that the two statements *mean* the same thing, and that the possibility of the useful falsehood would be conceptually impossible, just like that of the married bachelor. It may be the case that there cannot be useful falsehoods, according to the Mohists, but surely it is a matter of extension, and not intension. That is, there is simply nothing that is useful that is not also true (in the descriptive sense), even though being useful does not mean the same things as being descriptively true. What textual evidence do we have to show that the Mohists accepted (4) rather than (3)? The fact that they appear to interchangeably use normative and descriptive language seems to suggest an interpretation along the lines of (1).

Mozi 8.31.19[30] may give us reason for distinguishing the two so as to rule out interpretation (1). In discussing the effects of acceptance of ghosts on society, Mozi seems to point out that positive affects would obtain on our acceptance of ghosts *even if* ghosts did not in fact exist. If this is what is going on, (1) is ruled out. It is impossible to make this distinction if the "ghosts exist" and "we ought to accept the existence of ghosts" are the same in meaning. The relevant bit of 8.31.19 reads:

今絜為酒醴粢盛，以敬慎祭祀，若使鬼神請有，是得其父母姒兄而飲食之也，豈非厚利哉？若使鬼神請亡，是乃費其所為酒醴粢盛之財耳。自夫費之，非[1]特注之汙壑而棄之也，內者宗族，外者鄉里，皆得如具飲食之。雖使鬼神請亡，此猶可以合驩聚眾，取親於鄉里。

Now if we purify the wine and the grains in order to pay respects in our sacrificial rituals, acting as if the ghosts and spirits exist, and in this our fathers, mothers, and elder siblings drink and eat, how is this not a great profit? If the ghosts and spirits do not exist, it would be wasteful to use materials to purify the wine and grain. But considering this wastefulness, it is not the case that the materials are just thrown away. Rather, those within the family and those outside in the broader community all obtain drink and food. Thus, even if ghosts do not exist, acting in this manner can unify the multitude and create close relationships within the community.

Does this passage, however, rule out (2) as well? It turns out that this passage can be plausibly read such that it does not show that there might be counterexamples to (2). If ghosts do not exist yet one accepts that ghosts exist and thus attains the practical goals that the Mohists are concerned with, this might, on pragmatic grounds, suggest that one still *ought to accept* that ghosts exist.

This interpretation of the Mohist "standards" (*fa* 法 and *biao* 表) puts me at odds with a few other scholars who share my view that Hansen is wrong about the lack of a truth concept in Mohist thought, but reject that the "standards" have to do with truth, as I have argued above.[31] In particular, Chris Fraser and Frank Saunders Jr. have recent papers in which they argue against Hansen concerning truth in Mohist texts, but accept various features of his interpretation that I reject.[32]

Chris Fraser, following Hansen, interprets the standards as primarily intended to evaluate statements in terms of their pragmatic acceptability (distinct from truth concerns, as he understands truth), but as involving (necessarily) a conception of "semantic truth" as well.[33] Fraser recognizes the combination of descriptive and normative concerns in Mohist arguments, however, thus offering a more sophisticated reading of the Mohist evaluation of *yan* (statements). He still distinguishes the two concerns, but sees the Mohists as having them both, as a way of achieving their pragmatic goals. He writes:

> To call something "*shi*" is to endorse doing it and, normally, to be motivated to do or promote it. To call it "*fei*" is to condemn or reject it and to be motivated to refrain from doing it or to help prevent it. Since both the descriptive issue of whether something is a certain kind of thing and the normative issue of whether some activity is ethically right or wrong are conceptualized as a matter of distinguishing *shi* from *fei*, talk of *shi-fei* distinctions tends to mix descriptive and normative issues. Thus, as criteria for distinguishing *shi-fei*, the three standards apply to both empirical descriptions and normative prescriptions. The Mohists probably do not see them as standards specifically for evaluating empirical facts, moral norms, or social policy, but instead combine all three areas together under one rubric.[34]

Although Fraser recognizes this combination of the two concerns, and does accept that the Mohists did have a concept of truth, he goes on after this to claim that the Mohists were concerned with enacting the proper conduct *rather* than with truth. This, again, accepts a particular conception of truth associating it with descriptive content and perhaps a correspondentist property. When we understand truth in this way, it turns out that Mohists as well as many other early Chinese philosophers only had a minor concern with the concept.

Fraser's notion of the "primitive conception of correctness" at work in the *Mozi* is better explained in terms of a particular, and perhaps *pluralist*, conception of truth—one that will be further fleshed out by Wang Chong in the Eastern Han dynasty (whose theory we look at more closely below). While Fraser rejects the description of this concept as that of *truth* and instead discusses it in terms of *dao* (mainly because he seems to adopt the narrow conception of truth discussed above), it is unclear that he ought to do so. Why think that the *dao* focus, as he describes it here, is not exactly the Mohist conception *of truth*? Fraser rightly sees the normative and descriptive as combined for the Mohists, and says:

> This focus on *dao* leads them to merge the empirical question of whether ghosts exist with the normative question of whether we should act on and promulgate the teaching that they do.[35]

Why not read this as a theory of truth? Why the insistence on referring to the term (*dao* 道) in particular, and resisting the translation of it in this context as "truth" or the association of it with a theory of truth? Surely, there are key differences between the Mohist truth theory and that of a contemporary correspondence theorist, but then so are there massive differences between deflationists about truth and correspondence theorists, and we do not use this as a denial that the deflationist theory is a theory of truth or that they are concerned with truth when they offer their theories. Thus while Fraser offers a more satisfying interpretation of the early Mohists than those we looked at previously, he still associates truth with the narrowly descriptive and correspondentist conception of it, and thus misses some of what the Mohist view can tell us about their conception of the nature of truth in general, as well as how this influences later Chinese philosophical thought.

The later Mohist material complicates things. Almost all of the material is fragmentary, and for much of its history, scholars could make little sense of it. Recently, however, major breakthroughs such as that of A. C. Graham in reconstructing the later Mohist material have contributed greatly to our understanding of it. While some of what we find in this material echoes earlier Mohist views, there are also numerous ways in which the later Mohists develop their own unique positions. Given the terse, fragmentary, and unusually ambiguous nature of the material, however, there may be relatively little we can depend on in the later Mohist work to help us understand the theories of truth of the Mohists or other early Chinese thinkers. It is simply too vague and suggestive, and too condensed. Like much of Aristotle's work, it is akin to shorthand lecture notes. The later Mohist material gives interpreters lots to work with and draws them *because* it's so terse, unclear, ambiguous, and difficult, somewhat similar to the "School of Names" literature. While this may be great for those looking to solve the particular puzzles that this material presents, using this unclear material robustly to reconstruct wider views of concepts like truth, knowledge, and other related concepts in Mohist or early Chinese thought is problematic. It's compatible with a great deal. This is not to say, however, that it is of *no* assistance. There are certainly suggestions of positions that we can find in the material, which can help to lend additional support to arguments concerning more widely held views of truth.

In a recent article, Frank Saunders Jr. challenges Hansen's "anti-truth" position as it concerns the later Mohists in particular (much of Hansen's argument, as we have seen in chapter 1, relies on the Mohists).[36] He focuses on *dang* 當 and *he* 合 as offering something like truth concepts (or at least semantic adequacy concepts) in the later Mohist material.

Saunders attempts to show that the later Mohist distinguished between acceptable (*ke* 可) names and accurate names. If this is the case, he argues, then their concern cannot have been strictly pragmatic. While *ke* is a pragmatic concept, it was not only the acceptability (*ke*) of a *ming* on which it could be evaluated. Whether a *ming* was "fitting" (*dang*) or "tallying" (*he*) were additional considerations that were semantic rather than pragmatic. One important passage on which Saunders and Dan Robins comment is *Canon* B71 and its explanation: "Calling it a crane is acceptable *(ke)*, even though it is not a crane."

This speaks to the issue of using "borrowed" names. The acceptability of calling something a crane in this passage has to do with the use of the name as a proper name or lineage name, which is independent from a description or classification based on properties of a thing. This then, according to Saunders and Robins, boils down to the point that although proper names are not descriptive, there may be descriptive uses of them.[37] A person may have the family name "Cook" and yet not be a cook. Saunders thus takes *ke* (acceptability) as a pragmatic concept. The other two relevant concepts, *dang* and *he*, however, seem to work differently in the later Mohist material. *Dang* in particular, according to Saunders, is "the best synonym for 'is true' in classical Chinese philosophy."[38] While I have problems with this position, not least of which is that I don't think we can find a single term or concept that is *the* truth term or concept in early Chinese philosophy, I do think Saunders is right that *dang* does give us an important truth concept in Mohist thought.

One of the things that Saunders takes as problematizing the *general* understanding of *dang* as truth is that the Mohists appear to use it to evaluate *terms* rather than *sentences*. He considers *Canon* A74 in connection with this:

辯, 爭彼也。辯勝, 當也。(辯)。或謂之牛, 或謂之非牛, 是爭彼也。是不俱當, 不俱當 必或不當。(不若當「犬」。)

Bian is disputing about opposites. Winning *bian* is fitting. Explanation: Some say oxen, while others say non-oxen: this is disputing about opposites. Here, both do not fit. Not all fitting, some must not fit. (Not like fitting hound.)[39]

The explanation here, as in much of the later Mohist literature, is vague and difficult to make sense of. Saunders reads *dang* here as concerning words and application of terms rather than sentences, while A. C. Graham reads it as applicable to sentences, on the basis of this very same passage.[40] Saunders' insistence here that the disputing *(bian)* of A74 has to do with terms rather than statements seems to me to miss much of the import of *ming* 名(names) in Mohist thought and early Chinese thought in general.

The question here becomes: if the content of a name has to do with classification and application to other objects, how do we support the claim that a *ming* is not descriptive, and does not constitute a statement, evaluable for truth? That is, the first part of Hansen's thesis, which Saunders does not take himself to challenge, that the Mohists were concerned with *names* rather than *statements* or *sentences*, is effectively challenged. Since *ming* include descriptions and statements, perhaps similar to the way a nod of the head can entail a contentful statement "it is so" that can be evaluated for truth, it is unclear how we can deny that the Mohists are concerned with evaluating statements, whether they understand them as expressed by *ming* or something that we are more comfortable directly translating as "sentence" such as *ci* 詞. In his conclusion, Saunders writes:

> Semantic adequacy, the proper relationship between language and the world, was fundamental to their philosophy of language, as well as to their epistemology. However, this does not imply that the Later Mohists were working with a concept of truth as we would recognize it in the West. The Later Mohists had rather an array of terms that can best be described as evaluating either the semantic or pragmatic adequacy of their terms.[41]

I think Saunders himself has provided some reason to see the Mohist position concerning truth as applying to more than evaluating *terms*, but also *statements*. It is also interesting, and I think problematic, that Saunders is still hesitant to call these Mohists concepts concepts of *truth*. The title of the article itself suggests this. The Mohists were interested in semantic adequacy, but this falls short (or otherwise differs from) "truth as we would recognize it in the West." Therefore, is there no concept of truth? There are a few problematic things about this. First—it seems to take that the concept of truth is primarily determined by what we most philosophers in the West would be willing to accept as or recognize as a concept of truth. This is highly implausible, especially given that most Western philosophers (at least within the analytic tradition) construe truth so narrowly as to deny that the senses of truth outside the sense with which we are mainly concerned here are senses of truth at all. Thus, what most of the rest of English-speaking society thinks of as clearly matters of truth, the "true friend," "truth in general," etc. turns out not to be truth. I think we should be open to the possibility that the concept of truth outruns the bounds of the particular ways in which Western philosophers think about it, so that it might be possible that there are features of truth that *we* are unaware of, and thus our failure to recognize them as such shows not necessarily that they are *not* features of truth. Our recognition of something as truth cannot be the standard for its so being, if truth is something more than a provincial concept operative within our discipline of analytic philosophy. When we search for the nature of *truth*, we are surely searching for something more than *this* concept. We take ourselves to be seeking the nature of Capital T truth—the universal and important concept that everyone has reason to care about, and everyone uses. If this is the concept we're aiming to understand, Western recognition simply won't cut it as a standard. Understanding truth is understanding the ways in which it is conceived in a *variety* of places and traditions. Thus, insofar as the Mohist conceptions of semantic adequacy look different from the way Western philosophers understand truth (if they do, and I'm not convinced that they are as different as Saunders and others argue), what we should take from this is that the concept of truth is richer and more robust than Western philosophers generally take it to be.

I'm not sure what reason we have to resist calling this Mohist theory a theory of *truth* other than its failure to completely conform to the ways in which contemporary analytic philosophers think about truth. But, as I have mentioned before, on those grounds we also must reject almost all precontemporary Western philosophy concerning truth as about truth. From what I have discussed here, it is plausible that we should accord to the Mohists a theory (or multiple theories) of truth, whether it looks exactly like something that those Western philosophers would recognize or not.

NOTES

1. Hansen 1992: 95.

2. Graham 1978: 21. As we will see, Graham accepts an account of the Mohists in which they have a concept and theory of truth, while Hansen rejects this. I am in agreement with Graham on this point, even though I will outline the theory of truth represented in Mohist work somewhat differently than he does.

3. The first passage of the fragmentary Mohist *Yu jing* (Discussing the Canons) bluntly states this disagreement with the *Tianzhi* chapter of the *Mozi*. A. C. Graham outlines the objection thus: "Heaven, who rewards the good and punishes the wicked, is the ultimate sanction of all morality. But a fundamental difficulty has arisen, which is presented in the introductory section. Individualists are now arguing that since man's nature (*xing*) is ordained for him by Heaven, it is by following the dictates of his nature that he obeys Heaven. To 'expound a canon' the Will of Heaven merely encourages the selfish man to indulge in his natural egoism" (Graham 1978: 244).

4. Again there is tension between what we find in the "core" chapters of the *Mozi* and the later works, given that the opening section of the *Fei ming* chapter takes the authority of the sage kings to be one of the three "standards" (*san biao*) by which we determine the acceptability of a *bian* (distinction, statement).

5. Carine Defoort and Nicholas Standaert discuss various positions concerning this issue: in the introduction to their (Defoort and Standaert 2014). Clearly there are different hands behind the various sections of the *Mozi*, but perhaps all we can say with certainty is that *either* there are various schools represented in the sections *or* there are different stages of development or different time periods represented. For the "three schools" approach, see Graham 1985.

6. Or some particular Mohist school as opposed to another.

7. Fraser 2013.

8. The "standards" are explicitly discussed in all three parts of *Fei ming*. In the first section, they are called *biao* (based on the *gnomon* as sundial)—see McLeod 2016.

9. This question is at the heart of the Indian religious and philosophical text *Bhagavad Gita*, for example.

10. *Mozi, Fei ming* 1.2.

11. The Mohists seem to evaluate both *yan* (statements) and *shuo* (acts of saying). One way in which we *might* understand the relationship is that the *shuo* is an act that expresses a *yan*, which would render the *yan* similar to a "statement" or "proposition" in contemporary philosophy of language. Eventually, *yan* becomes the primary linguistic entity evaluated for truth, in Han dynasty texts. The scope of *yan* both in Mohist texts and in later work appears to be fairly broad—a *yan* can be a single statement, teaching, doctrine, etc. This immediately distinguishes any theory of truth connected with *yan* from contemporary theories of truth, as *yan* are not simple subject-predicate assertions primarily. Teachings or doctrines, in contemporary theory, would have to be evaluated on the basis of individual subject-predicate statements if truth-evaluable at all. We might thus take the "teaching of Confucius" as a conjunction of all of the particular individual statements of Confucius, and appraise it as true *iff* all of its conjuncts are true and false otherwise, etc. This is not the way *yan* are appraised in any of the early Chinese texts. A *yan* is not true or false on the basis of the truth or falsity of more basic constructions that comprise it through conjunction or any other relationship. We will see that there are very important results of this position concerning general theories of truth.

12. Alternatively, assertion of the existence of fate. *Yi wei* can signal belief ("taking it that *x*") or assertion ("maintaining that *x* is the case").

13. Hansen 1985.

14. Indeed, in considering the Mohist arguments against the anti-language positions of the *Zhuangzi* of *Canon* B 71, Hansen uses the example of truth paradoxes to make sense of the Mohist position. He quickly offers the caveat "the Mohists . . . do not formulate their criticisms of the antilanguage position as I did [truth paradoxes]. Instead of talking of *sentences*, *truth* and *falsity*, the Neo-Mohists speak of their more familiar *yan* (language). Instead of false, they use the term *bei* (perverse). They define *bei* as *bu-ke* (not permissible)" (Hansen 1992: 241). He then goes on to offer a translation of *Canon* B 71 that is almost exactly structurally parallel to the problem concerning truth that he discusses, with the only difference that the "truth" terms are substituted with these Mohist terms. If the most natural explanation of what the Mohists are doing here in English is discussion of truth paradox, and swapping terms like *bei* out with "false" and *yan* with "sentence" would give us exactly this, why not think that this is just a discussion of truth paradox? Of course the Mohists don't use the terms "truth," "falsity," and "sentence," because they were not writing in English. But given the way in which they use the terms they *did* use to express something structurally equivalent to discussion of truth *paradox* (even Hansen, the arch-rival of truth in early Chinese texts, seemed to have no more useful explanation than truth paradox), why shouldn't we simply think that those terms are meant to express truth concepts? Hansen's reasons for rejecting truth concern in Mohist texts rely on a very few and shaky passages and assumptions, but then he applies this such that it transforms passages most easily read as concerning truth into something else, simply because he has determined that the Mohists are not concerned with truth. A. C. Graham (1978:

446) reads B 71 straightforwardly as concerning truth paradox: "B 71 and 79 are essentially refutations of the propositions 'all propositions are false' and 'all propositions are true', similar to those of Aristotle in *Metaphysics* 1063b/30–35."

15. Graham 1989.

16. Fraser 2014: "The Mohists applied a pragmatic, non-representational theory of language and knowledge and developed a rudimentary theory of analogical argumentation." Also Loy 2011. While arguing that Mohists recognize a distinction between "semantic truth" and "pragmatic utility" (though I'm not sure he's right or why they would need to do so), Fraser also claims: "His focus on *dao* leads them to run together the empirical question of whether ghosts exist with the normative question of whether we should act on and promulgate the teaching that they do. The doctrine of the three models thus reflects the pragmatic orientation of their thought, in particular the assumption, common to many early Chinese thinkers, that the primary purpose of language and judgment is to guide action appropriately, rather than to describe facts."

17. Fraser 2014, Loy 2011: 657. Loy suggests that the Mohists move back and forth between the consideration of descriptive and normative claims, even in evaluating *yan* (statements) they take to be the same, thus possibly conflating the two. Loy reads "pragmatic" concern as distinct from "truth" concern, which seems to be a shared feature of pragmatist readings of Mozi. Loy also offers an interpretation in which there are *five* standards for appraising *yan* in the *Mozi*, based on different passages construing the *fa* or *biao* differently in the text.

18. Loy 2011: 657.

19. Loy 2011: 658.

20. Bryan Van Norden, A. C. Graham, David Wong, and Benjamin Schwartz all appear to accept versions of such a position.

21. Hansen, as we have seen, accepts such a view

22. Van Norden 2007: 160–161.

23. Fraser 2011.

24. Actually the third part of the chapter. The first two have been lost, and only the third is compiled in the extant version of *Mozi*.

25. *Mozi, Ming gui xia*, 2.

26. David Hume's arguments in *A Treatise of Human Nature* 3.1.1 concerning what he sees as an illegitimate move from "is" to "ought" is a key example of this.

27. Bilgrami 2010.

28. Some, such as Fraser (2011), have claimed that it is the Mohist position on *tian zhi* (the intention of heaven) that rules out the useful falsehood.

29. And we can of course generalize this to any entity, such that [*x* exists *iff* we ought to accept the existence of *x*], etc.

30. Following the book/chapter/section format.

31. Chris Fraser writes: "As framed in the text, then, the three standards reflect an explicit concern not with truth but with *dao*, the right way of individual and collective conduct and policy—including linguistic conduct, or verbal pronouncements" (Fraser 2012: 355).

32. Saunders' case is a difficult one. Although he rejects Hansen's position that the Mohists are interested in pragmatics and not semantics, he does not identify the idea

of semantic adequacy in the later Mohist work with "truth," apparently mainly for the reason that he thinks this conception of the Mohists is sufficiently different from the "Western" understanding of truth. I discuss this position further below.

33. Fraser 2012.
34. Fraser 2012: 354–355.
35. Fraser 2012: 357.
36. Saunders 2014.
37. Essentially, although it is kĕ (acceptable, pragmatically appropriate) to call something "Crane" if it is lineage-named "Crane," in this case the word does not (and must not) refer to actual cranes in that it does not denote an object of the kind "crane"; calling these "Cranes" is appropriate, but not accurate (Saunders 2014: 226).
38. Saunders 2014: 219.
39. *Mozi, Canon* A74, Saunders trans. in Saunders 2014: 220.
40. Graham 1978: 318.
41. Saunders 2014: 229.

Chapter 4

Xunzi

Xunzi is the early Confucian philosopher most clearly and explicitly concerned with issues of language, including truth. Thus it is no surprise that most of the scholarly literature surrounding issues of naming (*ming* 命), truth, and language is concerned with issues in the *Xunzi*.

Consideration of language in the *Xunzi* surrounds mainly the issue of *ming* (names), and their proper application. Part of the issue in understanding Xunzi's positions has been coming to terms with just what is signified by "*ming.*" Indeed, a large part of the contemporary debate surrounding interpretation of *zhengming* in early Confucianism involves disagreement surrounding the meaning and application of the concept of *ming*. While the etymologies of early texts such as the *Shuowen jiezi* and *Erya* can be dubious and misleading, they can also show us ways in which particular terms were understood during the period of the writing of these texts.

The entry on *ming* from the *Shuowen* reads:

名：自命也。从口从夕。夕者，冥也。冥不相見，故以口自名

"ming": Comes from "allotment" [ming]. From "mouth" [kou] and "night" [xi]. "Xi" means "hidden" [ming]. To be hidden is to be unseen, one brings forth names with the mouth.[1]

The *Shiming* entry on *ming* reads:

名，明也，名實事使分明也.

Names are "illumination." The cause of the distinction of name and actuality (ming-shi) is illumination.[2]

These definitions are of limited use, of course. But one thing they *can* offer us is a glimpse into at least one way of understanding the use of *ming* in the Han period, in which both the texts were compiled. Both the *Shuowen* and *Shiming* definitions suggest that *ming* is the means of revealing something otherwise unknown or inaccessible. The source or ground of this inaccessibility is impossible to discern from the contexts of these passages alone. Chen Bo reads the statement of the *Shuowen* as an assertion of names as "stand in" linguistic entities for objects, which play the role of objects when ostension is not possible.[3] While Chen's view that consideration of *ming* must have to do with a *cognitive function* of some kind must be correct, the above passages do *not* show that this cognitive function must be that of reference to objects absent ostension. While I am sympathetic to the view that, at least in the *Xunzi* and subsequent texts, *"ming"* refers to an identifying concept connected to particular objects or events in the world beyond roles (this is arguably less plausibly so in earlier material such as the *Analects*), this is too much to read into the very broad definition offered in the etymological texts of the Han.

The translation of *ming* as "name" and its corresponding treatment as akin to proper names is problematic. The main reason I translate it here as "name" is to be consistent with the most widespread practice. To treat *ming* as simply a name is to miss much, perhaps *most*, of its significance, concerning both its role in behavior modification and concerning the issue of truth. I suspect that some of the treatment of *ming* as consonant with names is the association of the two in contemporary Chinese languages. *Ming* is understood today in a far narrower way than it was in early Chinese philosophy. This narrow conception of *ming* leads to a number of problems, and it becomes difficult to make sense of the normative nature of the *zhengming* process and the idea of correct, good, or appropriate names (*shanming* 善名) if *ming* ought to be understood simply as name. Most scholars who have worked on the issue recognize that for Xunzi *ming* has this normative content, but this tends not to be then associated with a view that *ming* signifies something broader or altogether different from a contemporary understanding of names.[4]

Indeed, Jane Geaney has argued convincingly that *ming* should not be understood as names in the sense of labels or proper names.[5] Although her purposes in investigating the meaning of *ming*, as well as her conclusions on its meaning, are different than mine, I agree with Geaney that *ming* does not have the sense of name or label specifically in early Chinese texts. Geaney marshals a good deal of textual evidence demonstrating that various thinkers use *ming* in ways that seem inconsistent with *names*. In the discussion of *xu yan* 虛言 (false or empty statements) in *Hanfeizi* chapter 10, *ming* is contrasted with *shi* (as something like "actuality"), and is here seen as part of or associated with an empty statement (*xu yan*). The passage reads:

夫以實告我者秦也，以名救我者楚也，聽楚之虛言而輕誣強秦之實禍，
則危國之本也。

[The state of] Qin is harassing us in deed (*shi*), while Chu is rescuing us in name
(*ming*). If we listen to Chu's empty speech (*xu yan*) and make light of forceful
Qin's fulfilled (*shi*) calamity, this is the root of endangering the state.[6]

Geaney, in explaining this passage, explains that *ming* and *yan* are often
associated in early Chinese texts, as they appear to be in the *Hanfeizi* passage
here.[7] As she reads *yan* as having to do with speech or the spoken word in
particular, Geaney argues that *ming* likewise should be seen as a feature of
speech. I think there is a different conclusion that we should draw from this,
however. *Yan* certainly indicates speech. But, like the English term "statement," it has multiple senses. It can refer to a speech act, or alternatively the
content of a speech act. We see *yan* used in just this way in early Chinese
texts. In Wang Chong's *Lunheng*, *yan* are appraised for their truth value. This
cannot be done with a speech act alone—there must be linguistic content for
the entity to be appraised, otherwise one is considering the appropriateness of
the utterance of a particular noise—and why should one noise be improper if
another is proper? This is also consistent with the point I make about *ming* in
chapter 1. If *ming* is descriptive, then there is a natural association with *yan*
(which I translate as "statement" in part because *yan* is ambiguous in exactly
the same way as the English term). This perfectly fits with Geaney's reading
of both *yan* and *ming* as "things that are heard,"[8] though it focuses on the
thing heard as (in both cases) the linguistic content rather than the sound.[9]

Though the issue of *names* has not been a major concern in recent work
on the issue of truth, there are issues that approach the interests of the early
Chinese philosophers. As discussed in earlier chapters, one issue that comes
to the fore in a consideration of *ming* is that of *satisfaction* of descriptions
that can be taken to be identified by a particular *ming*. The most robust and
useful account of satisfaction and its relationship to truth is offered by Alfred
Tarski. Tarski's account of truth is still influential today, particularly among
those who endorse deflationary accounts of truth. A brief glance at Tarski's
account of satisfaction and its relationship to truth may help us to see some of
what *might* be going on in the early Chinese consideration of names.

Tarski took himself to be offering a way to account for truth in what he
called its "classical" sense as involving correspondence of sentences with
reality. Tarski's motivation for using satisfaction as the basic component of
his theory of truth was a formal constraint, particularly that sentences are
built from basic formulas (of a logical language), rather than from other sentences.[10] Although this constraint might strike us as outside of the concerns
of the early Chinese philosophers, it is surprisingly similar to a concern they

did have. *Ming* can be understood as basic predicative structures along the lines of Tarski formulas (first-order nonquantified formulas with free variables). A *ming* itself can be understood along the lines of Tarski's formula, and it is in *application* of the *ming* that we consider as the issue of satisfaction. We transform the formula associated with a *ming* into a *sentence* when all free variables are removed. Thus, when we consider whether "father" is a name properly applied to some class of persons, we ask whether the objects of this class satisfy the formula (*x* is a father), where father is defined by some description. A sentence is formed either when we substitute the variable with a particular or when eliminate the free variable through quantification. An additional concern of Tarski, according to Gila Sher, is giving some account of truth as correspondence. She takes this as one of the considerations grounding his reliance on satisfaction as basic (even though there seem to be problems with understanding his concept of satisfaction as explaining correspondence between language and world). Sher writes:

> The correspondence nature of Tarski's notion of truth is demonstrated by his choice of *satisfaction* as the central semantic notion of his method. Satisfaction is a relation between *objects* (sequences of objects) and linguistic entities (formulas of a given language), hence inherently a correspondence relation.[11]

Regardless of whether Tarski's account is ultimately successful at explaining such a correspondence relation, a desire to do so is clearly in the background. We see much the same thing in many of the early Chinese accounts of naming. The issue of whether names are appropriate or applicable often boils down to whether particular individuals satisfy the descriptions given by a name. Whether an individual or class does satisfy a description is never a matter of convention—the conventional aspect of naming is connected either with according of proper names or creating of classes based on description, and their association with particular words. None of the early Chinese thinkers, even the most radical such as Zhuangzi, take satisfaction of a description itself to be a matter of convention. And it is unclear how they *could* endorse such a view, absent a radical idealism even beyond that of Berkeley and his ilk, in which convention determines facts about events that take place in the world.

The theory of *ming* in early texts, including *zhengming* in the Confucian texts, makes more sense as a whole and is more plausible, I argue, if we understand it as involving descriptions rather than labels or proper names. But ultimately the textual evidence suggests that there is a theory of truth involved with the theory of *zhengming*, however construed. What makes for the theory of truth here is the notion of the adequacy of *ming*, and what it is that makes *ming* adequate. If Xunzi is correctly read as a realist or as a semi-realist (as

I read him), then the theory of truth on offer is a kind of correspondence theory, in which 名 *ming* are made true by their corresponding to *shi*. If Xunzi is correctly read as a conventionalist, on the other hand, his theory of truth becomes much more like a form of coherentism (perhaps blended with pragmatism), in which the *shi* created by *ming* are "truth-making" insofar as they cohere with one another in a system that has positive practical effects.

I argue here for the first of these options. Xunzi is, interestingly enough, not altogether distant from the *Zhuangzi* on the issue of truth. Both the *Xunzi* and the *Zhuangzi* adopt a view of truth on which it is necessary for a statement (or *ming*) to correspond with reality (whether understood in terms of *shi* 實 or *dao* 道). Both have views of objects, in which the way we "carve" the world is dependent at least in part on the mind. The difference between Xunzi and Zhuangzi here is that Xunzi holds that there are correct ways of "carving" the world, thus entailing that there are objective and universal truths, while Zhuangzi (as seen in the next chapter) rejects that there are *uniquely* correct ways of "carving" the world, which makes truth dependent (at least in part) on convention or perspective.

Perhaps the most clearly truth-oriented of the chapters of the *Xunzi* are the *Zhengming* 正名 (Rectification of Names) and *Lilun* 禮論 (Discussion of Ritual) chapters. Xunzi's views on *zhengming* are notoriously difficult to pin down, as what he says in the chapter lends itself to a number of possible readings, not all of which have much to do with language at all. It is here, however, that we see the first explicit theoretical interest in aspects of language in the Confucian tradition. By Xunzi's time, however, he would have had to engage in theorizing about language, as competing schools such as the Mohists, the School of Names, and Zhuangists all had sophisticated views concerning language and its applicability that Xunzi had to have a response to. It was no longer acceptable simply to ignore the issue of language, just as it had become no longer acceptable to ignore the issue of *ren xing* 人性 (human nature).

Certainly we see in the *Xunzi* the same kind of "truth talk" we see in other texts like *Mengzi*, a use of the concept of truth *de re* (to use Hansen's terminology). But in the *Xunzi*, unlike in earlier Confucian texts, we also see a *de dicto* concern with truth, and the beginnings of Confucian theorizing about, rather than just employing, the concept of truth. This concern is most clearly revealed in the *Zhengming* (Rectification of Names) chapter. While there has been much written about Xunzi's views and intentions in this chapter, I begin by offering what I take to be a plausible reconstruction of his views on the concept of truth contained in this chapter.

Names (*ming*), according to Xunzi, are established and applied to objects by the ruler, who is uniquely authorized to engage in the task of creation and rectification of names. From the beginning of the chapter, we see a concern with how things are called (*wei* 謂), which is connected to the distinguishing of actualities (*shi* 實). This is one of the earliest places in which we see the *ming-shi* construction, and this remains a major part of truth concern in early Chinese thought. The term *shi*, which we saw in consideration of Mencius (and will see in many other texts) as a term evaluating statements, is in this context what properly aligns with a correct name. A name is correct insofar as it matches and thus reveals the *shi* of a given thing. While this use clearly is different from *shi* as value of a statement, it is closely related to that use, and, I argue, should be seen as the extension of a truth concept.

It is in the *Zhengming* chapter that we most clearly find the emphasis on truth in *Xunzi*. It is also in this chapter that we find the most occurrences of the term *shi*, and the most extended discussion of it. We begin to get a clearer picture of what *shi* is, according to Xunzi, and its relationship with *ming*, through investigation of key passages of the chapter. The first mention of *shi* that we see in the chapter ties it to distinctions in things pointed out by *ming*:

故王者之制名，名定而實辨，道行而志通，則慎率民而一焉

Therefore the king institutes names. When names are established, actualities (shi) are distinguished. The way is practiced and (the king's) will is communicated, and this leads the people to be as one.[12]

The crucial part of this passage is toward the beginning. The ruler, in gaining success in fixing descriptions and the application of descriptions to things in the correct ways, enables the distinguishing (*bian*) of actualities. We see that this establishment of names is distinct from the ruler's devising of names that happens prior to this. This is what Xunzi means here by the "institution" (*zhi*) of names, which is discussed separately from their establishment (*ding*). The creation of a *ming* by itself does not help to distinguish actualities, as such distinction presumably requires the *acceptance* and *knowledge* of the name (description) by the people, who are the main focus of the ruler's action in rectifying names. The establishment (*ding*) of names in this sense then gives the people the ability to distinguish between things. So what does *shi* (actuality) have to do with this? It is *shi*, according to Xunzi, that the people are able to determine, and they would be unable to do so without the establishment of names. On the face of it, this seems a strike against a view of *shi* in the chapter as *reality* or *states-of-affairs*. It is difficult to see why we would need *names*, in the sense of description of anything else, to determine the differences between any given things in the world. Why would we be unable to determine the distinctions between objects that are distinct in the world?

If we adopt a conventionalist metaphysical stance, however, we can more easily see why the establishment of particular names would make a key difference in our ability to distinguish states-of-affairs in the world. Attributing something like a conventionalist metaphysics concerning names to Xunzi also can help us make sense of texts such as the *Zhuangzi*, which develop this conventionalism to its natural end, far beyond what Xunzi was willing to accept. David Elstein attributes to Xunzi what he calls a "modified conventionalism concerning language."[13] I too interpret Xunzi as holding what can be called modified conventionalism, but the conventionalism I have in mind and Xunzi's modifications to it diverge from Elstein's conception.[14] The key modification has to do with the notion of proper ways of distinguishing the world by language. According to Xunzi, even though names involve an ineliminably conventional element, there are normatively correct ways to determine names that the wise ruler understands in virtue of his grasp of reality or the way things are.

The discussion in the rest of this chapter aims at establishing that the Xunzian theory of names (名 *ming*) relies on and includes a theory of truth that, although for the most part is not explicitly discussed in the *Xunzi*, can be reconstructed here on the basis of a number of connected concepts, arguments, and claims of the text. In order to draw out the theory of truth on offer here, we must consider first the view of *reality* in the Xunzi, the basis of ritual and language in (mind-independent) reality, and finally the conventional nature of names/descriptions and the role reality (*shi*) plays in the justification of these names/descriptions.

REALITY AND RITUAL

The concept of ritual (*li* 禮)[15] is at the center of the thought of the *Xunzi*. There has been substantial disagreement among scholars, however, concerning Xunzi's view on the basis or ground of ritual (and we will see much the same is the case for language). Some things that Xunzi says seem to suggest that ritual is ultimately conventional—that it is fully created by sages and is mind-dependent. In other places in the text, however, we find suggestions that ritual is based in mind-independent reality, and that although the sages have a role in the institution and establishment of ritual, they do not create it, but rather make it clear or verbalize it. The difference between the two options can be subtle and complicated. Even on the conventionalist view, there will of course have to be a place for reality and the patterns of reality. The sage's creation of ritual, if indeed the sage so creates, will necessarily be constrained by both the nature of the sage, and also the nature of humans for whom the sage creates ritual. Given that the function of ritual is to create social harmony,[16] the sage in his construction of ritual has to understand and take account of human nature, and has to construct rituals that will have the requisite effect on human nature, which is necessarily a matter of mind-independent facts about nature. Thus, the conventionalist view does not attribute *pure* conventionalism to Xunzi concerning the rituals.

Likewise, the realist view of ritual also necessarily involves a conventional element. It is implausible to read Xunzi as claiming that the rituals are completely given mind-independently, in the same way that we may think that the ground of knowledge is independent of language and conceptualization,[17] or that metaphysical realists think about objects.[18] The reason for this is that Xunzi clearly claims at least that the sages have a role in determining certain essential features of ritual, which would not be possible were ritual to be properly construed as mind-independent in the metaphysical realist's sense. The question then becomes *how much convention* is involved in the construction of ritual? I think that the debate concerning conventionalism and realism regarding ritual in the *Xunzi* is concerned with the wrong question. We should not be asking "is Xunzi a realist or conventionalist concerning ritual?" but rather "which elements of Xunzi's view of ritual are conventionalist and which are realist?" We cannot make sense of Xunzi's position concerning ritual on a standard realist versus conventionalist picture, because Xunzi's position shares features with both, but ultimately fits well within neither.

Xunzi's discussion of ritual often assumes the convention-independent truth or acceptability of certain kinds of distinctions, as in the following passage concerning funerals from the *Lilun* chapter:

故喪禮者，無他焉，明死生之義，送以哀敬，而終周藏也

> Therefore the funeral rituals are none other than the illumination of what is appropriate in life and death, to send off (relatives) with sadness and respect, and finally to bury them.[19]

The wording chosen here is that of understanding, particularly *illumination* (*ming*). The rituals do not *determine* what is appropriate (*yi* 義) in life and death, but reveal it. The suggestion here is that what is appropriate in life and death is there—there are facts about it, even independently of our knowledge, and through ritual we come to remove the darkness, gaining understanding. The term *ming* 明 has the original sense of lighting or illumination. The character is comprised of a sun (*ri* 日) and moon (*yue* 月) together—the two celestial bodies that provide light. It is possible, of course, that what is appropriate can be "illuminated" in this case because ritual determines appropriateness, but this would be to make ritual the basis for appropriateness, in which case ritual could not be criticized or changed on grounds of appropriateness. While it is in the Mengzi that we find most of the discussion of *yi* as seemingly fundamental, Xunzi also distinguishes *li* and *yi* in numerous passages, in ways that suggest that it cannot be *li* that is the ground of or determinant of *yi*.

If this is the case, then what determines *yi*? While Xunzi never outright states what determines it, he does make claims that suggest a fundamental basis for *yi* that is based in *tian*, or nature. Another passage from *Lilun* reads:

禮者、斷長續短，損有餘，益不足，達愛敬之文，而滋成行義之美者也.

Ritual constrains the long and extends the short, limits the overabundant and increases the insufficient. It increases care and respect in patterns, and achieves the completion of appropriateness.[20]

This seems to involve more normative claims concerning what ought to be the case at a pre-ritual level. Ritual makes things the way they ought to be, which is identified with *yi*. It *completes* the expression of *yi*, rather than creating the standard of *yi*. It seems clear that *yi* is a distinct concept connected to, but not grounded in, *li*. *Yi* is grounded in nature, the way things are, or *tian*.[21] *Li*, on the other hand, is a combination of natural principle and the conventional effort of the sage. *Li* can be good or bad, acceptable or unacceptable, while *yi* simply *are*. There is a normative element to *yi*—that is, *yi* is construed as normatively binding, in terms of what we ought to do, but there is no *unacceptable* or *unjustified yi*. To be *yi* is to be acceptable. Ritual, as a matter of fact, may turn out to be completely acceptable (if it were not we would not call it ritual), but there may be a category related to ritual, perhaps *customs* (*su* 俗), that may be correct or incorrect. In the act of creation of custom/ritual, it is possible to *get things wrong*, presumably on the basis of lack of understanding. The sages, of course, don't get things wrong—this is one major reason they are sages, so the customs they create will all be ritual, will be proper. The sages seemingly still rely on natural features of the world, however—facts about the abilities and traits of things, about how the mind works, and about what will be effective in bringing about the desired states.

Xunzi argues for adherence to ritual on the basis of practical effects, but it is unclear whether these effects are *all there is to ritual* (so that ritual is a matter of convention, based on what things in a particular community or culture might play the relevant desire-constraining role), or whether these effects of ritual are based on more fundamental features of the world that privilege a particular set of rituals (namely, those of the Zhou).

As Sor-hoon Tan rightly points out, the little said in the Xunzi on the topic and the multitude of possibilities given Xunzi's practical view of ritual make it difficult to determine whether the Xunzi offers any metaphysical view at all, and if so, what it is. Of the options offered by contemporary scholars concerning Xunzi on the metaphysical status or source of ritual, I find the realist interpretation most plausible[22] (although as I mentioned above it is not completely accurate and I will offer key qualifications).

There are two issues here that need to be distinguished, although I will not here get into some of the interesting questions connected to this distinction, as my primary focus is on the connection between this issue and that of truth. There is the question of absolutism versus pluralism with respect to ritual, and there is the related question of realism versus conventionalism. Each member of one of these pairs, I believe, entails a member of the other pair, but it is important not to assume that if a historical (or contemporary) thinker holds one of these that he or she necessarily holds the other view that he or she is committed to (as discussed above). Paul Goldin does an admirable job at keeping these two considerations separate, and drawing one from the other, as I think is correct in the case of Xunzi. Xunzi is both an absolutist and a realist about ritualism, and his absolutism derives from his realism. Goldin writes:

> The rituals of the Sage Kings identify the natural order, and augment it, by confirming the distinctions that people are bound to make by nature. This is why there is only one set of legitimate rituals. There is only one Way. The Sage Kings apprehended it, and their rituals embody it. There is no other Way, and no other constellation of rituals that conforms to the Way.[23]

There are many passages in the *Xunzi* that one might point to in support of this view, including claims from the *Lilun* suggesting that the specific rituals established by the sages are unalterable, and that this is in part due to the perfect efficacy of these rituals:

三年之喪，何也？曰：稱情而立文，因以飾群，別親疏貴賤之節，而不可益損也。故曰：無適不易之術也。

Why must the mourning period be three years? My response is this: it is capturing the emotions and establishing the outward sign, in order to adorn the community. One does not neglect relatives whether rich or poor, and (likewise the mourning period) cannot be augmented or decreased. Therefore I say: it is without match and this method (of ritual) is not to be changed.[24]

We might take statements like this, however, to conflict with statements seeming to suggest that rituals are completely artificial, created by humans and based on human-dependent conventions. A number of interpreters, including Roger Ames and Kurtis Hagen, hold a view of Xunzi as endorsing a kind of ritual conventionalism and pluralism, in which rituals might be changed over time, or differ for different communities.[25] Hagen points to the following passage in *Zhengming*, for example, to support his conventionalist interpretation of ritual:

若有王者起，必將有循於舊名，有作於新名

If someone like the (sage) kings were to arise, they would necessarily adhere to the old names, and create (*zuo*) new names.[26]

Hagen takes this to show that Xunzi held a general view allowing for the malleability of traditional forms. This position is flawed in a couple of ways, however. First, there is an important disanalogy between construction of names and expression of ritual in Xunzi's thought. While a sage king may be able to 作 *zuo* (create) a name, he could never *zuo* ritual.

Another passage Hagen appeals to to support a conventionalist reading is this one from *Lilun*:

故喪禮者，無他焉，明死生之義，送以哀敬，而終周藏也

Therefore the funeral rituals are none other than the illumination of what is appropriate in life and death, to send off (relatives) with sadness and respect, and finally to bury them.[27]

He reads this as allowing for change in the rituals presumably because "what is appropriate in both death and life" seems malleable and applicable to time, circumstance, etc. In order to think this, however, we would *already* have to have reason to think that Xunzi is a conventionalist. Absolutists could easily say (and often do say) things like this. The difference for them that "what is appropriate" is not variable. It is the same, fixed, in situations of the relevant type. To explain the funerary rituals as expressing what is appropriate can simply be taken as a claim of the content and source of these ritual types. There seems nothing in this passage that could count as evidence in itself that Xunzi accepted as a conventionalist view of ritual.[28]

Sor-hoon Tan takes a different approach. She points out the seeming conflict between passages expressing realist/absolutist views and those expressing conventionalist/pluralist views in the *Xunzi*, and argues that it shows a fundamental inconsistency in Xunzi's metaphysical view of ritual. She argues that we should take this as reason to hold that Xunzi was not committed to any particular metaphysical view of ritual, and only offered the little he did as a way to support his practical theory of ritual action.

Whatever metaphysical assumptions there might be in the *Xunzi*, they serve to defend his theory of ritual. If the inconsistencies and ambiguities of the usages of *tian* are any indication, those metaphysical assumptions are probably unclear and apparently inconsistent. While he might not have been able to avoid metaphysical assumptions, Xunzi did not deem it necessary to have a viable, defensible metaphysical theory.[29]

Part of her argument for this final claim is that the little Xunzi does explicitly say about the metaphysics of ritual in passages like the opening of *Lilun* is consistent with a great number of theories advanced by scholars, and it is hard to privilege one of these as the correct view.

I think there is little reason to accept Tan's position, however. First, the fact that what little Xunzi says about metaphysics is consistent with a number of different theoretical possibilities is no indication that Xunzi intended his words to be ambiguous so as to avoid commitment. We should expect that anything about which not much is said will be consistent with a great many possible theories. Theories are only ruled out the more that is said about a subject, just as in experimental science many possible theories are consistent with just a sole observation.

Second, if Xunzi's sole concern was with the practical application of ritual, he need not have offered *any* metaphysical position, let alone the one outlined at the very beginning of his most direct discussion of ritual, *Lilun*. There are plenty of ritual texts from the period with no metaphysical statements whatsoever, including much of what is compiled in the *Liji*, so it would be strange that Xunzi felt that he had to say something about metaphysics up front if he had no worked-out theory and was not at all concerned with metaphysics.

Third, while the metaphysics indeed is intended to support Xunzi's practical views about ritual, in order to provide this support it needs to be fairly robust and defensible. After all, Xunzi is making quite extreme practical claims about the invariability of ritual. The ritual institutions cannot be changed (either through addition or subtraction), and cannot be abandoned. It's going to be important to have some kind of justification for this beyond simply the practical claim that ritual in its exact specificity is the only thing that works. If we are asked to adhere so stringently to ritual, we are owed an explanation as to *how* it works, and unless this explanation involves some unchanging features of nature itself, it looks like it will not be strong enough. Certainly, a conventionalist metaphysical explanation would not do the trick. I suggest, then, that Xunzi's discussion of metaphysics, specifically the source of ritual, is deemed necessary because his conception of ritual adherence is so much more demanding than that of other early Confucians, who seemed to allow for more variation in ritual than did Xunzi.[30]

In addition, there is good reason to think that the seeming statements of conventionalism about ritual that scholars like Tan (to some extent), Hagen, Ames, and others point to as contrasting with his "fundamentalist" claims[31] have been misread in the light of some common understanding of key terms such as *wei* (artifice, to create) and *zhi* (to institute, express).

Fung Yiu-ming argues that many interpreters have overlooked the fact that *wei* can have two different senses in Xunzi. Fung distinguishes the two senses on the basis of a distinction between external and internal. While Fung's discussion of these two senses is intended to put pressure on the standard view that Xunzi's theory of human nature assumes a completely corrupted *xing,* understanding this distinction can also help undermine a view of Xunzi as a ritual conventionalist. Fung explains:

> The customary view that "*xing* is internal while *wei* is external" is incomplete, if not wrong. The second sense of the term does refer to some kind of performance of external behaviors; but the first sense is about some kind of potential capacity, which includes thinking (or knowing) and activating (or willing) powers in humans, and which is the subjective power that can make the performance of external behaviors possible.[32]

Fung bases this on a seeming distinction made in the *Zhengming* chapter. If we read the *wei* (deliberate effort) here as following Fung's first, "internal" sense, we might read it as the power of *expressing* ritual, rather than *creating* it. This sense of *wei* makes possible a reading of *wei* as facilitation of the expression of ritual, the capacity within humans (sagely humans, at least) to give voice and expression to the rituals, which are themselves given as natural law, for anyone to discover.

The passage in question here comes from the opening of *Zhengming.*[33]

心慮而能為之動謂之偽；慮積焉，能習焉，而後成謂之偽。

To reflect and thus be able to enact a change is called deliberate effort (*wei*). Through collecting reflections and being able to practice, and thereby coming to completion is called deliberate effort.[34]

It is important to notice here that the definition Xunzi gives of *wei* both explicitly avoids the vocabulary of "creation," and also connects it with the term *zhi* used in the chapter to describe the sages' role in establishing correct language, which is analogous to their role in instituting ritual. The passages speak of "coming to completion" (*cheng* 成), making a "movement/change" (*dong* 動), and "reflection" (*lu* 慮), but never "creation" (*zuo* 作).[35] Instead, Xunzi describes the sages as *zhi* 制 (instituting, expressing) language and ritual, just as in the opening passage of *Lilun* cited above.[36] Why would this be? If we take the understanding of *wei* gained by a consideration of the "internal" sense outlined by Fung and read through the latter passage from *Zhengming* above, we can make better sense out of some of the claims of sagely "construction" of ritual given in chapters like *Xing e*, claims that are often taken by proponents of a conventionalist reading as being explicit claims of the human creation of ritual.

The key passage from *Xing e* reads:

凡禮義者，是生於聖人之偽

In each case ritual and appropriateness are derived from the deliberate effort
(*wei*) of the sages.[37]

We can see, if we take the reading of 偽 *wei* I describe above, that this
statement turns out not to be one privileging a conventionalist reading of
ritual, but rather a statement of the sages' necessary involvement in the
expression of ritual.[38] But how might we understand how ritual can be
something expressed rather than constructed, something construed in a
realist sense as *in the world* rather than dependent on human minds and
effort?

The "deliberate effort" that Xunzi discusses need not be thought of in
terms of innovation or creation (*zuo* 作)—indeed, a conservative ritualist like
Xunzi would likely be uncomfortable attributing the authority of ritual to the
decisions and creative powers of past individuals, however talented they may
have been. We might understand Xunzi's claim about *wei* as entailing that
the sages do not *create* ritual, but they reveal, expound, or give it voice. That
is, we might see the creative role of the sages as an *articulative* role. What
the sages did was to deliberate and express *li* based on their understanding
of *dao* (this in part involved correct application of 名 *ming* [names]), and
thus to articulate the implicit ritual structure inherent in the world. True, the
sages engage in *wei* 偽 (deliberate effort) to articulate the rituals, but this,
as explained in the last section above, does not necessarily entail a kind of
creation ex nihilo.

Presumably, when the sage brings something to completion (成 *cheng*)
through reflection, he accesses some features of the world that makes it possible, and correctly articulates this in formulated rituals. The sage is able to
access *dao* through reflection, to understand *dao*, and through practice is able
to discover the correct ways of articulating this *dao* through ritual. In order
to do this, the sage must be able to access facts about *dao* and express them
through language in a way that accurately reflects *dao* as it is. This is certainly
a matter of *truth*. The ruler's establishment maintenance of *ming* 名 (names)
is a matter in part of this insight into the *dao*.

REALITY AND LANGUAGE

The act of *naming*, for Xunzi, is, like the act of creating ritual, the task of the
ruler. A key difference between the projects of *zhengming* (rectification of
names) and that of the establishment of ritual, however, is that those properly
involved with ritual were the *sages*, whereas the ruler in general properly has

the role of rectifying names. Thus, it appears a less lofty activity than creation of ritual, even though it is of extreme importance.

Some, such as Eric Hutton, read *shi* 實 in the *Zhengming* chapter as signifying the "object" to which a name (*ming* 名) applies.[39] This reading of *shi* seems necessary only if we understand *ming* as approximating something like proper names or names, rather than descriptions. Xunzi, like other early Chinese philosophers concerned with *ming*, mean themselves to talk about descriptions as well as names when they discuss *ming* (as I argue in chapter 1). Indeed, reading *ming* merely as names of objects leads to the very difficulty that so many scholars aim to solve—how can merely accepting particular names for objects have the kind of broad effect that early Confucians claim for the establishment and acceptance of correct *ming*?[40] How can "noble and base" be distinguished and "like and unlike" be differentiated on the basis of names coined to refer to things? It is a difficulty that I have seen no good solution for, and I think part of the reason for this is that the problem assumes a conception of *ming* that is too narrow. If we understand *ming* in terms of fairly robust description (including normative description), the problem cannot even be formulated. It also turns out that the conception of *ming* that dissolves the problem also offers us a conception of *ming* and the act of and justification of naming that involves a particular theory of truth.

Lin Chung-I is skeptical that a move to an understanding of *ming* as involving statements dissolves the problem. He writes:

> Even if we allow the "name" to include not only terms but, extensively, also sentences and inferences (however they are to be conceived), the name-rectification still would not show its close relation to moral rectification under the language-refinement conception.[41]

I am less sure that this is the case. When we make a move from a view of *ming* as terms and names to one of *ming* as descriptions, the normative structure of *ming* becomes more clear. Lin agrees that *ming* must have some kind of normative structure, but I think that the normativity of *ming* is based in description, as it is very hard to see how it could be based in mere labels. Here, as in later thinkers, we can see that it is the inherent normativity of statements that plays a crucial role, and is essential for understanding early Chinese theories of truth. This does not of course rule out names as one kind of *ming*, but *ming* is a broader category than simply "names."

Xunzi, as I claimed above, is adopting a kind of metaphysical conventionalism, constrained by facts about the world that are perhaps prelinguistic.[42]

Robert Eno, reading Xunzi's view of *ming* as involving realism about objects, uses the term "true" (albeit in scare quotes), in discussing the Xunzi's position about the application and justification of *ming*. He writes:

> The notion of making distinctions (*bian*), which is no more than a "true" perception of natural divisions in the constitution of the world, is inextricably linked to the idea of creating proper order."[43]

Why does Eno use scare quotes around "true" here? Perhaps because he applies the term to *perception*? It is unclear at least on the face of it how one can have a true perception of a division in the natural world. Is it to see things as distinct that are in fact distinct? Without getting into the philosophy of mind here, we may ask the question "is this a matter of *perception*, or instead a perceptual *judgment*?" Is the distinction something we perceive? There would certainly be disagreement concerning this in the philosophy of mind, but I will bypass that issue here. Presumably we could take this at least as a claim that the truth of a statement, belief, or other entity that can take a truth value, is dependent on its matching the "natural divisions in the constitution of the world," or matching reality or states-of-affairs (without committing Xunzi or Eno to a particular metaphysics of states-of-affairs).

Bian, according to Xunzi, cannot be adequately made without proper *ming*. As mentioned above, the beginning of the *Zhengming* chapter contains the claim:

故王者之制名，名定而實辨

When rulers establish names, actualities (shi) are distinguished.[44]

It is not clear from this alone, of course, whether *shi* are distinguished because they are *constructed* by names, or whether they are distinguished because the correct names help us to accurately make these distinctions.

Ming should not be understood as proper names or labels. The category might *include* proper names, but even here the early Chinese thinkers do not understand proper names as simply being a tag or reference—every *ming* includes a descriptor. This is the only way in which one could make sense of the idea that there can be proper and improper *ming*. *Shanming* are those that facilitate the aims of the namer, which, although this does not necessarily involve a link with reality, does involve the creation of certain associations with the named thing. A proper name as such does not have any obvious effect on behavior or attitudes, unless we consider aesthetic issues or associations that people may have with a certain name. So perhaps people would be inclined to think poorly of a child named "Adolf Hitler" or "Pol Pot" for example, and think highly of one named "Mohandas Gandhi." But surely this cannot be what Xunzi is concerned with in his discussion of *zhengming*. For Xunzi, *zhengming* is central to governing and organizing human life at a fundamental level. The association of proper names with certain positive or negative memories cannot plausibly be held to have this kind of psychological power.

Descriptions, on the other hand, are another story altogether. There is a difference between "Adolf Hitler" and "murderer." The latter, even though it is a single term, is a description. When I say "*x* is a murderer," I am attributing certain actions and qualities to *x*. It means that *x* has killed a person or people, and in a way not consistent with self-defense, warfare, etc., but in an immoral way. This is a description. "Adolf Hitler," on the other hand, is a proper name, referring only to its referent, and its meaning is fixed by its referent. If I use it to name a child today, of course, it will take on the significance of an infamous referent of the same name. Presumably this is why in the contemporary world one is hard pressed to find any more people with the name "Adolf" or the surname "Hitler."

Notice that the example used above, "murderer," not only has descriptive content, it also has normative or evaluative content. It is built into the concept of the murderer that one has performed a morally wrong act. The description of some individual as a murderer, then, includes moral judgment. The question of whether the term is properly applied, then, will include the questions (1) whether the person in question killed someone, and (2) whether that act of killing was unjustified or morally reprehensible. If so, then the term "murderer" applies. We can certainly see how this will have implications for moral behavior and persuasion. Indeed, we dispute one another using names in this way all the time. Consider the contemporary debate in the United States surrounding abortion. What is not at dispute is whether the act of abortion is the willful elimination of a living thing—it clearly is. Rather, the nature of the dispute turns on the question of whether it is morally permissible for a woman carrying this unborn living thing to terminate its life. How we characterize a woman who makes such a decision will turn on how we read this moral permissibility or lack thereof. If it is permissible for her to have the abortion, then the term "murderer" certainly does not apply to her, while if it is impermissible, the term "murderer" does apply. This is why in some of the more heated rhetoric we hear antiabortion activists refer to abortion as "murder" and people who have had abortions as "murderers." This is a case in which the act of naming is in itself an act of both description and moral evaluation. To claim that "*x* is a murderer" is to claim that both *x* committed an act of killing, and that this act of killing was morally unjustified.

Staying with the theme of murder, we can see that there are two parts of establishing this *ming*. First, we must define what murder is—that is, we must supply it with a meaning. Next, we must define a class to which the term applies. One way of understanding this is in line with the Fregean notion of the *sense* and *reference* of a given term. Both of these must be established, according to Xunzi, and there is some element of convention involved in both projects, but this does not eliminate the need for a ground on which terms and statements are ultimately justified. Let us look to the statement from the *Zhengming* chapter most often taken as demonstrating the conventionalism of the *Xunzi* concerning names.

名無固宜，約之以命，約定俗成謂之宜，異於約則謂之不宜。名無固實，約之以命實，約定俗成，謂之實名。名有固善，徑易而不拂，謂之善名。

Names are without intrinsic appropriateness. Agreement on them is made through fiat. When there is agreement, they are established, and customs are completed, this is called appropriate. If there are disagreements, this is called inappropriate. Names are without intrinsic connection to reality. Agreement on them is made through fiat concerning reality. When there is agreement, they are established, and customs are completed, this is called giving reality to names. Names do have intrinsic goodness. If they are direct, simple, and non-trivial, they are called good names.[45]

This is a difficult passage that has been translated in a number of different ways, and has been the source of much debate.[46] My own translation here depends on a number of choices and assumptions about Xunzi's project, as most translations do. Bryan Van Norden understands Xunzi as advocating here what he calls a "weak conventionalism." The conventionalism endorsed by Xunzi is "weak" because it only applies to the coining of a name and the way the name is applied to particular objects in the world. This kind of conventionalism, unlike a more robust conventionalism in which objects in the world are in part *determined* or created by human processes of conceptualization or naming, has to do only with application of created names to realistically construed objects in the world.[47] Paul Goldin offers a more realist interpretation of the passage, in which Xunzi holds that how objects themselves are distinguished is not a matter of convention at all.[48] Eno, as we have seen, echoes the realist reading of Xunzi on reality.

Alternatively, we may read the above passage from *Xunzi* as offering a robust conventionalism, in which naming is responsible for the way we experience or make distinctions within reality, and is responsible for our apprehension of things in the world. Kurtis Hagen seems to endorse such a version of consequentialism, as do Hall and Ames.

While the above passage may offer the best evidence for the conventionalist reading, seen in the context of *Zhengming* as a whole, I think we have more reason to see it as advocating something like a semi-conventionalist realism. That is, names are constructed and instituted (*zhi* 制) by the ruler, but in such ways as to enable us to make proper distinctions, in terms of ones that exist in and mirror reality (*shi* 實). A number of passages suggest this reading. Early in the *Zhengming* chapter (before the passage discussed above), we find the claim:

故知者為之分別制名以指實.

Therefore the knowledgeable do this, separating, distinguishing, and instituting names, in order to pick out *shi*.[49]

This suggests that institution of names is linked with the ability to pick out or ostend (*zhi* 指) reality. There is no suggestion here that names play any role in the *creation* or determination of this reality (*shi*), but rather that they enable us to point it out. *Zhi* most literally means something like "to point with the finger." It can also stand for a finger itself. This is how the *Shuowen jiezi* explains the term (手指也 *shou zhi ye*). Reality here seems to be not determined, but referred to. Of course, if the right way to understand Xunzi's use of *zhi* here is along the lines of reference, and this is to be understood in a realist way, then there must be a standard of determining whether a name has properly referred to a thing. The descriptive capacity of names seems demonstrated here as well. If the purpose of the institution of names is to allow us to properly refer to reality and to correctly distinguish things, they cannot be mere labels. They must have some well-understood descriptive content associated with them. When we look at the examples that Xunzi offers of names properly instituted (by the past sages), this seems even more plausible the case. Names as they apply to persons and human nature, according to Xunzi, should be categorized in certain ways and have certain fixed meanings.

性之好、惡、喜、怒、哀、樂謂之情。

(Human) nature's goodness, badness, likes, dislikes, grief, or joy—call this emotion (*qing*).[50]

Xunzi also makes a claim that seems to cut even more deeply against robust conventionalism, that the "organs provided by nature" (*tian guan* 天管) are responsible for our ability to discriminate similarities and differences of things.

然則何緣而以同異？曰：緣天官

That being the case then what do we use to distinguish similarities and differences? I say: it is through the organs provided by nature.[51]

The chapter goes on to apply this to the process of naming. The establishment of *ming* takes place *after* this initial discrimination of similarities and differences using our natural abilities,[52] and it is this process that allows us to accurately distinguish *shi* (actuality/reality), or in other words, to grasp *the truth*. This understanding of *shi* as actuality gives us a ground against which we can determine truth, and the concept of *shi* itself later develops so as to itself become a concept expressing something like a property of truth belonging to statements.

Perhaps Xunzi's greatest contribution to truth theory was his definition of the concept of *shi*, which is adopted, elaborated on, and developed by later thinkers, especially in the Han period. While Xunzi uses *shi* in the sense of "reality," later thinkers (especially Wang Chong, discussed in chapter 6 below) understood it as a property of statements, and thus itself something akin to linguistic truth. *Shi* is sometimes translated in the *Xunzi* as "object,"[53] which assumes a certain view of the *ming* attached to *shi*. "Object" as translation only makes good sense if we assume that *ming* is something like a label or proper name. When we discriminate *shi* using our senses, however, it is not clear that we discriminate *objects* so much as the *contours of reality*, which is less about objects than about continually changing processes, events, and objects. Nonetheless, the specific ways in which Xunzi uses *shi* makes it problematic to understand the term as something like "reality" in general. Rather, we should see it as the aspect of things that ties them to reality, which we might call "actuality" rather than "object."[54] Xunzi writes:

知異實者之異名也，故使異實者莫不異名也，不可亂也，猶使同實者莫不同名也。

Knowing the different actualities support different names, one causes different actualities to have different names. There cannot then be disorder. It is like causing similar actualities to have similar names.[55]

I avoid the translation of *shi* as "object" here so as to leave open the breadth of the term *shi*. An object *can* be a part of reality or an actuality, but reality is more than simply objects. What is named is part of reality itself, and this need not be an object. Events, thoughts, abstract entities—these are all part of reality and thus manifest actuality (*shi*), but are not objects. In addition, rendering *shi* as an "object" seems to attribute to Xunzi a substance-based metaphysics in which the constituents of the world (or at least that we are able to pick out with the use of our senses) are discrete substances. The examples that Xunzi uses of the kinds of thing we pick out in the world via the "organs provided by nature" (*tian guan* 天官) seem very different than the kinds of thing we would generally specify as objects or substances. He mentions what we gain through sensation as example—sounds discerned by the ears, tastes by the mouth, scents by the nose, etc.

The concept of *shi* becomes the central truth concept in Eastern Han thought. The way in which it is understood by Eastern Han thinkers is heavily influenced by Xunzi's use of the concept, which represented a movement away from an understanding of *shi* as substance or fruit, and toward that of *shi* as reality itself, ultimately developing the concept of a broader notion of reality as property, of both things in the world and of linguistic entities.

This sense of *shi* is dominant after the Han. In discussions of the *Ming jia* 名家(School of Names) literature, later Confucians disparage these thinkers for their seeming lack of concern with truth in terms of *shi*. Chris Fraser writes:

> Gongsun Long's disputation is perceived as plainly not fitting "reality" (*shi*, also the "stuff" spoken of). It is an exercise in cleverness, a kind of trick performance in which the disputer attempts to make a case for a claim that everyone knows does not fit its object.[56]

I agree with these sentiments. Whatever the *Ming jia* thinkers are doing (and this material is even more impenetrable than that of the Later Mohists), they are likely not offering truth theory. Thus, while there is certainly much of interest going on in *Ming jia* texts, I pass over them here with minimal comment.

NOTES

1 *Shuowen jiezi* 835.

2. *Shiming, Yiyanyu* 48.

3. He writes: "The idea is: since we cannot see objects in the darkness, we are unable to refer to them via ostension. Thus, if we want to talk about objects in the dark i.e., use our mouths to refer to them, we must give them *names*. Thus, names represent objects in our speech and thought. Xu Shen was, therefore, concerned with the *cognitive function* of names" (Chen 2009: 107). Sun Zhenbin offers a somewhat similar but even less defensible account: "*Ming* means 'self-naming' or 'self-introduction.' Its form is a combination of two characters: *xi* (night) and *kou* (mouth). *Xi* signifies the nether world, and a person in the nether world cannot be seen by living people; therefore he introduces himself using his mouth, i.e., by words" (Sun 2015: 9). I am not sure of Sun's reasons for translating *ming* 命 as "introduction" and "naming," or *ming* 冥 as "nether world." The latter is especially awkward, given that the *ming* 冥 is understood in a more technical and philosophical way by even the early Han, for example, in its use in the *Lanming* 覽冥 chapter of *Huainanzi* (Major et al. 2010: 208).

4. Lin Chung-I (2011: 314) writes: "textual evidence shows manifestly that the referent of 'name' includes names of things in the normative domain."

5. Geaney 2010.

6. *Hanfeizi* 10, Geaney trans.

7. Geaney 2010: 257: "Examples in early Chinese texts often show *ming* substituting for *yan* and vice versa. Indeed sometimes the two appear together explicitly as things that are heard."

8. Geaney 2010: 257.

9. Geaney also discusses *Chunqiu Fanlu* 10.1 in offering evidence for her view of *ming*. As with the other passages she cites, it actually offers better reason for accepting a view of *ming* as the *content* associated with certain sounds. In particular, this passage seems to suggest that there is broader content to *ming* than names or labels would allow. "When the sages of old uttered cries in imitation of heaven and earth, those were what we call appellations; when they cried in giving commands, those were what we call names. *Ming* is, so to speak, *ming* (cry) and *ming* (command). *Hao* (appellation) is, so to speak, *xiao* (call out) and *xiao* (imitate). Calling out in imitation of heaven and earth is an appellation. Crying in commanding is naming. Name and appellation have different sounds but the same root—both cry and call out in order to achieve heaven's intent" (trans. Geaney 2010: 254).

10. Sher 1999: 152 ("What is Tarski's Theory of Truth?" *Topoi* 18 p. 149–166).

11. Sher 1999: 154.

12. *Xunzi* 22. 83/22/6–7. Citations here follow Xunzi Yinde, Harvard-Yenching Institute Sinological Index Series, Supplement no. 22.

13. Elstein 2004: "[Xunzi] defended a modified conventionalism concerning language: names were not intrinsically appropriate for the objects they referred to, but once usage was determined by convention, to depart from it is wrong. It would be a mistake to think of Xunzi's view as a kind of nominalism, however, since he is very clear that there is an objective reality that names refer to."

14. I don't disagree with Elstein's characterization of Xunzi's view on the acceptability of names, I am simply applying the phrase "modified conventionalism" to a somewhat different aspect of his thinking about language.

15. A concept distinct from the *li* 利 of the Mohists, which is spelled the same in Pinyin Romanization.

16. *Xunzi* 19.

17. A position famously attacked by Wilfrid Sellars, who calls it the "myth of the given" (Brandom 1997).

18. Elder 2004.

19. *Xunzi* 74/89/89–90.

20. *Xunzi* 73/19/63–64.

21. There are some complications, which I get to below, in passages in which Xunzi seems to suggest that both *li* and *yi* are dependent on the work of the sage. "Conventionalist" readings of Xunzi tend to rely on such passages, but I show how these can be made consistent with other readings.

22. Proponents of this interpretation include Paul Goldin, Bryan Van Norden, T. C. Kline, and P. J. Ivanhoe. I take Goldin's statement of the specific view, which

I endorse, concerning Xunzi's realism and absolutism about ritual to be the clearest, and the closest to my own position.

23. Goldin 2000: 73. T.C. Kline expresses a similar view: "The Dao of human beings that is manifest in the ritual and music created by the sages constitutes not simply a pattern of interaction that orders the state by keeping people out of conflict. It is not simply a prudential order. It is the proper set of practices and activities that bring human beings into harmony with their own natures as well as the patterns of the rest of the cosmos. The Dao is the moral order. It is the way in which human beings ought to pattern their actions" (Kline 2000: 165).

24. *Xunzi* 74/19/93–94. Watson reads the final line "It is a method that can neither be circumvented nor changed." Hagen takes this instead to be a claim that adhering to ritual is not negotiable, rather than that the specifics of this ritual cannot be changed. I think this reading stretches the text.

25. Hagen rejects an "absolutist" reading of Xunzi (a term I am fine accepting) in part on the basis that "traditional Chinese thinkers did not generally hold a world-view that would easily support a rigid absolutism" (Hagen 2003: 373). He cites A. C. Graham, Roger Ames, and others in support of this. I am not as sanguine as Hagen about the notion that we can generalize a worldview for the entirety of classical Chinese thought, which was certainly as diverse as any other tradition. While Mencius, Mozi, and perhaps even Confucius probably would not have given absolutism any quarter, Xunzi is a different thinker, and it's hard to believe that the thought of Hanfeizi as a development and expression of Xunzi's position on 法 *fa* (laws, standards) would have even been possible had not Xunzi been fairly absolutist.

26. *Xunzi* 83/22/11–12.

27. *Xunzi* 74/19/89–90.

28. Hagen also appeals to the passages where Xunzi describes the *wei* of the sage kings in establishing ritual. I discuss the issue of *wei* below.

29. Tan 2012: 173.

30. Compare the following two passages, for example: 立隆以為極，而天下莫之能損益也. (*Lilun*) 麻冕，禮也；今也純，儉。吾從眾。拜下，禮也；今拜乎上，泰也。雖違眾，吾從下。 (*Analects* 9.3). It is hard to imagine Xunzi allowing for innovations based on considerations of economy *or* popular use.

31. The difference between Tan and the others is that she takes this tension to show a fundamental incompatibility, while the others accept the conventionalist statements and try to explain away the realist-sounding statements. My attempt here might be seen as an acceptance of the realist-sounding statements and explaining away of the conventionalist ones. There is quite good reason, however, to think that it's the conventionalist-sounding statements that are the ones that *should* be explained away, and can easily be.

32. Fung 2012: 191–192.

33. I do not cite the entirety of the opening passage of *Zhengming* Fung discusses, as my interest here is purely in *wei*.

34. *Xunzi* 83/22/4.

35. Spoken about elsewhere in the *Xunzi*, and the kind of thing only sages can do, as is accepted throughout the period and well into the Han. Only in outliers like the

Eastern Han thinker Wang Chong do we see explicit resistance to the idea that *zuo* is something only to be engaged in by sages. Michael Puett discusses the various positions on *zuo* in the period in (Puett 2002). The interesting thing here is that Xunzi is explicitly discussing the role played by the sages themselves, the *xian wang*, and still does not claim that they were involved in *zuo*.

36. Xunzi commonly offers versions of the *Lilun* statement in various places in the *Xunzi*, such as this instance from the *Rongru* chapter: 故先王案為之制禮義以分之. ("Therefore the former kings engaged in *wei* and instituted/expressed ritual and appropriateness to distinguish [right from wrong].")

37. *Xunzi* 87/23/22.

38. Indeed, the purpose of this passage in the first place is to argue against the view that the source of ritual is within human nature, rather than external to it. This passage must be seen in light of the next sentence, 非故生於人之性也。 "They (ritual and appropriateness) are not, therefore, derived from human nature" (*Xunzi* 23.8).

39. Hutton 2014: 237 "Xunzi's word 'object' (*shi*) appears to include both the meaning and referent of a term, as distinguished by modern philosophers." He translates: "If the names and their corresponding objects are tied together in a confused fashion, then the distinction between noble and base will not be clear."

40. This is a problem numerous scholars have recognized. Lin (2011) discusses Chen (1954), in proposing a difficulty to what Lin calls the "language-refinement conception" of *zhengming*, noting that "the alleged close connection between normativity and name-rectification becomes dormant" (Lin 2011: 316) Chen proposes that "what Xunzi takes names to be is, in effect, something having more functions than those of concepts or terms" (Chen 1954: 121, Lin trans.).

41. Lin 2011: 316.

42. The Zhuangists wade even more deeply into this territory, but come to almost the opposite conclusion at Xunzi, that there are no uniquely determined statements.

43. Eno 1990: 146.

44. *Xunzi* 83/22/6–7.

45. *Xunzi* 83/22/25–27.

46. Hagen (2002) outlines a number of the different views on and translations of this passage.

47. Van Norden 1993: 376.

48. Goldin 2000.

49. *Xunzi* 83/22/14.

50. *Xunzi* 83/22/3.

51. *Xunzi* 83/22/15–16.

52. 然後隨而命之. "After this follow and command (*ming*) it."

53. Hutton 2014 uses this translation, and Hagen also endorses it.

54. John Makeham discusses this translation in Makeham 1994.

55. *Xunzi* 83/22/22–23.

56. Fraser 2009.

Chapter 5

Zhuangzi, Huainanzi, and Syncretists

While some scholars have seen the discussion of truth in early Daoist texts such as *Daodejing*,[1] I doubt if there is enough material there concerning the topic to understand the text as offering a coherent theory. In addition, the textual problems with reading the *Daodejing* as offering a consistent view of *anything* are perhaps the most difficult of any early Chinese text including the *Analects*. Although some of these difficulties plague the *Zhuangzi* as well, we have relatively good reason to think that the *Zhuangzi* at least offers us coherent views *within* chapters, if not consistency between the chapters.[2] The chapter of the *Zhuangzi* most famously (or infamously) concerned with language is the *Qiwulun*, on which I focus here. While the majority of the consideration of truth and other issues of language in the *Zhuangzi* are found in *Qiwulun*, there are also some discussions elsewhere in the text. While it is difficult to know the relationship between these other sections of *Zhuangzi* and *Qiwulun*, they occasionally may help to offer context or clarity on a position taken in *Qiwulun*. So the theory of truth that I outline here can be taken as one centered in *Qiwulun*, and which gets more or less support from other chapters of the *Zhuangzi*.[3]

It is good to keep in mind Bryan Van Norden's argument, backed up by an abundance of radically different interpretations of the *Zhuangzi*, that the text is "protean" and "almost like a Rorschach test: different observers see different things in it, and what they see there often reveals more about their own preconceptions than the *Zhuangzi* itself."[4] While this is certainly the case, much of this has to do with (perhaps misguided) attempts to make sense of the *Zhuangzi* as a unified whole—and the *Zhuangzi* is not alone in this. Other texts notoriously open to a seemingly endless multitude of interpretations are *Lunyu*, *Daodejing*, and the Zhou classics. Not surprisingly, it turns out to be these texts for which the issue of authorship and textual construction are the most problematic. I would contend that the *Zhuangzi* allows for such a multitude of interpretations for the main reason that there are many different, and not always compatible, views represented within the text. Different interpreters focus on different themes in the text, and then tend to read everything else in the *Zhuangzi* through the lenses of that theme. This is no different than the situation with other texts composed of disparate writings of different authors, such as the Bible.[5] It will be of use, then, to consider a number of different readings of the major themes of the *Zhuangzi* as they pertain to the investigation here of a view of truth that we may find grounded in *Qiwulun*.

The *perspectivist* position advanced throughout the *Zhuangzi* is well known and attested. It is in the *Zhuangzi* that we see the first robust appraisal of such evaluative concepts of *shi* 是 and *fei* 非, considering whether these evaluative concepts themselves are ultimately valuable. In texts prior to the *Zhuangzi*, there is consideration of truth and evaluation of statements (*shuo*, *yan*, or even *ming*), but this is the first place we see an explicit questioning of whether the assumption that discriminating (*bian* 辨) between right and wrong (*shi* 是 and *fei* 非) is itself a good thing. Prior to Zhuangzi, the attempt had been to determine *what* discriminations are proper, which are *shi*, which are *fei*, which can be considered permissible (*ke* 可), and which cannot. Determining the truth was an aim of these thinkers, and insofar as they thought about truth, and about how we attain it, they did so with the main goal of attaining it. The *Zhuangzi* not only questioned whether it is possible to attain the kind of objective truth that other thinkers aimed for, but also (more importantly, I think) challenged the efficacy and wisdom of the truth-seeking project itself. The first point may be taken as a *skeptical* point. But we see more than simply skepticism (of a Pyrrhonian or any other type) in the *Zhuangzi*, exemplified by the Renjianshi chapter. Truth, even if it were possible to attain it, according to the *Zhuangzi*, would simply not be the kind of thing we would want to have. That is, truth would be *stultifying*. The *Zhuangzi* in general presents us with an "anti-truth" message, of which skepticism is but one branch. The skeptical argument is one strategy in a larger toolbox that contributes to the overall position of Zhuangzi that we should reject the "truth-seeking" or rather "truth-making" project altogether. Of course, the *Zhuangzi* could not completely get away from truth. In its robust rejection of the concept, it offers us a number of interesting and important features of early Chinese thinking about truth. First, it shows us that at least a few of the extant theories of truth may have been based on the positions that the Zhuangists criticize. The Zhuangists, even more than their opponents in some senses, offer us fleshed out theories of truth that they attribute to contemporaries, and then offer up as piñatas to beat with glee. It is unlikely that these characterizations of other early Chinese theories of truth were completely out of the ballpark, even if the Zhuangist did mischaracterize them in certain ways.

One understanding of Zhuangzi's position concerning truth and reality is formulated best by Jeeloo Liu.[6] Liu interprets the *Zhuangzi* as accepting a kind of (internal) metaphysical realism, in which the (ultimately ineffable) *dao* represents reality as it is "in-itself." This may remind us of Kant's "noumenal". The parallels between this interpretation of Zhuangzi and Kantianism do not end there. As in the case of Kant, since the *dao* itself is ultimately free of conceptualization and necessarily distinct from individual human perspectives (the Kantian "phenomenal"), humans cannot access the *dao* (noumenal) through language. That is, we cannot express truths about *dao* through language, and thus we can have no *knowledge* of reality as it is in itself.

I find a basic problem with this interpretation of Zhuangzi. It requires a conception of a fundamental appearance-reality distinction that is based on the kind of representationalism about mental content that comes to the fore in early modern European philosophy, and which Kant inherits and has to explain (or explain away). The deep problems of Descartes in getting "behind the veil" of ideas to the real world set up the problematic that Kant ultimately chooses to solve by completely separating the noumenal and phenomenal realms, and in opting for a kind of "internal realist" approach in which what we understand as "reality" is the phenomenal world rather than the noumenal world in which it is grounded, and to which we can never hope to gain access. Even though there presumably is a way in which things are-in-themselves, we can never attain knowledge of this, as all of our experience is phenomenal.

In the *Zhuangzi*, however, it would be strikingly odd if the representational concern were an issue. Not a single thinker in early China whose texts we have access to posited anything like a Cartesian appearance-reality distinction that would require a Kantian or any other solution. It is at the least baffling that the authors of the Zhuangzi would invent and then take themselves to solve a problem that no one had ever worried about, and then to criticize opponents for their answers to this problem. Why would they take the attempt to describe "reality-in-itself" of other thinkers as misguided and a failure if other thinkers never attempted to do this? That would be like writing a diatribe criticizing Plato for getting evolutionary biology wrong. He never spoke about it nor even thought about the possibility. Surely, if the Zhuangist is attempting to actually engage in discourse with contemporaries, they must have been talking about, considering, and criticizing a practice that their contemporaries could reasonably be thought to have actually been engaging in. Thus, it is necessary to look outside of the *Zhuangzi* itself to understand what is going on in the *Zhuangzi*, particularly because so much of the text consists of criticism of contemporary positions and arguments.

Given what we have seen so far concerning theories of truth in early Chinese thought, hardly any text can be said to have endorsed a modern-style correspondence theory of truth. And although numerous thinkers do seem to have accepted a "way the world is," marked by *shi* 實 or *ran* 然, the truth of a *yan* (statement) did not, for any of the thinkers discussed, consist in a relation of correspondence between *yan* and the world directly. The closest we get to this conception is the Mohist view of *dang* 當 (fit)—but even here, it is not clear that statements *fit* insofar as they correspond to states-of-affairs or reality. It is possible that they represent the world in some metaphysically innocent sense (consistent with the "correspondence intuition" discussed in chapter 1 above). More importantly, however, even if other early Chinese thinkers did accept something like a correspondence theory of truth, we have even *less* evidence that they accepted the kind of appearance-reality distinction that the early moderns in the West are concerned about and which gives birth to Kant's phenomenal/noumenal distinction and his internal realism. This arises from an epistemological problem born from representationalism. There is no evidence that any early Chinese thinker viewed the mind or ideas as distinct from and representing a mind-independent world that served as ground.

Part of my initial argument in the first chapter of this book that the early Chinese philosophers must have had a conception of truth was that truth is basic, general, and fundamental in philosophy and human thought in general. This is not the case for the appearance-reality distinction and representationalism.[7] Absent good textual reason to think that a particular philosopher accepted such views, then, we should not assume that they must have. Given that we find these views nowhere in the pre-Qin Chinese literature, this puts pressure on the position that the *Zhuangzi* was criticizing other schools and thinkers for their solutions to this problem that none of them had actually considered.

So if the *Zhuangzi* is not concerned with *dao* as "reality-in-itself," a kind of Kantian noumenal, and the question of whether we can ever have knowledge about such a realm (certainly we can't), then how do we explain the arguments of chapters like *Qiwulun* which have appeared to so many contemporary interpreters to be making just this claim? And if the *Zhuangzi* is not doing this, as I claim, then how can I justify the claim that it presents an "anti-truth" position? Part of the answer here is that the "anti-truth" position that the *Zhuangzi* advocates is an anti-truth position concerning *early Chinese* views of truth, not Western views of truth. The truth claims and purported value of truth they are rejecting are based on the views concerning truth of the early Confucians and Mohists, which as we have seen are quite different from those of Plato, Descartes, Kant, Frege, or Russell. Now that I've given some outline (in previous chapters) of the extant theories of truth around the time that the *Zhuangzi* (particularly *Qiwulun*) was written, we can better understand just what it was that *Qiwulun* and its associated Zhuangist chapters were trying to do.

The issue of *perspective* and its centrality in making judgments and formulating *yan* (statements), which relies on the conceptualization and distinction of *shi-fei*, is a major one in the *Zhuangzi*, discussed in every chapter. The opening passage of the first chapter (*Xiaoyaoyou*) of the *Zhuangzi* makes a point about perspective in the *Zhuangzi*'s characteristically vague and cryptic way, through a story about mythical creatures.[8]

Others also read the following *Qiwulun* passage as a statement of perspectivism:

可乎可，不可乎不可。 道行之而成，物謂之而然。 惡乎然？然於然。 惡乎不然？不然於不然。 物固有所然，物固有所可。

The permissible is permissible, the impermissible is impermissible. In traveling the Way (dao) it is completed, and things in being called something are so. How is it so? By being so. How is it not so? By being not so. A thing has what inherently makes it so, and a thing has what inherently makes it permissible.[9]

First, a note about the language here. The author distinguishes 可 *ke* (permissibility) and 然 *ran* (being the case/being so), although the two are seen as closely related here. It is unclear that *ran* has any more semantic value than *ke*, however, though it might be the case. The concepts of permissibility and being so, however, even though they are both ultimately based on convention, are separable. Bryan Van Norden reads this passage as expressing the perspective-dependence of right and wrong, and presumably permissibility and being so.[10] If this passage is about the perspective-dependence of our conceptions, however, *which* concepts are so dependent? Are *all* of our concepts perspective-dependent, or only some proper subset of them? It appears from this passage that the author wants to make the *global* claim concerning not only all of our concepts, but even the most basic and general ones, such as permissibility and being so. That is, in employing the concepts of *ke* and *ran* in this case, the author of the passage seems to want to make a point about *truth*, as the most general and foundational of human concepts. If *truth* is ultimately perspective-dependent, then all human concepts are so. So is this then a statement of radical perspectival relativism?

What would have to be the case in order for this to represent a relativist position? Zhuangzi appears in the above passage to endorse the position that simply asserting or *so-ing* something makes it so, such that not only the acceptability or assertability of a statement relies on the individual perspective, but the *truth* or "so-ness" of a statement also so relies on perspective. A. C. Graham argues that this perspectivism in the *Zhuangzi* is indeed entrenched, such that anything that can be said can only be said "from a lodging place."[11] Not only does this seem the case, however, but it appears that the standards for acceptability or *truth* of a statement can only be within perspective as well, according to this passage.

At the same time, there are very different things said about statements, even within the *Qiwulun* chapter itself. While the above passage suggests a kind of radical relativism, other passages in the chapter seem to suggest that certain statements and even certain perspectives are better than others, presumably on some ground independent of either the perspectives in question or the perspective of the author who appraises them. The discussion of "greater knowledge" (*da zhi* 大知) and "lesser knowledge" (*xiao zhi* 小知) seems to suggest this.[12] For instance, the author of *Qiwulun* writes:

大知閑閑，小知閒閒；大言炎炎，小言詹詹。

Greater knowledge is leisurely and vast, while lesser knowledge is constrained. Greater talk (*yan*) is penetrating, while lesser talk is merely verbose.[13]

There are also other passages in which the author praises the summation of knowledge of the ancients, which consisted in a certain attitude toward statements in general:

古之人，其知有所至矣。惡乎至？有以為未始有物者，至矣盡矣，不可以加矣。

As for the ancients, their knowledge had that in which it was exhausted. In what was it exhausted? In holding that there had never begun to be things, (their knowledge) was exhausted and complete. There could be nothing added to this.[14]

This suggests that the Zhuangist position in *Qiwulun* is not a thoroughgoing relativism, but that there are certain perspectives that are better, in that they are more expansive, more effective, or more *accurate* than other perspectives. The distinction between greater and lesser knowledge and statement is certainly meant as a normative distinction. We *ought* to aim to have greater knowledge rather than lesser knowledge, and if this is the case, then we have to have reason independent from our current perspectives, whatever they are, to attain, generate, or retain great knowledge and abandon or remain free of lesser knowledge. Throughout *Qiwulun* there are stories, claims, and exhortations regarding people whose knowledge was or is not up-to-snuff, who missed things crucial to attaining a proper understanding. This seems hard to square with a thoroughgoing relativism. There are some options, however, for the relativist here.

Jeeloo Liu argues that the position of the *Zhuangzi* as a whole is a meta-physical realism combined with semantic perspectivism.[15] She suggests that a kind of Putnam-like (or Kantian) internal realism is at work in the *Zhuangzi*, in which the reality is composed by the individual perspective. It is not just that *any* statement is permissible or true, then, but that those sufficiently coherent with the beliefs and experiences of the overall individual perspective are true. This position seems to amount to a coherentist theory of truth within particular perspectives. If this is right, then the relativism endorsed in the *Zhuangzi* is not a radical relativism, but a more "tame" relativism. Still, this seems to conflict with the passage from *Qiwulun* above. It is not *just* in the speaking of a *yan* that the *yan* is true or acceptable, it is with its coherence with the overall worldview or perspective of the speaker. The problem with this is that although the *Zhuangzi* (including the *Qiwulun* chapter with which I am concerned here) says things perhaps suggestive of this, it never clearly says anything that entails such a reading, and the objectivist leanings in the text seem clearly to be linked to extra-perspectival considerations.

Dao does, on the other hand, appear to be something about which there are mind-independent facts, even if we cannot ultimately express those facts in a language outside of perspective. Though we *might* be able to. A number of passages in *Qiwulun* make statements about the *dao* that have the sense of objective, perspective-independent statements that are presumably supposed to be true of the *dao* itself, not just of the *dao* (*Zhuangzi*). Because why should I care about the *dao* (*Zhuangzi*), rather than the *dao* (*Alexus*), or the *dao* (*Anyone else*)? Consider the following passage:

夫道未始有封，言未始有常，為是而有畛也。請言其畛：有左，有右，有倫，有義，有分，有辯，有競，有爭，此之謂八德。六合之外，聖人存而不論；六合之內，聖人論而不議。

The *dao* had not yet begun to achieve recognition. Words had not yet begun to have constancy. When they do, then boundaries are created. We can state the boundaries: there is left, right, order, appropriateness, division, distinction, contention, argument. These are called the eight potencies. Outside the six directions (the world), the sage exists and does not engage in discussion. Inside the six directions (the world), the sage engages in discussion yet does not discourse.[16]

Surely this is more than just a statement from and dependent for its truth on the perspective of the author, which none of his readers can be expected to share. Presumably the author here is trying to express *truths* about *dao*, and about how language came about, and how our conceptualization led to problems and movement away from knowledge.

One possibility, raised by Karyn Lai, is that the focus on relativism in the Zhuangzi is intended not to make a universal or wide-ranging point about the semantic or metaphysical status of statements, but rather to foster cultivation of recognition of the limits and contingent nature of one's own perspective, so as to create more fruitful interactions between persons. Lai writes:

> The recognition of difference and plurality is, for Zhuangzi, the critical first step in debate. Those who acknowledge the plurality of perspectives are more likely to enter into debate with a view to negotiate rather than a view to dominate.[17]

This point is well taken, but I would go even further than this, given some of the things we see in *Renjianshi* and *Qiwulun*. The conversation near the beginning of *Renjianshi* between the Zhuangist version of Confucius and his student Yan Hui[18] suggests that even debate itself is something to be avoided and subverted. It is perhaps that the recognition of the limitation of the individual perspective makes one more likely to *give up* debating, and to aim for *harmonization* rather than domination or negotiation. This may be part of what Zhuangzi's Confucius means by *xin zhai* 心齋 ("fasting of the mind"), which aims at completely undermining one's self-conception. Confucius explains to Yan Hui that traveling to Wei in an attempt to reform the way of its king is not only a fruitless task that will end in death, but it actually has a different aim than the one Yan Hui claims it does. The suggestion is that Yan Hui is being less than honest here. At a key point in the exchange, Confucius says:

且若亦知夫德之所蕩，而知之所為出乎哉？德蕩乎名，知出乎爭。名也者，相軋也；知也者，爭之器也。二者凶器，非所以盡行也。

And it is as if already know that virtue has been lost. And do you know how virtue is lost? It is lost by gaining a name (*ming*). Knowledge is lost through argument. Having a name is a way for people to smash one another. Knowledge is a tool for argument. These are both deadly weapons, and cannot be used to maximize conduct.[19]

Contention (*zheng* 爭) should be understood here to include debate, because this is presumably what Yan Hui intends to travel to the state of Wei to do. Confucius expresses the seemingly cynical view that knowledge is for the sake of contention, and virtue is for the sake of making a name. If Yan Hui seeks to actually make a difference, or actually has a concern for social harmony, he should, Confucius suggests, engage in *xin zhai* 心齋 and give up his conceptualization of *shi-fei*. That is, he should *recognize the limitations* and the contingency of his own perspective. Only then will he be able to both recognize and make use of the *tian li* 天理 ("natural propensities").

The overall *strategy* of *Qiwulun* and related chapters may be important here. As with *Daodejing*, it may not be the case that Zhuangists hold that there is *no place* for perspective-independent truth or that we cannot know anything perspective-independently, but rather that since we constantly focus on the perspective-independent, we miss the reliance of most of what we say and do on individual perspectives. That is, we tend to see the world in terms of objectivity and universality, when it is actually fraught with subjectivity and in most ways we are bound by perspective. Even "perspective-independent" truths, if such exist, are only understood from within perspectives—they simply hold from *all* perspectives. The last sentence of the *Renjianshi* chapter expresses this well:

人皆知有用之用，而莫知無用之用也。

Everyone knows the use of the useful, but no one knows the use of the useless.[20]

It is not that the "useful" really has no use, but we need not talk about the use of the useful, because everyone knows it, and they cannot recognize the usefulness of anything else. Zhuangists constantly extol the virtues of the conventionally "useless" then because *this* is what we always miss. It is only this that we need to be taught. Similar points can be made for positions in the *Daodejing* concerning the overwhelming concentration on *yin* (陰), the low, dark, yielding, and passive. It is not that *yin* is superior to *yang* or always overcomes it, or that we should absolutely reject *yang* and constantly adhere to or act consistently with *yin* (this would presumably be just as bad as being constantly *yang*). Rather, it is because everyone already knows the power of *yang*, and we are all constantly stuck in *yang*. We don't need to be shown that *yang* can be effective. *Yin*, however, is subtle and easy to miss (and perhaps even more effective in an age in which everyone is obsessed with *yang*). I think a plausible interpretation here is a hybrid. We should resist, I think, the tendency to read *Zhuangzi* as accepting an overarching position concerning all language and knowledge meant to apply to *everything*. Indeed, having such a position would itself seem to violate key Zhuangist positions, including recognition of the limitations of an individual perspective and view. One way of understanding the view represented in the *Zhuangzi* (for purposes here limited to *Qiwulun* and similar passages and chapters) is that *many*, perhaps even *most* of our statements and beliefs are perspective-dependent, and that we rely on these perspective-dependent positions in our interactions with others, most often without recognizing their contingency. There is *also*, however, perspective-independent truth, most often having to do with features of the *dao*, and to have *knowledge* of these truths requires seeing the limitations of our individual perspectives and gaining distance from these perspectives (thus the "fasting of the mind" enjoined in *Renjianshi*, to eliminate the "self" perspective). This is not just *another* perspective, the "perspective of the *dao*," if you will, but rather is a transcendence of perspective.

This is a controversial interpretation, of course. A number of scholars read the *Zhuangzi* in general as offering an "anti-truth" message.[21] Insofar as truth is something that can only be understood as a property of assertoric linguistic entities, *perhaps* there is an anti-truth message in the Zhuangzi. And in one sense, as I explain above, the *Zhuangzi* is offering an anti-truth message. They are rejecting earlier conceptions of truth and attempting to replace them with something very different. The *Zhuangzi* does very similar things with other concepts, such as that of personhood. It radically rejects the Confucian and Mohist conception of the person, even going so far in its playful language as to suggest that we should strive not to be persons at all.[22] But what is at the root of this is not a complete rejection of the concept of personhood, but rather a reenvisioning of personhood altogether. The Zhuangist is in essence saying: "If that's what you mean by 'person' then we should not be persons. If that's what you mean by 'truth', then there is no truth."

I think a better way to understand what is going on in the *Qiwulun* chapter and in Zhuangist thought in general is that it offers a *localism* about truth, which truth can be expressed in differing, perhaps even contradictory, ways within different perspectives. This does *not* amount to a thoroughgoing relativism, because what *makes* a statement ultimately true is not its consistency with individual perspectival standards, but rather its consistency with *dao*. The reason differing and even contradictory statements can be consistent with the *dao* is that the *dao* can be expressed *multiply*. That is, *dao* is not something that privileges only specific descriptions from specific perspectives. It is perhaps easiest if we think of truth here as something like "correspondence with *dao*," although it is far from clear that the Zhuangists have anything in mind like a correspondence *dao* theory of truth, where *dao* plays the role of states-of-affairs in correspondence theory. I mainly use the idea of correspondence here because it will be one familiar to most of us, and reduces the complication of my explanation. We can replace correspondence here with whatever connection between *yan* and *dao* the Zhuangists had in mind (if any at all), and the rest of the theory should remain intact. What is at least clear is that the Zhuangists held that truth is a matter of some accurate representation of or connection with *dao*. Part of the difficulty is that the *Qiwulun* chapters (at least in parts) seem to argue that one can give no accurate representation of *dao* using language.

But not so fast. Can one not give *any* accurate representation of *dao* using language, or simply no *complete, final,* or *universally* accurate representation of *dao* using language? That is, what the Zhuangists may be doing in *Qiwulun* is arguing for a semi-relativism. What makes statements true is *dao*, which is single and unchanging (that is, the same *dao* makes my statements and your statements true), perspective and individual-independent, and can be accurately or inaccurately represented. However, *dao* does not privilege a *single* description of the world from a single perspective, but allows for the truth of descriptions from within numerous perspectives, that may contradict or otherwise clash with each other considered *across* perspectives.[23] What most often causes us to reject statements is their inconsistency with truth as determined from our own perspectives. But what the Zhuangist theory shows is that inconsistency with truth as determined from any perspective does *not* entail falsity, insofar as this means lack of consistency with *dao*. What is false within one perspective will be true within another perspective. Are there then two different senses of truth and falsity at work here? A true (perspective) and true (*dao*) and similarly for falsity? I don't think this is what is going on. Any true statement is true only within a perspective, but it is made true within that perspective by perspective-independent standards, namely the *dao* itself. The *dao* is "multiply-corresponding," if you will—the same *dao* makes true statements from within different perspectives that may contradict one another. If truth of a statement is understood in terms of correspondence with the *dao*, it is the nature of the *dao* that tells us whether there will be different and contradictory corresponding statements within perspectives or not. While a standard correspondence view might suggest that *reality* or states-of-affairs can be described in perspective-independent ways, *this* is the main position that the Zhuangists reject. *Dao* can only be described from within a perspective, and thus the limitations of our perspectives also limit the scope of the truth of our statements, in much the same way that human thoughts can only be expressed through language, but there is no one language that expresses the single thought that every human has signifying a shared and universal idea.[24] *Dao* can only be ultimately expressed free of perspective in a nonlinguistic manner, such as a kind of skilled activity (like Cook Ding's magnificent carving of oxen in *Zhuangzi* chapter 3). Shang Geling describes a view very much like the one I offer here, paired with the view that the Zhuangists' main goal in their discussion of truth and language was "achieving enlightenment":

In contrast to Laozi, Zhuangzi did not reject language as the means of expressing Dao. Laozi points out that Dao cannot be talked about, but he talked at length about it. This paradoxical situation does not bother Zhuangzi; instead, he takes this paradox as the feature of Dao language, a new way of expressing Dao how it is. This is what he called "speaking of what cannot be spoken of" or "speaking without language" (*yanwuyan* 言無言). For Zhuangzi, language could become a twofold means to approach the ultimate Dao of liberation: (1) by deconstructing language through and within language itself (2) through the recognition that language as an instrument to express things as indispensable, so long as we are aware of its limitations and do not mislead ourselves into taking it as having ultimate reference to Dao. It is even possible that we can use language to reveal some kind of meaning that may help us in achieving enlightenment.[25]

This recognition of the limitations of language that we find in *Qiwulun* and other chapters of the *Zhuangzi* need not be understood as a rejection of *truth* or the possibility of truth, knowledge, and related concepts, unless we assume that there must be *perspectiveless* truths, as Zhuangzi's opponents do. Such truths, according to Zhuangists, are impossibilities in part because all human concepts are ultimately tied to perspective, whether individual perspectives or a broader human perspective, which still does not exhaust or perfectly correspond to *dao*.

This is the main point of a few of the arguments made in *Qiwulun* concerning comparative and boundary concepts. Two arguments in particular that are notoriously difficult to interpret concern what we might call "boundary concepts," and show that statements relying on such concepts have a fatal flaw when it comes to being considered as universal or summative of truth:

有始也者，有未始有始也者，有未始有夫未始有始也者。有有也者，有無也者，有未始有無也者，有未始有夫未始有無也者。俄而有無矣，而未知有無之果孰有孰無也。今我則已有謂矣，而未知吾所謂之其果有謂乎，其果無謂乎？

There is a beginning. There is a not yet beginning to be a beginning. There is a not yet beginning to not yet beginning to be a beginning. There is having. There is not having. There is not yet beginning to not have. There is not yet beginning to not yet beginning to not have. And suddenly there is having and not having, and I do not know of having and not having which is having and which is not having. And now I have said it, but still do not know whether what I have said is something that can be said, or something that cannot be said.[26]

The problem with these statements is that because they employ concepts like that of a "beginning" (*shi* 始) or "existing/having" (*you* 有) that are dependent on boundaries. Because of this, they cannot ultimately make sense of an *unbounded* reality. Zhuangzi may be understood here as doing something very similar to what Immanuel Kant is doing in the Antinomies in his *Critique of Pure Reason*—showing that the very concepts themselves preclude proper ways of thinking about them, and thus engaging in a reduction of metaphysics (in Kant's case) or *universal* or *perspectiveless* truth (in Zhuangzi's case).

SHI-FEI

The discussion of the concepts of *shi* 是 and *fei* 非 in *Qiwulun*, and the *Zhuangzi* in general, is not (unlike those found in some Confucian and also in later Han texts) one concerning truth. The Zhuangist authors use *shi* and *fei* mainly in their subject-marking determinative sense (*it is this/it is not-this*), as well as in their moral sense (*right/wrong*). *Shi* (this) is also used in opposition to *bi* 彼 (that) in the text, suggesting that the Zhuangist concern with *shi* is that of how things in the world are *picked out* or determined, rather than issues of truth. There are issues of truth connected to these uses, of course, but there are some other ways of employing *shi* and *fei* such that they represent truth terms. We do not see this in *Qiwulun*. This is in part because the main concern of the Zhuangists seems to be with our insistence on and attachment to the way that we individually (or communally) make discriminations (*bian* 辨), which is based on the process that we might call "conceptualization," which is to distinguish things through *shi* (this) and *fei* (not-this). Distinguishing any object from the world-stuff in general is an act of *shi*, and also at the same time an act of *fei*.

Indeed, in *Qiwulun*, *shi* 是 is considered alongside *ran* 然 (being the case) in an answer to the question of how we harmonize views based on *tian* (nature). The passage reads:

是不是，然不然。是若果是也，則是之異乎不是也亦無辯；然若果然也，則然之異乎不然也亦無辯。

Right or wrong, the case or not the case. If right is actually right, then what is different from right is not distinguished from what is wrong. If what is the case is actually the case, then what is different from what is the case is not distinguished from what is not the case.[27]

Here, we see a couple of things going on. There is, according to this passage, a problem with the way we generally employ both *shi* and *ran*. These are perhaps best taken here as *(morally) right* and *true*. The problem here is that what is determined as morally right or true *in a full sense* (*guo shi* or *guo ran*) rules out the moral correctness or truth of anything else (presumably anything contradictory at least), and sets up a situation in which we are committed to the extra-perspectival context of *dao* and describing it. Is it even possible to do this? The final sentence in the passage seems to consider what would have to be possible for us to make these extra-perspectival exclusive claims about *shi* and *ran* according to *dao*. We have to "forget the year" and "forget righteousness," and consider that which is not *bounded* by these concepts. But if we do this, of course, it becomes plausible that we will not be able to linguistically express rightness or truth. The *Qiwulun*, like the *Zhuangzi* in general, seems to accept that there is truth, but perhaps that there are multiple levels of truth, just as we see in some philosophical schools of Buddhism in India and later in China. Surely, the author(s) of *Qiwulun* take it that the claims they make about the limitations of language or the inadequacy of certain types of claims to capture the *dao* should not be seen as true only from the author's perspective. Nor should they be seen as merely inviting us to take the perspective from which these statements are true. Rather, they present them as statements with authority and normative pull on us. Such normative pull could only come from a statement that is true either perspective-independently or equally true within all perspectives. But there would be little practical difference between these two alternatives.

Consider claims in *Qiwulun* like the following:

物無非彼，物無非是。自彼則不見，自知則知之

Things are not without a "that," things are not without a "this."[28]

This is surely meant as something true universally. If it is not, then there is little point to the passage. The various things that the Zhuangists say about *dao* or knowledge are similar, as are the numerous claims they make about the inefficacy of conceptualization or devaluation (which is a necessary corollary to valuation). How do we make sense of this on the kind of semi-relativist or hybrid perspectivalist view that I attribute to the Zhuangists as represented in *Qiwulun*? These meta-level claims seem to be intended as universal by the author(s). We cannot take them as meta-level claims about perspective *formation*, or we are committed to the existence of some perspectiveless perspective. If all statements can only be made and appraised from some perspective, this must additionally be true for these meta-level statements, and thus there must be some perspective conceptually prior to the construction of perspectives. Why not simply hold that it is *this* perspective that is the authoritative one, and those things that hold true from this perspective are universally true?

The Zhuangists are not making this obvious mistake, in my opinion. To say that *yan* are true only from within perspectives *does not* entail that there can be no *yan* that are true across multiple, most, or even all perspectives. Those *yan* that are true are so because they correspond to *dao*, but at a certain level of generality, certain features of *dao* may be expressed similarly across perspectives. Thus, for example, complex statements like [the sky is blue] may be voiced very differently across languages, while the now almost universally used "okay" is exactly the same across languages. "Okay" is a word in Hindi and Japanese as much as it is in English. Thus, the Zhuangists can make sense of claims like the above as true from within a variety of, or perhaps all, perspectives that it is possible for humans to have. The Zhuangist do not, nor do they need to, say that such claims hold from *every* perspective. It is imaginable that there are certain perspectives (perhaps perspectives not possible for humans to achieve) from which they do not hold true. These claims are justified here, however, as long as they are true from within the perspectives we do and generally could be held to occupy.

SKEPTICISM

Sometimes the claim is made that the *Zhuangzi*'s perspectivism has a basis in skepticism. That is, perspectival differences are based on what we fail to see or know, which is a matter of conceptualizing the world in certain ways. Chad Hansen writes:

> The main target of doubt in these passages is conventional wisdom, especially our shared, conventional patterns of discrimination or distinction making. A key claim is that any time we make a discrimination, we fail to see something.[29]

When we consider a skeptical position, there are a number of alternatives. The skeptic in general denies that we *have* or at the limit that we *can have* knowledge, but skeptics may differ on the basis of their skeptical claims. Are we in a position lacking knowledge because we lack proper *justification* for our beliefs? This justificatory skepticism has been the overwhelmingly influential kind in Western thought, from Montaigne and Descartes' evil genius to Putnam's "brain-in-a-vat." But one might also adopt skepticism on the basis of a rejection of the application of truth values to statements—through a robust rejection of the possibility of truth. After all, if knowledge is true belief plus some grounding feature, whether that be justification, epistemic context, reliability, etc., elimination of the possibility of either of the other two components, belief and truth, will also leave us in a skeptical position. If Zhuangzi is a skeptic, then, he is a very different kind of skeptic from those in the Western tradition, in that he is not (at least mainly) concerned with issues of justification, with the question of "what turns a true belief into knowledge?"—and on concluding there is no ground for this pronouncing skepticism. Rather, his main concern is the question "is any statement *true?*"—and answering this in the negative, at least for *most* statements that humans make and can make, skepticism is declared. There seems to me no very good evidence that Zhuangzi was a radical skeptic, who rejected the possibility of knowledge and even the category of truth, as Soles and Soles have argued. Not only is the textual evidence more compatible with the view that Zhuangzi rejected the possibility of knowledge or truth in *certain kinds* of common statement, but the kind of radical skepticism and epistemological nihilism that Soles and Soles attribute to the *Zhuangzi* would leave Zhuangists unable to respond to the standard problem for the skeptic: isn't the claim that we have no knowledge a knowledge claim?

Soles and Soles argue that the Zhuangists are aware of this objection, and that it has no force for them, that they have a ready response. They write:

> In characterizing his own position as a dream, in describing his own words as the supreme swindle, Zhuangzi is warning his audience not to suppose that his words are drawing perspective-free distinctions.[30]

And later:

> The conclusion is that the man of far reaching vision has no use for categories. The point is that all attempts at categorization fail. And if all attempts at categorization fail, to categorize a judgment as true, even true from a perspective, is to attempt what cannot be done, and it is to miss the whole point of Zhuangzi's nihilism.[31]

These attempts do not solve the problem. First, if the Zhuangists' own words should be taken as perspective-dependent and "the supreme swindle," then what reason do we have to let ourselves be thus swindled? The Confucian or any other opponent can merely respond: "If you're right, then you're wrong! And if you're right, then my insistence on the Confucian *dao* is no more problematic than your own 'swindle words.' So what reason do I have to follow your teachings and not those of Confucius?" Second, any points being made about what the "man of far reaching vision" does or the necessary failure of categorization must be understood itself within perspective and as also ultimately not universally true. So again, why can't we simply reject it? If any point Zhuangists are trying to make is only as perspective-bound, conditional, and ultimately *untrue* as any point Confucians or Mohists make, why should we take Zhuangists any more seriously than we take them? What reason do we have to follow the Zhuangist path rather than the Confucian or Mohist path? The Zhuangists would be rendered as inert as a radical skeptic who claims "all statements are equally false." This is a necessarily false statement. Because if it is true, it itself is false. And if it is false, it is false. There is no way that this statement can be anything other than false.

Reading the Zhuangists as offering a perspectivist theory of truth in which only universally applicable or *dao-correspondent* statements are unproblematically true offers us a more sensible picture of the Zhuangists. It also makes it easier for us to understand the difference between *xiao zhi* and *da zhi*. Lesser knowledge is a matter of knowing narrowly perspectival truths—ones that only hold as true from within certain perspectives, and not across them. Greater knowledge is a matter of knowing the much smaller set of truths that transcend perspective (even though they may still only be expressed perspectivally). This Zhuangist understanding of truth is developed minimally in the *Zhuangzi* itself. It finds a fuller expression in the later text *Huainanzi*, which develops many themes of the *Zhuangzi* in general. In my opinion, philosophers have spent far too much time investigating the *Zhuangzi* and far too little investigating the *Huainanzi*, in which many of the positions of the *Zhuangzi*, including its position concerning truth, are refined and improved.

HUAINANZI AND SYNCRETIST TEXTS

The early Han text *Huainanzi*, which was deeply influenced by numerous chapters of the *Zhuangzi*,[32] offers a similar theory of truth to that of the *Qiwulun* chapter, but one that extends and develops the ideas of the *Qiwulun* in new ways. Thus, although the *Huainanzi* was compiled in the second century BCE, some hundreds of years after the *Zhuangzi* was likely compiled,[33] the theory (or rather theories) of truth advanced in the former text may be closely related to that in the latter. On my interpretation of one major theory of truth offered in the *Huainanzi*, we see a further development of the basic structure offered in the *Qiwulun* chapter of *Zhuangzi*, and thus a consistent overall theory that we might call the Zhuangist-Huainan theory of truth.

The overall project of the *Huainanzi* has been the subject of some debate. While clearly the text has a political purpose, as evidenced by the compilation of the text by Liu An and its presentation to Emperor Wu of Han,[34] it also has philosophical, religious, and other goals, consistent with the positions of its authors and possibly also of Liu An himself. As with the *Zhuangzi*, it is best to consider the positions expressed by the Huainanist authors (for lack of a better term) on a chapter-by-chapter basis. There seem to be some things advocated in certain chapters that are rejected in others,[35] and at the same time there is a certain cohesiveness to the text in general. This cohesiveness, at least, must be in part due to the project of Liu An's court, including the selection of sources and compilation of the text, and the construction of descriptive and synthesizing chapters such as *Yuan dao* and *Yao lue*, which also relied on earlier sources.

The theory of truth in the *Huainanzi* that can be seen as consistent with that presented in the *Qiwulun* and affiliated chapters of the *Zhuangzi* is most apparent in a cluster of "*dao*-based" chapters of the *Huainanzi*, at the beginning and end of the text, especially the first two chapters, *Yuan dao* 原道 (Origins of the Way) and *Chu zhen* 俶真 (Activating the Genuine).

The overall theme of the text is *unification*, of schools, teachings, political systems, peoples, states, and every other aspect of human life. One of the things that the *Huainanzi* suggests is that disparate systems of thought, such as those of the Daoists, Confucians, Mohists, and Legalists (among others) can be seen as *aspects* or *perspectives* that each capture some particularity of *dao*. The primary conceptual relationship that the *Huainanzi* uses to make sense of this synthesis is that of *ben-mo* 本末 ("root and branches"). The *ben* is commonly identified with *dao* (when it is identified at all), and the branches are the myriad teachings, schools, states, political systems, and all other aspects of the human world that the *Huainanzi* aims to unify. Each of the chapters either deals with the difficult task of characterizing the *ben*—that is to say, the *dao*—which presents a challenge because *dao* is ultimately prior to all conceptualization according to the *Huainanzi* (just as in the *Zhuangzi*), or with describing the various *mo* (branches), and their connections to the root.

One position we see maintained throughout the *Huainanzi* is that the key to understanding how we can both make sense of the various branches as all acceptable (even in the face of apparent contradiction) and equally valuable in differing situations is understanding *dao*. One who understands *dao*, the sage (*sheng* or *sheng ren* 末 聖人), will be able to understand and employ any of the branches when the time calls for it. It is perhaps the *Huainanzi* that offers the best case for those who argue that the concept of *dao* in early Chinese thought comes closest to the Western concept of truth,[36] yet strangely the *Huainanzi* is seldom invoked in this capacity. Part of the reason for this, perhaps, is the general neglect of Han dynasty philosophy by philosophers. By far most philosophical attention to early Chinese thought has been on Warring States' thought, and philosophers seem to have accepted the prejudice popularized by Zhu Xi in that Han thinkers were primarily interested in interpretation, and that they misunderstood the thought of the early philosophers.[37] Nonetheless, *dao* as something like a truth concept, although perhaps beneath the surface in the *Zhuangzi*, is more fully developed in the *Huainanzi*.

We find the issue of truth as a concern in the discussion of expression of custom (*su* 俗) and ritual (*li* 禮) in the *Huainanzi*. In the *Qisu* 齊俗 ("Balancing Customs") chapter, a picture of the relationship between the acceptability of a set of customs and *dao* is described. It is perhaps no coincidence, as Andrew Meyer points out, that the title of this chapter seems to play on the *Qiwulun* of *Zhuangzi*, both in employing similar terminology and in its similar phonetics. The term *qi* 齊 (balancing) is the same in both titles. *Qiwu* 齊物 ("Balancing things") in the *Zhuangzi* becomes *Qisu* here. And we find similar considerations in the two chapters as well, including their seeming positions concerning the connection between the *way things are* or reality and human constructions such as language (in the case of *Qiwulun*) and ritual or custom (in the case of *Qisu*).[38]

Because *Qisu* deals primarily with ritual and custom and their acceptability (or lack thereof), it may appear strange to claim that this chapter tells us anything at all about a conception of truth. But the consideration of the grounding of ritual and custom in *dao* in this chapter gives us a clear illustration of how the author(s) view the general acceptability of human conceptual constructs through something like a correspondence with *dao*. Their views on language turn out to be the same as those on ritual and custom. The *Huainanzi* is clear throughout its chapters that human constructions such as language, ritual, morality, and law are all ultimately inadequate to perfectly express *dao*, which is ineffable and preconceptual (a view shared with Zhuangists).

This necessary separation of human concepts (expressed in both language and ritual) makes all expressions neither equally permissible nor equally expressive of *dao*. While *dao* cannot be completely captured in language or expressed by ritual,[39] it is possible to speak properly or construct proper rituals based on the understanding of *dao*.[40] That is to say that language and ritual *can* correspond to *dao*, even though this correspondence itself does not fully capture or express *dao*. This is a critical difference between the *Huainanzi*'s version of "correspondence" and that of contemporary correspondence theories of truth.

The concepts of *shi* and *fei* are discussed in *Qisu* 11.15 in a way that does not completely deconstruct these concepts as we see in *Qiwulun* or other chapters of the *Zhuangzi*.

天下是非無所定，世各是其所是而非其所非。所謂是與非各異，皆自是而非人。由此觀之，事有合於己者，而未始有是也；有忤於心者，而未始有非也

In the world, "right" and "wrong" have no immutable basis. Each age affirms what it deems right and rejects what it deems wrong. What each calls right and wrong is different, yet each deems itself right and others wrong. Seen from this basis, there are facts that accord with one's self, yet they are not originally "right." There are those that are repellent to one's heart, yet are not originally "wrong."[41]

The problem here, according to the author(s), is that there is no justification for particular discriminations of right and wrong independent from the perspective of the individual. There are "facts that accord with one's self," and such facts do not warrant *universal* claims of right and wrong, as many tend to make, including the texts of the various schools. Why should we not simply read this as a statement of (at least moral) relativism, and leave it at that? In this same chapter, there is a great deal of discussion about the "proper or orderly state," the "standards" attached to *dao*, righteousness, proper rituals, appropriate conduct, and a host of other moralist Confucian concepts. The chapter takes a positive stance on these concepts, unlike what we see in Zhuangist texts. If the most we can say about right and wrong is that they are relative to facts about individuals and nothing else, there is no way to make sense of the kinds of sweeping claims concerning what makes ritual and morality acceptable that we see in *Huainanzi* and the *Qisu* chapter in particular.

Fortunately, the *Huainanzi* offers us a way of making sense of the relativistic sounding claims along with the universalist sounding claims about proper ritual, governance, etc.[42] The fundamental distinction between root (*ben* 本) and branches (*mo* 末) established in the *Huainanzi* is meant to serve as a bridge between *dao* and individual perspectives. In this way, *Huainanzi* offers us a more theoretically sophisticated version of what appears to be going on in the *Qiwulun* chapter of *Zhuangzi*. The Zhuangists do not (and cannot, if their words are to be taken at all seriously) reject the possibilities of truth, justification, or knowledge. If this were the case, their words would be no more significant than barking in the wind. And although some passages seem to suggest that is just what the Zhuangist words amount to, they cannot mean this seriously. Because Zhuangist barking in the wind would be no more significant, true, or even different from Confucian, Mohist, or Legalist barking, and there would be no purpose of the *Zhuangzi* other than to add yet more barking to the already overflowing pot of barking. Given the Zhuangist criticisms of empty or unjustified statements in *Qiwulun*, this is not likely. Yet in the case of the *Zhuangzi*, even though there does seem to be some suggestion that *dao*-language, however we might understand this, is justified in some sense, the authors do not explain what this justification consists in, other than to say that when we understand or otherwise attain *dao*, we speak properly, and recognize the limitations of language.

The *Huainanzi's* general distinction between root and branches gives us a way to make sense of the connection between statements and *dao*, and the particular understanding of the relationship between ritual and customs and *dao* in *Qisu* is useful here, as well as some more general discussions in the first two chapters of *Huainanzi*.

禮者, 實之文也 ; 仁者, 恩之效也

Ritual is the patterning of substance, humaneness is the application of kindness.

義者, 循理而行宜也 ; 禮者, 體情制文者也

Rightness is following the patterns and doing what is appropriate; ritual is embodying feelings and establishing a design.[43]

There is a proper way of expressing and constructing ritual (*li* 禮), which is clearly, according to the Huainanist authors, conventional, but also based on and grounded in a particular relationship with *dao*. That is, what makes the difference between a proper and justified ritual and an improper one is whether it corresponds to or properly expresses *dao*. This can be made sense of even in the face of the perspectivism adopted by *Huainanzi* when we recognize that *dao* can only be properly expressed within particular perspectives, and never from some universal perspectiveless position or a super-perspective. This does not, however, mean that there is no unique way that *dao* is. It simply means that every *expression* or statement about *dao* will be true about *dao* from within a particular perspective, even though it is made true by correspondence with *dao*.

The first two chapters of *Huainanzi* offer a more general explanation of the connection between *dao* as root and the numerous schools, arts, rituals, and statements as branches. 1.13 explains the connection between *dao* and the "myriad things" thus:

故音者，宮立而五音形矣；味者，甘立而五味亭矣；色者，白立而五色成矣；道者，一立而萬物生矣

As for tone: when the *gong* note is established, the five tones all take shape; as for flavor: when sweetness is established, the five flavors all become fixed; as for color: when white is established, the five colors develop; as for the Way: when the One is established, then the myriad things all are born.[44]

The myriad things, just as in the case of statements from within perspective, are connected to *dao*. Those statements that can be taken as justified within perspective, then, are those that accurately express or correspond to *dao* in a way other statements do not. Even though all statements *arise* from *dao* (just as *all things* arise from *dao*), not every statement properly *corresponds* with *dao*. And here we have a criterion for truth, albeit one that looks much different from truth on a non-perspectivalist account, since there is ultimately no statement that can be true from every perspective or extra-perspectivally.

CONVERGENCE

The *Huainanzi* shares with the *Zhuangzi* the view that various statements or teachings may correspond with *dao* but contradict (or appear to contradict) one another. We uncover the overarching understanding of truth in the text in consideration of the *method* advocated throughout the text. The *Huainanzi* offers what I refer to as a "convergence" view of truth, in which we attain truth via a method that we can refer to using the same name.

There are two early texts beside the *Huainanzi* in which we find formulations of a convergence model of philosophical method: the Warring States texts *Shizi* and *Lushi Chunqiu*.

One may object to use of the *Shizi* to explain an important methodological position in late Warring States and early Han philosophy. *Shizi* might seem a difficult case, as it is likely that much of the text is later than its claimed

Warring States' origin, with the text probably having been written sometime during the Han. The syncretistic nature of the text would certainly lend support to the view that it was constructed in large part during the Han. The convergence model is on display here and heartily endorsed. Given that my purposes here are not primarily historical, however, but rather philosophical, the issue of the *Shizi*'s dating is not essential. It certainly fits the intellectual trends we see in the early Han, but regardless of its date(s) of construction, it not only develops a convergence model explicitly, but also offers explicit reasons for rejection of exclusivist models, going even further in this than other convergence texts. *Shizi* is helpful here in particular because it offers an explanation of what is problematic about the exclusivist model of philosophy.

From an investigation of the three texts mentioned, we can discover a coherent view about what in general is the problem with the exclusivist model, which forms part of the reason for endorsing a convergence model as an alternative. The *Shizi* offers a clear and potent statement:

> 墨子貴兼，孔子貴公，皇子貴袁，田子貴均，科子貴別囿。其學之相非也，數世矣而已：皆夆於私也。天，帝，皇，后，辟，公：皆君也。弘，廓，宏，溥，介，純，夏，嘸，冢，睅，昄：皆大也。十有餘名而實一也。若使兼，公，均，袁，平易，別囿：一實也，則無相非也。

> Mozi valued impartiality, Kongzi valued public-mindedness, Huangzi valued centeredness, Tianzi valued equanimity, Liezi valued emptiness, Liaozi valued dispelling closed-mindedness. Their schools mutually denied each other, only stopping after several generations: but all were trapped in selfishness. Heaven, thearch, sovereign, monarch, governor, lord: all are words for "ruler." Immense, wide-open, vast, wide, broad, large, spacious, encompassing, supreme, eminent, big: all are words for "great." More than ten names but the actuality is one. If one makes impartiality, public-mindedness, emptiness, equanimity, centeredness, peace, and dispelling closed-mindedness one actuality, then there will be no mutual negating.[45]

Here it is "selfishness" (私 *si*), or attention to one's private and personal views and concerns, that the *Shizi* describes as the problem with the one-sided views of the various schools, and it is for this reason that they are unable to see that their own positions represent only a part of the broader truth/actuality (*shi*). When we obtain *shi* as we ought, we make the way of all of the various schools into one, unifying them such that there is no exclusion. According to *Shizi*, the fact that there is "mutual negating" shows then that there is selfishness, and to overcome one is to overcome the other.

Very similar things are said about exclusivism in the *Lushi Chunqiu*. A passage from the *Quyou* 去尤 ("Dispelling Partiality") chapter of Book 13 of the *Lushi Chunqiu* reads:

世之聽者，多有所尤，多有所尤則聽必悖矣。所以尤者多故，其要必因
人所喜，與因人所惡。東面望者不見西牆，南鄉視者不睹北方，意有所
在也。

Among this generation there is a great deal of partiality. When there is a great
deal of partiality, then one's opinions will be in error. The reasons for this abundance of partiality are many, but its primary and essential causes are the likes
and dislikes that people have. One who faces east cannot see the western wall,
while one with a viewpoint from the southern country cannot see the northern
lands. Ideas have location."[46]

Because of the *locatedness* necessarily inherent in any particular idea,
when we become attached to a particular idea, we become partial (*you* 尤),
and this partiality leads to error (*bei* 悖). According to this passage, the
attachment that leads to partiality has its ground in what we like and dislike.
We desire a certain thing or event, and this leads us to privilege one idea over
another. The final part of this passage tries to give an example of location that
makes it seem very much like *perspective*. If I am looking to the east, my
perspective is such that I see only the things in the east, and nothing in the
west. This does not mean that the west does not exist or is unimportant, but it
is outside of my field of view. To be concerned *only* with what is in my field
of view, however, is to be shortsighted, just like a person who is concerned
only with the present because this is the only time period he inhabits, and thus
spends all his money on a lavish feast and goes hungry thereafter because he
didn't think of saving money for food in the coming days. To see only the
east is *not* to see all that there is, and the suggestion here is that to have an
expansive, unified, proper view of things is to see (or at least recognize) the
value of *all* sides—north, south, east, and west, regardless of what is pres-
ently in one's field of view. In order to have such an expansive view, we must
rid ourselves of partiality (*you*).

Another passage in the *Changjian* 長見 ("Farsightedness") chapter of
Book 11 of the *Lushi Chunqiu* further suggests that shortsightedness is an
additional deficiency of perspective leading to exclusivism. The passage
seems to suggest, however, that we can be or become farsighted, and that this
is a matter of having a more expansive knowledge (likely understood in terms
of convergence). The passage in question reads:

智所以相過，以其長見與短見也。今之於古也，猶古之於後世也。今之
於後世，亦猶今之於古也。故審知今則可知古，知古則可知後，古今前
後一也。故聖人上知千歲，下知千歲也。

Whether or not one exceeds others in wisdom is a matter of whether one is
farsighted or shortsighted. The present is like the past, just as the ancient times

were like ages to come. The present is like the ages to come, just as the present is like the past. Therefore in examining and knowing the present one can know the past, and knowing the past one can know the ages to come. Past and present, earlier and later, all are one (*yi*). Therefore the sage understands the thousand years that have gone before, and the thousand years to come.[47]

Knowing the present well, if we connect this to the previous passage above, has to do with attaining a unity of positions, of various perspectives, converging on the truth (*shi* 實) discussed by the *Shizi*.[48] Here we do not have an explicit statement of doctrinal positions, but the idea of understanding different *ages* (*shi* 世) as unified strongly suggests it. Once again, the exclusivist is maligned as shortsighted, partial, and only in command of a tiny bit of the truth, and it is for this reason that the exclusivist is partisan.[49]

The *Huainanzi* has plenty of its own to add to this litany of criticisms of the exclusivist model. As in the *Shizi* and *Lushi Chunqiu*, *Huainanzi* presents the criticism that the exclusivist only sees part of the full picture, and that taking their limited perspective as the whole is ineffective at best, and dangerous at worst. The opening chapter, *Yuandao*, of the *Huainanzi*, explains:

夫臨江而釣，曠日而不能盈羅，雖有鉤箴芒距、微綸芳餌，加之以詹何、娟嬛之數，猶不能與網罟爭得也。射鳥者扞烏號之弓，彎棋衛之箭，重之羿、逢蒙子之巧，以要飛鳥，猶不能與羅者競多。何則？以所持之小也。

Now if someone spends an entire day pole-fishing along a riverbank he will not be able to fill up even a hand basket. Even though he may have hooked barbs and sharp spears, fine line and fragrant bait, and, in addition, the skills of Zhan He or Juan Xuan, he would still be unable to compete with the catch hauled in by a trawling net. Or suppose a bowman were to stretch out the famous Wuhao bow and fit it with the fine arrows from Qi and add to this the craft of Yi or Feng Mengzi. If he wanted to hunt birds in flight, he would still be unable to match the amount caught by a gauze net. Why is this? It is because what he is holding is small by comparison.[50]

The problem with the exclusivist described here is continuous with what we see in the other two texts discussed. The problem is not that the exclusivist has the *wrong* view, any more than we can say that the person looking to the east has the wrong perspective on the world. The problem is that the exclusivist takes his own limited view as uniquely authoritative, which is to be like the person looking to the east holding his own field of vision to be determinative of all that is within the world. Here in *Yuandao* we see a statement that the limited view of, say, the Confucian, or the Mohist, may be effective and in some sense true—that is, it may be like a pole that will catch one a few fish—but no such limited view could hope to compete with the expansive and unified view attained through convergence of the many perspectives. This unified view is here likened to the trawling net, drawn wide and sweeping across the whole river, rather than sticking to a point, in one spot. The spot where the Confucian and the Mohist drops his "line" will be covered by the trawling net, as will all the other spots on the river—so not only will the trawler catch those fish that the Confucian and Mohist may have caught, but will also catch all the others, and the expansive catch of the trawler will lead to a yield so large as to overflow the boats, compared with the tiny haul of even the most skilled pole fisher. The exclusivist here is thus the pole fisher who looks for a good spot on the river, while the convergence theorist is the trawler who collects fish from *all* spots.[51]

In the second chapter, *Chuzhen* 俶真 of the *Huainanzi*, a hierarchy of persons is described, and a continual degradation from the earliest times of unity to the contemporary period of chaos and disunity is described, in which we can see further explanation of the problem with exclusivism and its link to one-sidedness and the specific positions of existing schools. It explains that in the golden age at the beginning, the age of "utmost potency," unity was complete, intact, and unproblematic. There was no need for convergence, as everything remained in this primordial unity. The suggestion seems to be that this state can no longer be achieved. The chapter goes on to describe even lower levels of degradation, and by the time we get to the third level, during the age of Shennong and Huangdi, we see something relevant to our consideration of the exclusivist model:

剖判大宗，竅領天地，襲九竅，重九熱，提挈陰陽，嫥捖剛柔，枝解葉貫，萬物百族，使各有經紀條貫。于此萬民睢睢盱盱然，莫不竦身而載聽視。

They split and sundered the Great Ancestor, examining and directing Heaven and Earth, enumerating the Nine Vacancies, and demarcating the Nine Boundaries. They clasped yin and yang, kneaded the hard and the soft, split the branches, and sorted the leaves. The myriad things and hundred clans were each given structure and rule. At this, the myriad people all were alert and awake, and there were none who did not straighten up to listen and look. Thus they were orderly but could not be harmonized.[52]

With further degradation comes exclusivism:

施及周室之衰，澆淳散樸，雜道以偽，儉德以行，而巧故萌生。周室衰而王道廢，儒墨乃始列道而議，分徒而訟，於是博學以疑聖，華誣以脅眾 . . . 是萬民乃始慲觟離跂，各欲行其知偽，以求鑿枘於世而錯擇名利。

Coming down to the house of Zhou, decadence dispersed simplicity; people deserted the Way for artifice; they were miserly of Potency in conduct; and cleverness and precedence sprouted. When the Zhou house declined, the kingly Way was abandoned. The Confucians and Mohists thus began enumerating their Ways and debating, dividing up disciples, and reciting. From then on, broad learning cast doubt on the sages; elaborate deceit tyrannized the masses [. . .] the myriad people first forgot the trail and abandoned the path; all wanted to practice their own knowledge and artifice, seeking to force conditions on the age and crookedly acquire fame and profit.[53]

The teachings and "divisions" of *Ru* and *Mo* began when things degraded to an almost irretrievable point, and part of the problem here was that everyone wanted to follow *their own* knowledge alone. Part of the idea developed here and in previous passages seems to be that one's own limited perspective, ability, knowledge, etc. is insufficient to capture *dao* in its fullness, and thus insufficient to capture truth (*shi* 實). Part of what the exclusivist does not recognize is that his or her own perspective, knowledge, understanding is necessarily only a limited part of a possible unified whole.

With this discussion of the general problems with exclusivism comes a positive view concerning the convergence model in these texts. But before detailing the positive conception of the convergence model itself, it is important to clarify two related issues concerning syncretism and pluralism in the texts in question.

TWO CONCEPTIONS OF PLURALISM: ESSENTIAL AND INESSENTIAL

We have to be careful here, when considering the convergence model, to distinguish between a familiar kind of pluralism in the contemporary Western context and that of the dominant conception of pluralism in the Han dynasty convergence texts.

Today, pluralism is best known in its religious guise, and one popular view is a "one-within-many" position, which is different from the view endorsed by the Han convergence model texts. The view of multiple viewpoints, positions, or religions as manifesting a single and shared truth is a popular one. John Hick offers a succinct statement of such a view of religious pluralism: "An infinite transcendent reality is being differently conceived, and therefore differently experienced, and therefore differently responded to from within our several religio-cultural ways of being human."[54]

Note that this is *not* the conception of pluralism endorsed by the Han convergence model texts. Given what we have seen above, it is not that the different schools and viewpoints, Confucianism, Mohism, Daoism, etc. are seeing and differently representing *the same thing*, that they are all expressing a single *dao*. Rather, it is that the *dao* itself is a unification of the multiple perspectives, viewpoints, etc. The fishing passage from chapter 1 in *Huainanzi* expresses this best. The trawling net does not represent a single truth that *everyone* has—indeed, no one has such a perspective. The view from the individual is necessarily limited, thus the only way to gain full understanding is to unify one's own perspective with those of others. Part of the difference here between the Han convergence theorists and contemporary pluralists is a difference in belief about what is possible for the *individual*. According to most contemporary pluralists, I as an individual within a tradition can conceive of the "infinite transcendent reality," as Hick claims. The Han thinkers reject this, however. An individual is necessarily limited by individual perspective, abilities, and understanding. I can only ever access part of the *dao*, just as I can only see what is in the direction of my visual field, and not the entire world. Attaining unity is a matter of constructing the proper *communities*, not simply a matter of individual viewpoint.

The *Lushi Chunqiu* takes up this issue in Book 17, in the *Zhidu* 知度 (Knowing Measure) chapter. It advises even the ruler to know his place, reminding him that even the loftiest person in society cannot have complete understanding, cannot see everything.

明君者，非遍見萬物也，明於人主之所執也。有術之主者，非一自行之也，知百官之要也。知百官之要，故事省而國治也。明於人主之所執，故權專而姦止。姦止則說者不來，而情諭矣；情者不飾，而事實見矣。此謂之至治。

A ruler who is enlightened does not observe the entirety of the myriad things. His enlightenment consists in having a plan to command and employ people. One with the techniques to command does not take on everything himself, but knows how to delegate things to his officials. Because he knows how to so delegate, his dealings with affairs are infrequent yet the state is ordered. Because his enlightenment consists in having a plan to command people, he consolidates his power and duplicity is ended. When duplicity is ended, then persuaders don't come around, and states of reality are manifest. When states of reality are not obfuscated, then the truth (*shi*) about affairs can be seen. This is called consummate order.[55]

Insofar as the convergence model is a kind of pluralism, it is an *essential* rather than an inessential pluralism. Hick's religious pluralism, mentioned above, is an inessential pluralism. The difference between the two surrounds the *basis* of the pluralism. Hick's religious pluralism, notice, is based on the view that there is a single reality that is understood in multiple ways, and that ultimately what is perceived within one perspective is the same entity, the "infinite transcendent reality" that is perceived within another perspective. What is "inessential" about this pluralism is that there is no *necessity* of multiple viewpoints or perspectives. One can discover that transcendent reality within any given viewpoint—one does not need to understand or accept other viewpoints into a coherent worldview in order to access this transcendent reality. Indeed, one will have no additional insight into this transcendent reality if one gains knowledge about new viewpoints—one will simply gain insight into the ways that other people with other perspectives perceive this infinite reality. One need never accept, investigate, or even know about other perspectives in order to access the transcendent reality.

Inessential pluralism is not the pluralism of a unity created from disparate viewpoints or perspectives, and because of this, such a pluralism does not *require* methodological syncretism. Note that the descriptive syncretists discussed above, such as the Han philosophers Dong Zhongshu and Yang Xiong, might embrace inessential pluralism, while still rejecting the convergence model of philosophy. The reason for this is that if methodology is a matter of the kinds of intellectual practice that enable us to access truth, reality, *dao*, or whatever it is we're after, an inessential pluralist view will not require any kind of methodological syncretism, as being syncretic in philosophical approach (system building) will not aid one in accessing the fundamental truth within *each* perspective. To return once again to Hick's pluralism, understanding the "infinite transcendent reality" accessed within each religious perspective will not be facilitated by learning about or using all available religions. The proper method to access or understand such a being will not require a robust (or *any*) synthesis, as this reality is accessible in *each* religious perspective. Indeed, this is part of the point of Hick's pluralist view, from which one can claim that a particular religious experience and life within one single religious tradition would be sufficient—one can access the transcendent reality without needing to leave the confines of one's own religious perspective.

Essential pluralism, however, of which the Han convergence model is a variety, holds that pluralism is necessary and ineliminable in any account of truth or reality—any acceptable account of the world. It is not that *the same reality* is understood differently in different perspectives, but that there are different *things* perceived in different perspectives, and to have an accurate understanding of the whole, these different perspectives must be somehow unified. Thus, we cannot discover the truth or reality within any single perspective, because it is not there. One must rely on others and the viewpoints and perspectives of others in order to have a full understanding of the world. Without pluralism, without *convergence* in this case, we simply cannot accurately or properly understand the world, and cannot then successfully do things like govern (which the Han texts are very concerned with). This kind of pluralism will *require* methodological syncretism, because if the unification of perspectives is necessary for proper understanding of the world, the method for system building will have to facilitate such unification, which the convergence model does.

A passage from *Huainanzi* on relative abilities lends itself to such an interpretation:

湯、武，聖主也，而不能與越人乘幹舟而浮於江湖；伊尹，賢相也，而不能與胡人騎騵馬而服駒騟；孔、墨博通，而不能與山居者入榛薄險阻也。

Tang and Wu were sagely rulers, but they could not compete with the men of Yue in navigating little boats and sailing on the rivers and lakes. Yi Yin was a worthy minister, he could not compete with the Hu people in riding horses from Yuan and breaking wild steeds. Confucius and Mozi had broad understanding, but they could not compete with mountain-dwellers in entering overgrown thickets and hazardous defiles.[56]

Paul Goldin takes this passage as evidence of what he calls "insidious syncretism" in the *Huainanzi*,[57] holding that it shows that even so-called sages like Confucius and Mozi are limited and so should only be used by the ruler for what they can offer the state. I disagree with this reading, and think the passage fits much better into an interpretation like my own, where this constitutes part of an argument for the necessity of convergence.

First, why point out the shortcomings and weaknesses of people you remark on elsewhere as having understood some essential portion of the *dao*? If there is an implicit criticism in this passage it seems to be that what made Confucius and Mozi *exclusivist* was their lack of full ability and understanding, their ultimate failure of openness that would have allowed a synthesis of their thought. It is no accident that Confucius and Mozi (*kong mo* 孔墨) are used here. As Goldin himself points out, Confucius and Mozi were taken as arch-opponents, and *Ru-mo* 儒墨 was often used as a complex to identify these views by opponents, not adherents.[58] Why does the *Huainanzi* use Confucius and Mozi in this positive way? Surely not just to point out the limitations of concentration on virtue. The use of these most opposed of rivals would have surely been intended to make a broader point about why they ultimately fell short, even if sagely, and more importantly how their thought might be unified—following with the major interest of the convergence theorist with unity.

Secondly, there are other passages in *Huainanzi* that seem to echo the sentiments of the above passage but lend themselves much more to a convergence model interpretation, such as 1.9:

木處橷巢，水居窟穴，禽獸有芁，人民有室，陸處宜牛馬，舟行宜多
水，匈奴出穢裘，於、越生葛絺。各生所急，以備燥濕；各因所處，以
禦寒暑；並得其宜，物便其所。由此觀之，萬物固以自然，聖人又何事
焉？

Tree dwellers nest in the woods; water dwellers live in caves. Wild beasts have
beds of straw; human beings have houses. Hilly places are suitable for oxen and
horses. For travel by boat, it is good to have a lot of water. The Xiongnu pro-
duce rancid animal-skin garments, the Gan and Yue peoples make thin clothes
of *pueraria* fabric. Each produces what it urgently needs in order to adapt to the
aridity or dampness. Each accords with where it lives in order to protect against
the cold and the heat. All things attain what is suitable to them; things accord
with their niches. From this viewpoint, the myriad things definitely accord with
what is natural to them, so why should the sages interfere with this?[59]

In addition, Goldin does not mention the various other places in HNZ and
also in LSCQ that Confucius and Mozi appear in much the same fashion as
in the *Qushu*. There are passages in LSCQ that are phrased almost exactly the
same as this passage, for example, as there are in the HNZ, and examination
of these passages seems to fit a reading of them as advocating the convergence
model as I suggest, expressing that unity can be achieved by overcoming partiality (*qu you* 去尤) in the *Lushi Chunqiu*, or prioritization in the *Huainanzi*.

Goldin argues that the "syncretism" of the *Huainanzi* is ultimately in the
service of undermining philosophical debate and thought altogether, putting
in its place a hierarchization in which each person plays his or her own role
and does nothing more. Goldin says:

the *Huai-nan-tzu*'s syncretism . . . does not mean taking ideas from every conceivable corner. It means taking ideas that sound as though they come from
every conceivable corner, but weaving them into the justification of a political
state that subdues all philosophical disputation. The *Huai-nan-tzu* is a "school"
all to itself: it is the autistic-paternalistic anti-intellectual school.[60]

I think there are deep problems with this position. First, it takes an altogether too cynical view of what is actually said in the *Huainanzi*. I don't
believe we have any special reason not to read philosophical texts at face
value, regardless of what their authors or patrons may have thought would
be the further political value of these texts. Goldin's view seems to commit
the mistake of thinking that if Liu An ultimately had in mind the position of
ordering the state by subduing debate, that the *Huainanzi* could not also have
honest theoretical reasons for advancing the convergence position arising
from theoretical concerns such as attaining full understanding of the Dao.
Second, there is a large gap between what Goldin shows, the seeming desire

of the *Huainanzi* to undermine disputes and differences, and the conclusion that its aim was to undermine philosophical debate as a boon to the ruler. How, indeed, would philosophical differences even be seen as in any way relevant to maintaining order in Liu An's time? Philosophical "schools" never had such power in early China (or indeed in any period of Chinese history). As the passage from the *Hanshu* above shows, rulers in the period seemed much more interested in attaining philosophical unity as a perceived *benefit* than as a way to undermine dangerous philosophical difference. Such differences were seen as problematic not insofar as they made political unity more difficult (they didn't).

Passages such as the ones above ultimately offer more evidence, I suggest, that the Han convergence theorists were advocating a kind of essential pluralism about methodology—a necessary feature of the convergence model.

WAYS OF UNITY

We have seen that the *Huainanzi* and other convergence texts take it to be necessary for a proper understanding of the world that disparate viewpoints are unified, but what method is used for the process of this unification? That is, in what does such a unity consist, how do we achieve it, and what is the method through which we can achieve it?

Fortunately, these texts have a great deal to say on these points. In the *Lushi Chunqiu*, a great deal is said about the "One" (*yi* 一), as guiding principle and organizing strategy. Convergence is by means of the One, and utilizing this will enable one to utilize any or all of the individual aspects of the One.

凡彼萬形，得一後成。

Each of the myriad semblances is completed after attaining the One[61]

先王不能盡知，執一而萬物治。使人不能執一者，物感之也。

Because the former kings were unable to have exhaustive knowledge, they adhered to the One and the myriad things were ordered. If people cannot adhere to the One, things will confuse them.[62]

What is it to attain or hold to the One? Given what we have seen of the *Lushi Chunqiu* passages above, especially those maligning the exclusivist, attaining and holding to the one is a matter of at least in part accepting and knowing how to employ various disparate viewpoints and perspectives, even if they are not one's own. Indeed, the best ruler recognizes his own limitations, the fact that he necessarily occupies a single limited perspective, and thus allows the perspectives of others to make up for these deficiencies. Thus, attaining and holding to the One (used interchangeably with *dao* in some places in *Lushi Chunqiu*[63]) must be a matter of holding close, or at least not rejecting, these other perspectives. But, according to both the *Lushu Chunqiu* and the *Huainanzi*, attaining this unity is a matter primarily of internal cultivation, of conditioning oneself such that one will have the proper responses to the various viewpoints and perspectives. Unity, or attaining the one, is only possible in the context of recognizing one's own place (one's limited nature) and giving up the partiality discussed above. The *Lunren* 論人 chapter of Book 4 describes "returning to the self" (*fan zhu ji* 反諸己) thus:

> 何謂反諸己也？適耳目，節嗜欲，釋智謀，去巧故，而游意乎無窮之
> 次，事心乎自然之塗，若此則無以害其天矣。無以害其天則知精，知精
> 則知神，知神之謂得一。

> What do we call "returning to the self"? It is to make suitable the ears and eyes, to restrain preferences and desires, let go of wisdom and plan making, abandon skill and purposiveness, and wander among the multitude of limitless ideas. Affairs of the mind become spontaneous, and if you are like this nothing can harm your nature (*tian*).[64] If nothing can harm your nature, you know the essence. If you know the essence then you know the spirit, and if you know the spirit, this is called "attaining the one" (*de yi*).[65]

This is reminiscent of the *Qiwulun* chapter of *Zhuangzi*, in which the Zhuangist version of Confucius enjoins Yan Hui to undergo a "fasting of the mind" (*xin zhai* 心齋) in order to perfect himself.[66] The consummate person, according to Zhuangzi, has no self.[67] What he means by this is that all those things that we conventionally take to distinguish oneself from another, namely characteristics, desires, roles, etc., are limiting in that they tend to generate the kind of *partiality* mentioned above, that will not accept anything outside of its own perspective. The partial person in this sense is incapable of appreciating different perspectives, and this leads to the kind of rejection of alternative viewpoints that are characteristic of the Confucians and Mohists, for example.

Chapters 4 and 5 of Book 3 of the *Lushi Chunqiu* have a great deal to say about attaining the One and the skills and powers of a person who attains the One. For our purposes here, most importantly it makes it clear that attaining the One does unify disparate viewpoints and perspectives (凡彼萬形,得一後成 "each of the myriad semblances are completed after attaining the One"[68]), and it also describes the discriminative abilities of the person who has attained the One, who has been emptied of the kind of partiality that blinds one to the value of any given perspective. [69]

The *Huainanzi* also includes a number of statements presenting *dao* as playing this unifying role, and describing the attaining of *dao* as the result of the process of unifying divergent viewpoints and perspectives. *Huainanzi* speaks more in terms of *dao* than of "the One"[70] Attaining knowledge of or realizing *dao* leads to the kind of unity discussed in the *Lushi Chunqiu*, in which one becomes able to accept, value, and more importantly *utilize* a multitude of viewpoints and perspectives.

是故無所喜而無所怒，無所樂而無所苦，萬物玄同也。無非無是，化育
玄耀，生而如死。

If you realize the Way, there is nothing to rejoice in and nothing to be angry about, nothing to be happy about and nothing to feel bitter about. You will be mysteriously unified with the myriad things, and there is nothing you reject and nothing you affirm. You transform and nourish a mysterious resplendence and, while alive, seem to be dead.[71]

Perhaps one of the most potent descriptions of unity in the *Huainanzi* is given in chapter 2, which discusses the structure of the unity that I have been discussing, and will allow us to make better sense of just what "attaining the One" or realizing *dao* will enable.

百家異說，各有所出。若夫墨、楊、申、商之於治道，猶蓋之無一橑，
而輪之無一輻。有之可以備數，無之未有害於用也；己自以為獨擅之，
不通之於天地之情也。

The Hundred Traditions have different theories, and each has its own origins. For example, the relationship of Mozi, Yang Zhu, Shen Buhai, and Lord Shang to the Way of Governing is like that of an individual umbrella rib to the whole canopy and like that of an individual spoke to the whole chariot wheel. If you have any one of them, you can complete the number; if you are missing any one of them, it will not affect the utility of the whole. Each one thought that he alone had a monopoly on true governing; he did not understand the genuine disposition of Heaven and Earth.[72]

Here we see that unification or convergence is a matter of structuring the various viewpoints and perspectives into a whole that uses the strengths of all parts. The unified whole, however, is more than simply the sum of the parts, and none of the parts is in itself essential and necessary for the whole. The umbrella and rib metaphor is particularly potent here, as it shows the necessity for unification without holding the necessity of any given viewpoint or perspective. The individual perspective of, say, Mozi is an important part of the structure of a unity, but is not essential to this unity, just in the same way that the rib of an umbrella is important but not essential. If enough ribs were removed, there could be no structural integrity and the umbrella would collapse. But any *one* rib could be removed with minimal or no effect on the whole of the umbrella. Thus, unification of disparate viewpoints and perspectives is a matter of not just being able to accept the value of these various perspectives (by ridding oneself of partiality, as described above), but is also a matter of recognizing the ultimate *inessentiality* of any given viewpoint. This combats the tendency to partiality discussed in *Lushi Chunqiu* 13/3.1 above, which is based on "like and dislike," or to speak in terms reminiscent of the *Zhuangzi*, value and disvalue. "Dislike" can be overcome by recognizing the need for unity, while "like" can be overcome by recognizing the inessentiality of any given perspective.

Other passages in the *Huainanzi* discuss the convergence model as involving something like the Zhuangist ability to accept transformation and delight in the "transformation of myriad things" (*wanwu zhi hua* 萬物之花). There is a clear statement of this at the close of the *Yaolue* chapter, and the *Huainanzi* as a whole, as stock is taken of the project of the *Huainanzi*, and the authors offer a final statement of what they believe themselves to have accomplished:

以統天下，理萬物，應變化，通殊類，非循一跡之路，守一隅之指，拘系牽連之物，而不與世推移也。故置之尋常而不塞，布之天下而不窕。

We have thereby unified the world, brought order to the myriad things, responded to alterations and transformations, and comprehended their distinctions and categories. We have not followed a path made by a solitary footprint or adhered to instructions from a single perspective or allowed ourselves to be entrapped or fettered by things so that we would not advance or shift according to the age. Thus, situate this book in the narrowest of circumstances and nothing will obstruct it; extend it to the whole world and it will leave no empty spaces.[73]

Truth as representation of *dao* is consistent with seemingly contradictory or mutually exclusive teachings or statements. As with the *Zhuangzi*, even though truth is not bound to perspective, truth can only be expressed perspectivally, and expressions of the truth (a matter of the content of *dao*) will take numerous and sometimes conflicting forms. Having a full understanding of *dao*, according to the *Huainanzi*, is to have an understanding of how the various true teachings and statements all represent this fundamental *dao*, which is to have an understanding of the *root* rather than merely of the branches. The *Huainanzi* thus in the end offers us the most robustly developed "*dao*-based" theory of truth of early (pre-Buddhist) Chinese philosophy. It advances the positions of the *Zhuangzi* in an ultimately more satisfying and consistent manner than does the *Zhuangzi*, and offers a clearer explanation of the *dao*-based theory of truth than the more suggestive and metaphorical language of the *Zhuangzi* allows.

NOTES

1. Jeeloo Liu adopts such a view in Liu 2003.
2. Liu 1994.
3. One sometimes sees discussions of the views of "Laozi" or "Zhuangzi" as if these represent single individuals and their thought. The vast majority of the evidence cuts against this—there was likely *no* historical individual who can be associated with Laozi (the "old master"), and though there *may* have been a historical Zhuang Zhou, it cannot be the case that the chapters in the *Zhuangzi* represent his thought. See Liu 1994. I do not get into the textual sources and evidence here, as I am concerned with theories of truth rather than issues of authorship, but this explains why I use the term "Zhuangist" here rather than "Zhuangzi"—and even this must be understood as pertaining primarily to *Qiwulun*. "Zhuangist" refers to the position of whoever was responsible for *Qiwulun*, whether single individual or philosophical committee.
4. Van Norden 1996: 247.
5. Van Norden considers the possibility that the difficulty of giving a unified interpretation of the Inner Chapters of the Zhuangzi may have to do with multiple authorship, but claims "it seems worthwhile to attempt to reconcile apparent contradictions before we start making efforts to explain why they are there" (Van Norden 1996: 247). This seems to me reasonable if there is no independent textual and historical evidence to suggest that the text should be read as representing a coherent system of thought. But it is far from clear to me that we have this in the case of Zhuangzi. In recent years, a great deal of evidence has been offered that the Inner Chapters are not a coherent single-authored text. See Chris Fraser's criticisms of Liu Xiaogan (Fraser 1997), Graham 1986, as well as Esther Klein's arguments that the "Inner Chapters" did not exist before the Han (Klein 2010). In addition, David McCraw's techniques in McCraw 2010 seem compelling. McCraw writes: "Lately experts have gradually moved away from a "book-author" paradigm to a recognition that many diverse, short texts proliferated between -350 and -200, but most of them neither match with received 'books' nor have any identifiable author. Yet you still see most writers on Zhuangzi (hence, Zz) attributing large parts to one 'Zhuang Zhou' and speaking as if large parts of the Zz have textual integrity. Plenty of evidence exists to falsify such notions, but students of lexical measures have lacked statistical expertise, and no one has examined Zz's abundant rhyming evidence to help unravel the text" (McCraw 2010: 1).
6. Liu 2013. Interpretations like this are also offered by Karyn Lai (Lai 2006) and David Loy (Loy 1996).

7. Indeed there is good reason to think that this distinction is an *exception* rather than the norm in philosophical thought.

8. *Zhuangzi* 1.1.

9. *Zhuangzi* 4/2/33-34. Zhuangzi citations here refer to Zhuangzi Yinde, Harvard-Yenching Institute.

10. Van Norden 1996: 251. He writes: "Whether something is beautiful or hideous, benevolent or unbenevolent, or righteous or unrighteous depends on one's perspective."

11. Graham 2001. Karyn Lai also suggests that if this reading is right, we must take the text to be presenting a kind of radical relativist position. She writes: "If Zhuangzi is correct, all claims have an *ad hominem* characteristic; they are ultimately reflections of the self rather than expressions of reality. This view seems to have relativist overtones: if all views are ultimately lodged in their own perspectival reference frames, then the criteria for assessing them must be derived from within each perspective. A relativist solution is, of course, another way to deal with the issue of perspectival plurality" (Lai 2006).

12. There is also a counterpart of greater and lesser *statements* (*da yan* 大言/*xiao yan* 小言).

13. *Zhuangzi* 3/2/9–10.

14. *Zhuangzi* 5/2/40–41.

15. Liu 2003.

16. *Zhuangzi* 5/2/55–57.

17. Lai 2006: 371.

18. The authors of the chapter here are playing on the relationship between Confucius and the person he saw as his best student, in the *Analects* [6.7, 6.11, 9.20, 11.7, 11.10.] Zhuangzi's version of Confucius in *Renjianshi* is very un-Confucian, more like a Zhuangist mouthpiece, and he upbraids Yan Hui, who is caught in Confucian thinking. The whole story should be considered a *parody* in an important sense. See McLeod 2012.

19. *Zhuangzi* 8/4/5–7.

20. *Zhuangzi* 12/4/90–91.

21. Soles and Soles 1998.

22. See McLeod 2012.

23. It is important to note the distinction here between a perspectival view of *judgments* and a perspectival view of *truth*, a distinction that Soles and Soles (1998) rightly point out. I do not conflate the two here. Zhuangists offer a theory of truth in which truth can only be expressed within perspective and is *partially* perspective-dependent, but also dependent on *dao*, which is perspective-independent. Thus, there are both perspective-dependent and independent aspects of truth.

24. So, for example, the thought that [I am hungry] is expressible only in a particular language, even though this can be said to be a universal human thought. But the English "I am hungry," German "Ich bin hungrig" and Chinese "我饿" are all expressions of that thought. We cannot, however, access the thought in some "universal language" below the level of the individual local languages in which it is expressed. Even if scholars who argue for a "Language of Thought" are correct, such a language

does not constitute an expressible, communicable language capable of taking truth values.

25. Shang 2006: 39.

26. *Zhuangzi* 5/2/49–51.

27. *Zhuangzi* 7/2/90–91. I translate *shi* 是 and *bu shi* 不是 here as "right" and "wrong" rather than "this" and "not this" as they are sometimes also used in *Qiwulun* and the *Zhuangzi* more widely, because I take the point here to be one concerning morality.

28. *Zhuangzi* 4/2/27.

29. Hansen 2003.

30. Soles and Soles 1998.

31. *Ibid.*

32. There are some arguments that the compilation *Zhuangzi* itself as we have it today was a construction of the *Huainanzi* project of Liu An in the mid second century BCE. Harold Roth considers the possibility in Roth 1991, and Esther Klein offers further argument for the "Huainan" hypothesis in Klein 2010. John Major, on the other hand, questions this, given the use of different metaphors in both texts: "The scarcity of tool metaphors in the *Zhuangzi* relative to the *Huainanzi* and the negative tone of the tool metaphors in the Primitivist chapters [of *Zhuangzi*] suggest that the borrowing was overwhelmingly unidirectional. It may well be . . . that the *Zhuangzi* was edited into its received form by scholars at the court of Huainan; but if so, the work was definitely editorial rather than compositional. The *Zhuangzi* contains few passages that can be said to show the influence of the *Huainanzi*'s characteristic use of tool metaphors" (Major 2014: 195).

33. Though there is controversy about this. See Roth 1991.

34. It has been argued and suggested that Liu An's primary purpose in having the Huainanzi compiled was to encourage Emperor Wu to avoid taking direct control over Liu An's territory of Huainan. Major et al 2010. If this was the goal, Liu An failed magnificently, being forced to suicide in 122 BCE (Seventeen years after presenting the *Huainanzi* to Emperor Wu) after which the territory of Huainan came under direct authority of the Han court.

35. Ritual (*li* 禮) is disparaged in early chapters, while it is praised in chapters such as *Zhu shu* 主術 (The Art of Rulership) and other later chapters.

36. Mou 2006, Xu 2010, Graham 1989: 3.

37. In actuality, neither was the case. The prejudice persists to this day. Chad Hansen calls the Han a "philosophical dark age" (Hansen 1992: 7, 15). He suggests that beginning in the Han thinkers no longer innovate, and focus instead on, (badly) interpreting earlier texts. While there was a focus on tradition in much of Han thought, this is misleading, because there was no less a focus on tradition in Warring States and earlier thought. Indeed, a famous passage from the Analects attributes to Kongzi the statement "I transmit and do not create" (*shu er bu zuo*), and the Warring States and earlier texts are replete with interpretations of earlier texts and appeals to tradition. Han thinkers were no *more* tradition bound than those of earlier periods. And indeed, in the Eastern Han, with thinkers like Wang Chong, Wang Fu, Xu Gan, and Xun Yue, we see far less reliance on tradition and authority than we do in the Warring States texts.

38. Andrew Meyer writes: "The title 'Qi su' is a clear allusion to that of chapter 2 of the *Zhuangzi*, the 'Qi wu lun', variously translated as 'The Discussion of Making All Things Equal' or 'The Sorting That Evens Things Out'." Major et al. 2010: 391–392.

39. The Huainanist authors accept the necessity of and usefulness of ritual *li* 禮, while the Zhuangists for the most part reject it. While they diverge from the Confucians in that they reject the view that ritual is *ideal*, it is still *necessary* in a less than perfect world. There is lack of clarity on this point, however, as some *Huainanzi* passages also seem to suggest that in the ideal times of the past ("Grand Purity" or "Utmost Essence"), ritual was still employed. *Huainanzi* 9.8 (Major et al. 2010: 302).

40. This may be a point (one of many) on which the Huainanists diverge from the thought of Zhuangists. While much attention has been paid to the use of *Zhuangzi* in the *Huainanzi*, and even the ways in which the organization of the *Zhuangzi* text may be due to Huainanists, relatively little has been paid to the numerous ways in which Huainanist authors use Zhuangist and other material in ways that seem directly opposed to Zhuangist and other Daoist views. This in itself provides some reason for seeing the *Huainanzi* not as a "Daoist" text, but as a syncretistic one engaged in its own attempt to synthesize schools through the terminology and broad conceptions of Zhuangist thought. Thomas Michael argues (Michael 2005) that *Huainanzi* fits squarely within a "Daoist" tradition based on its conceptual concerns and terminology, but the views expressed on such issues as ritual and language are far closer to Confucians than Zhuangists. In addition, claims of the organizational chapters of *Huainanzi* such as 1 and 2 set out a synthetic vision that very nearly outright claims to be an attempt at combining all schools.

41. *Huainanzi* 11.15 (trans. Major et al. 2010: 417).

42. A discussion of the orderly state in 11.19 demonstrates this.

43. *Huainanzi* 11.8 (trans. Major et al. 2010: 408–409).

44. *Huainanzi* 1.13 (trans. Major et al. 2010: 65).

45. *Shizi* 10.2, Fischer, trans (Fischer 2012). Fischer notes about this passage, in his translation and study of the *Shizi*, "This passage in particular shows why Shizi would later be called a syncretist. It is notable for attempting to bring together various philosophical traditions, as well as for having the nerve to put Kongzi second on the list after Mozi." Fischer 2012: 140.

46. *Lushi Chunqiu* 13/3.1.

47. *Lushi Chunqiu* 11/5.1.

48. The use of *shi* in the *Shizi* passage above may actually constitute evidence for a relatively late composition date for the passage, given that it coheres more closely to the use of *shi* in Eastern Han texts such as *Lunheng* and *Zhonglun* than it does to the use of *shi* in the Warring States texts. On the other hand, such a blatant statement of methodological syncretism and the convergence model would be extremely out of place in the Eastern Han. The dating of the *Shizi* remains a difficult issue, and one I cannot solve here.

49. Knoblock and Riegel point out a related passage describing one-sidedness: ("Yongzhong" 4/5.6) "In the world there are no completely white foxes yet there are completely white fox fur coats" (Knoblock and Riegel 2001). This suggests that what

causes people to go astray is to fail to be comprehensive, developing only a part of what is inherent in things, is part of the *Dao,* is true. The making of completely white fox fur coats means that one must ignore all the non-white in the fox and neglect it, but all of that is part of the *authentic* fox, part of the Dao. The person who ignores this is not wrong in their claims of whiteness, but is *one-sided.* They are not wrong to claim that the fox is white, but they are wrong to claim that the fox is *only* white.

50. *Huainanzi* 1.6, trans. Major et al. 2010.

51. *Lushi Chunqiu* 17/2.1 makes a similar point, albeit a positive one, concerning rulership. "Nowadays, even in constructing a chariot, one has to make use of the expertise of several different specialists before it is completed. How can governing a state be as simple as constructing a chariot? A state relies upon a large number of wise and able men. It cannot find security simply by using a single thing or a single method" (Knoblock and Riegel 2001: 50).

52. *Huainanzi* 2.10, (trans. Major et al. 2010: 99).

53. *Ibid,* 2.10 (99).

54. Hick 1993: 140.

55. *Lushi Chunqiu* 17/5.1.

56. *Huainanzi* 9.8, trans. Goldin 1999.

57. Goldin 1999.

58. Goldin 1999: 175, "Well into the third century, the Confucian and Mohist lineages saw in each other their most sophisticated intellectual opposition. Certainly the term *Ru-Mo* (Confucians and Mohists) existed long before the *Huainanzi,* but it was typically used by thinkers who did not consider themselves members of either group in passages ridiculing both." While this is true for the most part, Goldin neglects to mention the instances of the structure in the earlier text *Lushi Chunqiu,* used in the same positive sense as that of the HNZ. Indeed, in LSCQ, *Ru-mo* is used in the pejorative sense *alongside of* the seemingly positive evaluation of Confucius and Mozi (LSCQ 15/3.1).

59. *Huainanzi* 1.9, trans. Major et al. 2010: 56. Similarly, (trans. Major et al. 2010: 433): "If you heed the arguments of a multitude of individuals as a means of ordering the state, it will be endangered in no time. How does one know this is so? Lao Dan esteemed softness, Confucius benevolence, Mo Di wholeness, Master Guanyin purity, Master Lie Yukou emptiness, Tian Pian equanimity, Yang Zhu the self, Sun Bin strategic position, Wang Liao going first, and Ni Liang going last. There are bells and drums to unite their ears; solidarity with law and regulation to unite their minds; keeping the wise from being clever and the stupid from being clumsy to unite the troops; and not permitting the brave to go first nor the timid to go last to unite strength. Where there is unity, order results; where there are differences, chaos ensues; where there is unity, security results; and where there are differences, danger arises. Surely it is only the sage who can unify the myriad differences so that the stupid and the wise, the skilled and the clumsy, exhaust their strength and tax their ability as if they emerged from a single cave. Wisdom that lacks proper techniques and ability that is undisciplined—even with reliance on strength, nimbleness, experience, and practice—are insufficient to bring about success."

60. Goldin 1999:182.

61. *Lushi Chunqiu*, 3/4.2.

62. *Lushi Chunqiu* 25/3.5.

63. 3/5.2, 5/2.4.

64. Notice the difference from the common 性 *xing*. I read the above as in the sense of "what we have received from *tian*," which is our nature.

65. *Lushi Chunqiu* 3/4.2. Trans. Knoblock and Riegel 2001: 106.

66. *Zhuangzi* 4.8.

67. 故曰：至人無己，神人無功，聖人無名。"Therefore we can say: the consummate person has no self, the spirit person has no achievement, the sage has no reknown" (*Zhuangzi* 1.8).

68. *Lushi Chunqiu* 3/4.2.

69. *Lushi Chunqiu* 3/4.2 B. Indeed, this is also a major theme of much of the *Zhuangzi*, which constantly enjoins us to recognize the "use of the useless" and to do away with our attachment of value to only particular perspectives over others, a tendency that comes hand in hand with having an "identity" or "self," and thus characteristic concerns, preferences, values, and behaviors. For the *Zhuangzi*, ultimately even the categories of "true" and "false" themselves are simply problematic ways of devaluing certain experiences and perspectives. This point is most eloquently made at the end of the *Qiwulun* chapter, in the story of Zhuangzi and the Butterfly. *Zhuangzi* 2.49.

70. And in LSCQ it seems that "the One" may be the personal or graspable aspect of *dao*—Dao as cognized by human beings.

71. *Huainanzi* 1.19, trans. Major et al. 2010: 72.

72. *Huainanzi* 2.7, trans. Major et al. 2010: 92–3. This passage also provides further criticism of the exclusivist model. The failure here, of Mozi, Yang Zhu, etc., according to the author, is not that any of these men had the wrong way, but that the way each possessed was not the *conclusive* way, and that the partiality and exclusivism of each made it such that each of them took his own single perspective to be *the* way itself.

73. *Huainanzi* 21.4, trans. Major et al. 2010: 867.

Chapter 6

Wang Chong and Xu Gan

The two philosophers considered in this chapter offer theories of truth far more robust than the ones we have seen in much of the previous material. It is in the Eastern Han specifically that we find increased reflection on the categories of language in play in the early tradition, including semantic and associated concepts, such as truth. By this time, although there are still a cluster of terms that roughly play the role of our concept of "truth," one term in particular, *shi* 實, achieves ascendancy as expressing the foundational concept of truth. Sometimes the origin of a foundational truth theory like those familiar in the West is attributed to the influence of Buddhism, the schools of, had conceptions of truth at the very core. Such a view then commits us to the position that it is not until the Wei-Jin period at earliest that truth becomes a concern in Chinese philosophy. China required the importation of "truth-concern" from South Asia before they worried about these issues. But it turns out that this position gets things backward. It was the linguistic and truth concern developed throughout the Eastern Han that laid the foundation for Buddhism. Buddhism may not have even been possible in the Chinese context without the philosophical developments concerning truth and other concepts by Eastern Han thinkers.

We know that in its Chinese guise, Buddhism first gained hold as a "boutique" religion of the upper classes, rather than rising from the masses as did a number of popular Daoist religious movements.[1] The earliest mentions of Buddhism that we see in Chinese texts are from the fifth-century *Hou Han shu*, a chronicle of the history of the Eastern Han. The text mentions statues and idols of the Buddha in the imperial court, and makes suggestions that the ruler at least at one point understood himself as an adherent of the Buddha's teachings—whether or not he accurately knew what that entailed.[2] The traditional story at least is that the Eastern Han emperor Ming was responsible

143

for the official establishment of Buddhism in the Han Empire, including the establishment of the *Baima si* 白馬寺 (White Horse Temple) in the capital Luoyang, a clear statement of endorsement or at least acceptance.

The ruling and upper classes were just the ones who had been exposed to the philosophical literature of the scholars of the Eastern Han. The concern with language and truth in the work of these philosophers certainly had at least some purchase in the minds of their readers, and it was into this fertile climate that Buddhism took root. Thus, although I do not argue for this here, I think there is a good argument to be made that it was not the introduction of Buddhism in China that brought truth to the fore in philosophical thought, but rather the shift of philosophical concern toward truth and metaphysics that made it possible for Buddhism to take root. Some of the innovations of the Eastern Han philosophy were likely necessary in order to make Buddhism appear as a "live option" rather than as an unintelligibly foreign ideology. The latter, of course, could never have taken hold in China.

The developments of Western Han syncretist texts such as *Huainanzi* paved the way for the concerns of the Eastern Han thinkers with language and method. Some new concerns also arise during the Eastern Han period. Some scholars attribute the changes in Han thought (and early Chinese thought in general) to political situations. In the case of Eastern Han thought, the development of concern with the distinction between *name* and *actuality* first considered in the *Xunzi* comes to the fore. Some scholars suggest that this is related to the collapse of political power in the Eastern Han, and the corruption inherent in the system of recommendations and promotion in the period, which scholars saw as routinely passing over talented individuals.[3] While these are certainly relevant considerations, sinologists can sometimes put too much emphasis on them, and see them as more central than they actually were.[4]

For likely a variety of reasons, including political and economic reasons, as well as internal philosophical reasons, language, method, and reality become major concerns in the Eastern Han. While there are a number of views relevant to our topic throughout the period, two philosophers in particular develop positions on the concept of *shi* 實 that offer us innovative and interesting theories of truth. I think we can go as far as to say that the theories of truth offered by Wang Chong and Xu Gan can be taken as the summit of pre-Buddhist Chinese thought on the concept of truth. It is in the work of these thinkers that we find the most reflective and well-developed theories of truth. Thus, it is these thinkers with whom I conclude my consideration of early Chinese theories of truth, leaving the scene just before the entrance of Buddhism into the now fertile intellectual soil of the declining Han Empire.[5]

In most Eastern Han texts, *shi* 實 is understood roughly in the way we see it in Xu Gan's *Zhonglun*, considered as connected to *ming* and the process of correctly formulating and using descriptions. Terms such as *ran* 然, *dang* 當, and *shi-fei* 是非 function generally in the same way that we see them work in earlier texts, suggesting a kind of folk theory of truth or correctness. The central truth-related concept in the Eastern Han period is that of *shi*, which is developed in two major ways, most fully in the work of Wang Chong and Xu Gan. Both of these developments concerning the concept of *shi* can be seen as developments of earlier theories of truth, especially that of Xunzi, and while there is some overlap in the two understandings, Wang Chong and Xu Gan have both somewhat different purposes in their considerations of *shi* and different positions concerning what *shi* is and what role it plays in an overall theory of truth.

WANG CHONG'S THEORY OF TRUTH

Wang Chong's theory of truth is complex, and connected to his overall methodology. The *Lunheng* 論衡, his only known work,[6] was intended to aid Wang's contemporaries in appraising the statements and teachings of current and former figures, including the works of the "sages." Wang understood the overall project in terms of attainment of truth. That is, in appraising statements and teachings (which fall under the category of *yan* 言), it is truth that we should seek. We should accept true statements and reject false ones. Part of the difficulty inherent in understanding Wang's theory of truth in the *Lunheng* is that he does not always use the same terms for this concept of truth when it appears throughout the text. When he discusses truth as a topic, offering more explicit theorizing about the concept, he generally uses the terms *shi* 實 and *xu* 虛. In many other places, however, Wang uses terms such as *ran* and *fou* or *shi* and *fei* to express the concepts of truth and falsity. In a sweeping statement of the purpose of the *Lunheng* in the autobiographical *Ziji pian* 自己篇, Wang writes:

況論衡細說微論，解釋世俗之疑，辯照是非之理，使後進曉見然否之分。

The *Lunheng* uses precise language and detailed discussion, to reveal and explain the doubts of this generation of common people, to bring to light through debate right and wrong principles (是非之理 *shi fei zhi li*), and to help those who come later clearly see the difference between what is the case and what is not the case.[7]

Here Wang uses both *shi* 是 and *ran* 然 to discuss truth, which he puts forward as the primary concern of his text. While these terms could be used to express the truth concept, for Wang Chong, the term *shi* 實 played the central role, in that it was used whenever the concept of truth itself was discussed. When we ask the question "what does it mean for a statement to be *ran*?" Wang's answer is that the statement is *shi* 實. In chapter 4, we saw through a consideration of the concept of *shi* in the *Xunzi* how the concept came to be understood as a central concept in what we might call the "cluster" of truth concepts in early Chinese thought.[8]

The concept of *shi* has a rich and complex history in early Chinese thought, some of which we have seen in chapter 4. According to the Han etymological text *Shuowen Jiezi* 說文解字 of Xu Shen, *shi* is understood as *fu* (富), or "fortune, wealth." It is broken into the *mian* (宀) ("roof") radical and beneath it the character *guan* (貫), which is explained as coins (*bei* 貝) strung together on a thread.[9] This led to its early use in a sense close to our "substance"—the substantial or valuable part of a given thing. This could be a property of any-thing—persons, governments, or teachings. It is not limited to an appraisal of language.[10] A couple of other glosses Xu Shen makes are relevant here as well. He uses *shi* to describe both *shi* 室 (hall) and *he* 覈 (investigation). Makeham reads the first case as meant to suggest that "a room is that which is filled."[11] Makeham does not mention the gloss of *he* as *shi* (he had the misfortune of writing his book in the years before online term searches and websites like the Chinese Text Project, to which I am deeply indebted). Here, we may find something even closer to Wang's eventual use of *shi*. Xu, after offering *shi* as the description of *he*, continues:

考事，兩笮邀遮，其辭得實曰覈

Considering matters, things being covered up and one's sentences/statements achieving *shi* is called investigation.[12]

Xu also glosses *ri* 日 (sun) as *shi*, suggesting fullness of filling (of light, in this case). In each of these cases, *shi* seems to be given the sense of a filling, fullness, or substantiality. *Shi* fills a room or is what a room can be filled with, represents the fullness of the sun, and can fill an investigation. Makeham writes:

From this primary meaning arose the extended meanings of "replete," "com-plete," "solidness," "substantiality," "filled out." These meanings share the common sense of "substantial manifestation." *Shi*, meaning "fruit," is derived from this sense of substantial manifestation.[13]

I would add to this another point, however, arising from the gloss of *he* that Makeham does not mention. In this passage from the *Shuowen* in par-ticular, *shi* seems to have a veridical content absent from the other senses.

It can still be understood as substantiality or "substantial manifestation," but the manifestation here seems to include the sense of "how things actually are." An investigation is completed when the investigator obtains not just some explanation or other, but one that matches the actual events, or states-of-affairs, one that mirrors the way the world actually is. A *true* explanation.

This broad understanding of the terms *shi* and *xu* gives rise to Wang's more particular understanding of the terms as truth terms, just as *you* and *wu* become particularized in texts such as Zhuangzi to refer to "things" (*wu*) or conceptualization in general. In the *Mengzi* we see a use of *shi* as flagging a property of *yan* (saying, teaching), very similar to what we find in *Lunheng*. 4B45 reads:

言無實不祥。不祥之實，蔽賢者當之。

Words without truth are inauspicious. The truth or essence of inauspiciousness is to cover over the propriety of the sages.

In the first sentence, *shi* seems to perform much like a truth property. Words that are without *shi* are not auspicious. If *shi* is to be read as "fullness" here, just as *you* is read "to have," what is it that auspicious words are full *of*? Certainly not *shi*. That which would make words auspicious, effective, or otherwise of positive value would most likely be, for Mengzi, those words that contribute to cultivation of virtue. Whether or not this use of *shi* commits Mengzi to a property of *yan* such that these *yan* assert things *as they are*, or whether there is some other property marked here that makes words valuable, it is certainly the case that the point is being made here that there is some property words can have or lack, and the obtaining of this property makes the difference between valuable and valueless words. This sounds a whole lot like a truth property, and there are few other properties that could plausibly stand in this relation between words and value.

The second sentence here, however, does not help to clarify things. It seems to attribute *shi* to inauspiciousness—the *shi* of inauspiciousness is enacted by those who obscure sageliness. The fullness of inauspiciousness is a possibility here—*shi* in this sense would be close to *cheng* 成 (completeness). There are a number of other places in the *Mengzi* where *shi* is clearly used in its sense of "fruit" or "fullness." We can see movement, however, toward the truth-value sense in which Wang Chong uses the term.[14] A passage in the *Xunzi* also seems to signal this move toward Wang's understanding. Xunzi, criticizing the teachings of non-Confucian schools, argues that in being one-sidedly concerned with a particular value, they each rejected an important consideration. For example, he says that in Zhuangzi's concern with *tian*, he neglected *ren*. In Mozi's concern with usefulness, he rejected culture, and,

惠子蔽於辭而不知實

In Huizi's over-concern for manipulating words he did not understand shi.[15]

This reading of *shi* contrasts it with *xu* 虛 (empty, false). Wang Chong, as mentioned above, does not get into the issue of the relationship between *ming* 名 and *shi* 實, although he certainly does deal with the issue at the core of this debate in the work of thinkers like Xu Gan. There is a simple terminological difference between Wang and thinkers like Xu. As Makeham explains, Xu Gan's general purpose in discussing *ming* and *shi* in the *Zhonglun* is to distinguish between the names and positions that people attain in government and the substance or talents of the persons, which often, he argues, come apart. Both Wang and Xu criticize their times as ones in which people without talent, without substance, can rise to lofty positions in government, simply due to flattery, corruption, or manipulation. While Xu tackles this problem by considering *ming* and *shi*, Wang also deals with it, but in a different way. According to Wang, differences in *ming* 命 (destiny) are responsible for the different levels of success of persons, which is independent from the person's talent or quality, which is a matter of *qi* 氣 (vitality) and *xing* 性 (nature). Wang is much more concerned with the distinction between nature and destiny than he is with the distinction between actuality and name. We see Wang as engaging in some of the same reasoning, however, in his considerations of nature and destiny, that we see later, thinkers like Xu Gan and Wang Fu engage in concerning name and actuality. Indeed, we might ask the question of whether these thinkers were influenced by Wang's discussion of this topic, and if so, why they shifted the terms of the debate toward *ming* and *shi*, especially given that Wang's concern with *shi* was so specific and linked to the core of his philosophical method.

The sense of *shi* that we find in Wang Chong's work is that of *shi* as "reality" or "actuality." *Shi* used in this way has a history itself, part of which I discussed in chapter 4. It developed from the early uses in pre-Qin texts[16] to become something new in the late Warring States and early Han, in part due to the developments of the *Xunzi*. The Xunzian sense of *shi* is further developed in the work of Wang Chong and later Xu Gan (170–217 CE). When we consider the use of *shi* as "actual properties" to evaluate sentences, as Wang often uses the term, we find that the most plausible interpretation of his use of *shi* in various linguistic contexts is as a theoretical basis for truth claims. If we examine the connection of the linguistic evaluative terms *shi* (是) and *fei* (非), as well as *ran* (然) and *fou* (否) to Wang's *shi* as "actual properties," we begin to see the shape of a fairly robust theory of truth underlying his philosophical method and his discussion of language and the teachings of earlier philosophers.

One of the features of this use of *shi* is its reference to *linguistic entities*, such as names, rather than physical objects, as in other uses of the term.[17] The reason that this term becomes linked with consideration of names (*ming* 名) is that it is consideration of *shi* that is connected with the appropriateness of fundamental and basic descriptions of the world. Wang sees *shi* not as primarily connected with *names* in this sense, but rather with the wider category of *sentences*. This is why the majority of his discussions of *shi* are connected with *yan* (言 "words," or "what is said") rather than *ming*—Wang is attempting to make clear that the contents of what is said in statements[18] (or teachings) can be *shi*.[19]

John Makeham considers the correlative thought of the early Han (especially that of Dong Zhongshu) to be a major source of the view of *shi* as justifying the application of names to things, locating there what he calls a "correlative theory of naming."[20] For Dong, it is the intentions of *tian* (天) which justify certain names, rather than *shi* (實) (which Makeham argues is an innovation of Xu Gan's). In Dong's work, we see a movement toward correlative theories of naming based on the connection between *tian* and names. Names, on this view, gain their applicability or acceptability based on their correlation with (or, one might say, *correspondence* with) certain features of the world—in Dong's case, features of *tian*.[21]

I agree with Makeham that this is a major source of the transformation of the *shi* concept from that of something similar to "essence" or "substance" to a higher-order concept expressing actual properties of discussed entities (whether linguistic or otherwise). However, I do not think that Xu Gan was the first thinker to use *shi* as justificatory for naming (or the acceptability of sentences or other linguistic entities), or the basis for names. The earlier philosopher, Wang Chong, used *shi* as a way to evaluate linguistic entities whether (sometimes) names or (more often) sentences, teachings, and beliefs.[22] One of Wang Chong's innovations was to apply *shi* to a wider range of entities, including statements or teachings.

Even though "truth" is an acceptable rendering of *shi*, we should see its scope as larger than that of the concept of truth discussed in much contemporary philosophical literature. Non-assertoric utterances can be *shi* or *xu*, for example. Take the sentence, spoken by someone: "Hello, how are you doing?" This is a perfect example of something we would generally take to lack truth value, but it can be either *shi* or *xu*, and is so based on the authenticity of the speaker. These words can be uttered even while the speaker lacks genuine concern proper to the normal utterance of these words. Thus, *shi* and *xu* link to the normative expectations of ritual as well. A greeting such as the above, according to ritual standards, is properly given only when the words and gestures are followed in the spirit appropriate to them. If such a greeting is uttered without the proper gestures and/or spirit, then, this lack of authenticity constitutes a lack of *shi*. Such a greeting is *xu* (empty), and thus false. Thus, *shi* and *xu* have a larger scope than our "truth" and "falsity," but we can see how the aspects of *shi* and *xu* clearly and plausibly contain the ideas of assertoric truth and falsity. It is this aspect of Wang Chong's theory of *shi* (not wholly unique to Wang) that allows him to develop what I call a "pluralist" theory that we might take to solve many of the problems with contemporary theories of truth, and the obstacles they seem to inevitably stumble over. Many of these difficulties may arise, we will see, because of the use of conceptions of truth that are merely properties of assertoric linguistic entities. Our "commonsense" understanding of truth is more in line with Wang's understanding of *shi*, but we cannot square this with technical accounts of truth as the narrow property described. Wang's theory of *shi* might help us to think about how we might develop technical theories of truth that square with the "folk" conception of truth, and take us away from the idea of truth as a narrowly linguistic property, while offering accounts that make sense of the manifestation of truth properties in assertoric linguistic contexts.

SHI IN THE LUNHENG—A PLURALIST THEORY OF TRUTH

In calling Wang's theory of truth a "pluralist" theory, I intend to invoke contemporary theories of pluralism about truth, with which Wang's theory shares a number of features. Although Wang's theory of truth diverges from contemporary pluralist theories in a number of ways, its basic insights fit it within the category of pluralist theories by contemporary determinations of what such theories are.

Pluralism about truth is relatively recent to the contemporary (post twentieth century) debate about truth, although it has predecessors throughout the history of Western, Chinese, and Indian philosophy.[23]

Contemporary pluralist theories of truth can generally be seen as a reaction to the perceived failure of "monist" theories of truth. Monist theories of truth generally take the concept of truth to express a particular *single* property belonging to certain linguistic entities—whether propositions, sentences, statements, or something else.[24] Monist theories of truth differ with respect to what they identify as this truth-making property. Contemporary monist theories have generally come in three loosely defined types: *correspondence* theories, *coherence* theories, and *pragmatic* theories.[25] All such theories are *monist* theories of truth, because they take truth to be a single property expressed by the concept of truth, such that anything which is truth-apt is so in terms of the possibility of having this single property. The only way things can be true is to have the single property that the theory equates with *the* property of truth, for example, correspondence with states-of-affairs, coherence with beliefs or general worldview, etc.[26]

Pluralist theories of truth are not necessarily in full disagreement with monist theories of truth on specific properties. One of the main features of pluralist theories is that they hold that the predicate "is true" expresses different properties in different domains or discourses (or however we define the relevant context). A pluralist might hold, then, that "true" in discussions of physics or metaphysics, for example, expresses a property of correspondence, while "true" in discussions of ethics or aesthetics expresses a property of coherence with other beliefs and one's general worldview.

One important feature of pluralist theories of truth is the notion of the requirements that particular concepts must meet in order to be a concept of *truth*. Pluralist theories are in a difficult position in some sense. They offer ways to understand the concept of truth, and as such purport to be offering us an explanation of a *single* concept. The concept of truth itself is not plural—there is *one* concept of truth—on this much they agree with monist theories of truth. The key to pluralist theories is that the single concept of truth can *express* different *properties* in different domains or linguistic contexts, whereas monist theories hold that the single concept expresses one single property in all linguistic contexts in which there are truth-apt linguistic entities. The monist, however, has an easy way of defining the *concept* of truth— as the concept that expresses the particular property that they identify with the truth property. The pluralist does not have this option. We cannot specify a univocal concept of truth by the properties it expresses if there are numerous properties it expresses, dependent on context. For example, to do this we would have to think of the concept of truth defined by a disjunction including all the various properties in different domains or contexts that the truth predicate expresses (i.e., "x is true" *iff* x corresponds with states-of-affairs when x is a statement of physics, or x coheres with a general worldview when x is a statement of ethics, etc). It is not, however, the *disjunction* that makes a statement of physics true, but the *single* property of correspondence. So with the disjunctive response there has been a failure to explain what it is about correspondence and about coherence (or whatever multiple properties of truth exist in the theory) that they have in common which make them *truth properties*. They certainly don't share the *disjunction* in common.

There are a few different ways in which one might answer the objection that pluralism theories cannot express truth as univocal. The different pluralist theories will turn on these answers. One way to make sense of the univocality of truth is to offer as a description of the concept of truth a set of *platitudes* about truth that any property must meet in order to count as a property of *truth*. In this way, we are able to have a univocal concept of truth, but one that will pick out a number of different properties in different domains or contexts, as different properties in these contexts will meet the requirements of the platitudes about truth. Crispin Wright famously takes this tactic, and offers a number of features of a truth property that we might take to be plati-tudes about truth, which any property must meet to count as a truth property.

Wright proposes a list of platitudes as descriptive of the concept of truth (features that any property must meet in order to be a truth property), includ-ing "transparency"—"that to assert is to present as true"; "opacity—that there are some truths we may never know or are incapable of coming to know"; and "correspondence"—that for a proposition to be true it has to (in some sense) correspond to reality.[27] The platitudes that Wright mentions are negotiable—as we learn more about truth and how it works in different domains, we may find that some of the "platitudes" are unreasonable or otherwise wrong, and we may discover that there are other things that should be added to the list of platitudes.

Another way to capture the univocality of truth has been offered by Michael Lynch, who defines truth as a functional property. There is a par-ticular property picked out by the predicate "is true" across contexts, but this property is relatively thinly specified, and is supplied by different particularly robust properties in different contexts. This move avoids commitment to truth as a second-order property such as "the property of having a property that meets the truth platitudes," which Lynch sees as problematic, and I discuss further below.

Bo Mou has offered a different way to understand a pluralist concept of truth. According to Mou, the general thesis that truth "captures the way things are"[28] can be represented in different ways in different "perspectives," through elaborations within given perspectives that are principles (fixed to perspective) expressing this basic thesis, such that the nature of truth itself is represented differently in different perspectives, while there is still a unified conception of truth underlying all of these perspective-based principles.[29]

Wang Chong's conception of *shi* (實) as a tool for appraisal of teachings and linguistic entities offers us a detailed and explicitly pluralist theory of truth that operates differently from the pluralist alternatives above, although in certain key ways it is closest to Crispin Wright's view, as it does take the truth property to be a second-order property, but one based on basic facts about what humans do and should look for in statements, rather than on a list of platitudes concerning truth.

SHI AS NORMATIVELY POSITIVE PROPERTY

Two essays in particular in the *Lunheng* offer us the greatest insight on Wang's view of *shi* as a pluralist concept of truth. The *dui zuo* 對作 ("Defending Cre-ations") and the *wen kong* 問孔 ("questioning Confucius") chapters show us how Wang uses *shi* to appraise teachings and sayings (言 *yan*).

The *dui zuo* chapter shows us *shi* (實) connected with the oppositions *shi* (是)/*fei* (非) and *ran* (然) ("what is the case")/*fou* (否) ("what is not the case"). *Shi* (實) is contrasted with *xu* (虛) ("falsity," "merely apparent properties," "empty [talk]").[30]

The main purpose of the *dui zuo* chapter is twofold: One purpose is to demonstrate that corrections *dui* 對 are needed to the classic texts (everything which has come before him) and to contemporary writings and teachings based on "unfounded or empty assertions" (虛言 *xu yan*). Wang does something similar in the beginning of the 問孔 *wen kong* chapter. There he offers reasons for the "criticisms" of Confucius that he goes on to deliver, along with a method for appraising teachings or statements in general (which he discusses and uses in the *dui zuo* chapter as well). Wang's other purpose in this chapter is to defend his own work insofar as it is a "creation" (作 *zuo*) rather than a "relation" or "tradition" (*zhuan* 專 or *shu* 術), and the usefulness of "creations" in general.[31] The dominant view of the day, as Wang recounts in the chapter, is that only the sages were justified in creating (*zuo*) and that those who are merely worthies should concentrate on transmitting (*shu*) the creations of the sages.[32] Wang here attempts to defend the usefulness of innovation by less than sagely people such as himself. Wang is basically defending himself for his "innovations" here, arguing that "creations" such as the *Lunheng* have become necessary because corrections are needed to the traditions, which have perpetuated falsehoods and exaggerations.

In the *dui zuo* chapter, because it is both a defense of Wang's work and an explanation of the efficacy of "corrections" (*dui* 對), there is some consideration of the concept of *shi* (實) and the related concepts of *shi-fei* (是非) and *ran-fou* (然否). In the early part of the chapter, Wang discusses *shi* (實) and explains how certain writings were historically necessary, due to the failure of the common people to recognize the truth:

眾事不失實，凡論不懷亂，則桓譚之論不起。

If the multitude in their works had not gone astray from truth (shi), and some discussions had not gone bad and become disordered, then Huan Tan would not have written his works.[33]

It is for similar reasons that Wang Chong wrote the *Lunheng*. As he explains near the end of the chapter:

論衡九"虛"，三"增"，所以使務實誠也

In the Lunheng the nine chapters on "falsity" and three chapters on "exaggerations" are meant to create in people the impetus to strive for truth (實 shi) and sincerity (誠 cheng).[34]

We see here that the critical problem that Wang is trying to address is the ignorance of *shi*, which he thinks is endemic in his society and in the writings of contemporary scholars. *Shi* is opposed with *xu* (虛), which is translated often as "emptiness" or "falsity." The sense of *xu* as "false" grows out of its meaning as "empty," and in Wang's writings it has the sense of "*merely apparent* qualities." This way of understanding *xu* helps us to make sense of the passages in which Wang talks as if *xu* words or teachings as *xu* are naturally attractive. Understanding *xu* as "falsity" does not give us an explanation of the attractiveness of *xu* things, according to Wang. Statements that are simply *false* do not necessarily attract us, unless they have some other attractive features—such as making us feel better about ourselves, etc. It is not the *falsity* of certain propositions that leads us to assent to, believe in, live by, or otherwise adopt them, but rather some other attractive feature. With the concept *xu*, however, there does seem to be a built-in attractiveness *xu* entities possess.

Wang mentions the seemingly attractive features of *xu* entities in the *dui zuo* chapter, in his discussion of *shi* (實). He says of the "common people"[35]:

俗之性，好奇怪之語，說虛妄之文。何則？實不能快意，而華虛驚耳動心也。是故才能之士，好談論者，增益實事

It is the nature of common people to enjoy strange stories and sayings, to delight in empty (xu 虛) and absurd writings. Why is this? The truth (shi 實) isn't easily [or quickly] believed, but flowery and empty speech astounds the hearers and excites their minds. This is why scholars with talent, who enjoy discussion, add things to and exaggerate the truth (shi 實) about affairs.[36]

Xu statements are (or at least can be) flowery, ornate, and naturally appealing to the "common people" (with the intimation that those of high talent will not find *xu* statements compelling). There seems to be a necessary link between *xu* and flowery statements, as the "floweriness" of *xu* statements serves as the reason that the common people tend to accept such statements. At first reading, it seems that Wang has failed to consider two possibilities: that there might be (1) true statements that are flowery; and (2) false or empty statements that are not flowery and appealing. But if we take Wang to be claiming that there is something inherent in *xu* statements that makes them appealing, we can show that he is not making this (seemingly elementary) mistake. *Xu* statements are appealing partly because they *appear* to be true, even when "appearance" is thought of in terms of tendency to accept (something we easily accept may be thought to, in this way, *appear to us* as true). Does this mean then that Wang thinks of *shi* statements as appearing false, and thus being rejected by the "common people?" If we take "appearing" true as linked to appeal to imagination, or being "easily (or quickly) believed" (*kuai yi* 快意), then the fact that the truth is not quickly or easily believed, or is unappealing to the "common" does show that it, in a sense, does not appear true. Of course, it will appear true to those above the common, who possess some wisdom, and it is thus the responsibility of such people to write works promoting the truth, to stir up energy in the common people to seek the truth. And it can *come to* appear true to the common people given proper instruction by more wise people (such as Wang Chong and others whom he praises).

Does something appear to be true simply because someone asserts it, for example? Think of a statement like "Confucius was ten feet tall." To assert this (in a serious way, outside contexts of joking, fiction, or semantic ascent) is to assert it *as true*, even though it is in fact false (one might be lying, ignorant, or misinformed). In most normal contexts, a sentence such as this would be uttered so as to inform or convince another person of certain features of Confucius, namely that he was ten feet tall. Assertion of x is to present x as true. It would be naïve, we might think, to take assertion as grounds for belief, but if we consider the normal case, this is often what we in fact do. We generally take a friend's assertion that "it is 11:30 am" or "Bill isn't here yet" or "Bill has grey hair" as acceptable grounds for assenting to the statement asserted. At more removed levels, we accept the assertions of experts of all kinds when they say things like "smoking causes cancer," or "Jupiter's upper atmosphere is 90 percent hydrogen." The mistake common people (俗人 *su ren*) often make, according to Wang, is failure to be reflective. They accept what is asserted by people around them as true, even though these people are often either ignorant, misinformed, or dishonest.

Xu statements, then, can be thought of as false statements that we are somehow inclined to believe. So *why* are we inclined to believe them? Is it due to the mere fact of their being asserted (in the right context)? Or is there some more robust explanation? The above seems to suggest that there is something extra that *xu* statements have.

Xu statements are not only the ones we would be *inclined* to believe due to assertion, but they have some other compelling quality—common people delight in them and they appeal to the imagination. Thus, common people are more likely to imagine these statements as possessing the properties that would make them *shi*, based on wishful thinking. We can see how this might work. Human psychology is such that it is far easier to get someone to believe something they would like to be true than something they either have no interest in or do not want to be true. This facet of our psychology can be and has been used to great effect by those wishing to deceive in various ways.[37] But how about in cases of ignorance or misinformation? The statement "Bill is six feet tall" may be false, and I may believe and thus assert this statement, to inform a friend about features of Bill. I may have been misinformed, however, having never met Bill. In fact, say, Bill is only five feet seven inches tall. There is nothing intrinsically compelling, beyond my assertion, about the statement "Bill is six feet tall." This is not something we would expect to "appeal to the imagination" or be believed due to a human inclination to accept the fantastic. Rather, it will generally be accepted because I assert it and the listener has no reason to doubt that what I say in such cases is true. So is this statement *xu*?

For Wang, statements of this kind *are not-xu*. There are statements, like my example of "Bill is six feet tall," that are *not-shi* but are also *not-xu*. The reason Wang does not speak about this kind of statement is that he is mainly concerned with *xu* statements *as compelling to su ren*. *Xu* statements are most problematic. We can and do easily correct our mistakes when they involve things that we have no general inclination to accept. My friend might believe me that Bill is six feet tall, but when he gets different information from someone else, he will likely come to doubt what I told him, and remain agnostic about Bill's height until meeting him. However, *xu* statements are much trickier than this because cognitive bias is involved. We are hesitant to give up belief in statements that we would like to be true, for example, and often hold to them even in the face of overwhelming evidence that they are false.

Shi 實, as the opposite of *xu*, is being used to flag *actual* properties (the actual possession of the properties that we seek when appraising statements) as opposed to merely *apparent* properties (the mere apparent possession of these properties) of statements, teachings, or whatever can be *shi*-apt. To see what these properties are, we have to look to Wang's discussion surrounding the concepts related to *shi* and *xu*.

In the *dui zuo* chapter, there are two dichotomies discussed in relation with *shi* and *xu*—namely *shi-fei* (是非) and *ran-fou* (然否). In the *dui zuo* chapter, *shi* (是) and *fei* (非) when discussed as concepts rather than verbally used, seem to be connected to ethical or normative contexts. Alfred Forke, in his translation, noticed this and translated *shi* (是) and *fei* (非) in the *dui zuo* chapter as "right" and "wrong," respectively, in all the places where they are discussed as evaluative properties. We see *shi* and *fei* mentioned along with *ran* and *fou*, "is the case" and "is not the case" in discussions of *shi* (實) in the chapter. Two passages in particular show us the two dichotomies discussed together:

明辯然否，病心傷之，安能不論？ . . . ［孟子］引平直說，襃是抑非

Those who can determine what is the case and what is not the case feel an ail-ment in their hearts which pain them [at the thought of truth being subverted by the "common people" and flowery scholarship] . . . [Mengzi's] language was straight and to the point, according high place to the right (是 shi) and sup-pressing the wrong (非 fei).[38]

One may find it curious that *shi* and *fei* are translated here as "right" and "wrong," which suggests moral normativity, while *ran* and *fou* are translated in more clearly truth-evaluative terms as "what is the case" and "what is not the case." What is the justification for the difference? Are we given any reason to read *shi* and *fei* as I do in the above passage? A consideration of some other instances of *shi* and *fei* in this chapter may help. The following passage is crucial for understanding the normative use, as well as for understanding how Wang may be seen as a pluralist about truth.

況論衡細說微論，解釋世俗之疑，辯照是非之理，使後進曉見然否之分

> *The Lunheng uses precise language and detailed discussion, to reveal and explain the doubts of this generation of common people, to bring to light through debate right and wrong principles (是非之理 shi fei zhi li), and to help those who come later clearly see the difference between what is the case and what is not the case.*[39]

Here, we see *shi* and *fei* connected to the "principles" (*li* 理) that Wang aims to uncover. His purpose in the *Lunheng* is to reveal *shi* and *fei* principles and to help people distinguish between what is the case and what is not the case. What is the reason for using two different formulations here, *shi-fei* and *ran-fou*, if he means something like "truth and falsity" in both cases? It is implausible that this should be seen as simply using synonyms to mean something like "truth and falsity," so that he is saying that he wants to (1) uncover true and false principles, and (2) help people distinguish between what is true and what is false. This point is strengthened by his use of *li* (理), by which Wang means something like "*moral* principle." This is far from the Song Neo-Confucian use of *li* (理) to express a foundational metaphysical concept. The above mentioned is the only occurrence of *li* in the *dui zuo* chapter, but if we look to the *wen kong* ("Questioning Confucius") chapter, in which consideration of argument and method is a central theme,[40] we learn more about how Wang uses *li*.

難 孔子，何傷於義？誠有傳聖業之知，伐孔子之說，何逆於理？ . . .

> *[If we] challenge Confucius, how is this injurious to moral appropriateness? If, sincerely attempting to transmit the knowledge of the sages' teachings, one attacks Confucius' words, how does this oppose principle (li)?*[41]

This is clearly a view of *li* as either the collection of moral norms or the ground of moral norms. Wang's second sentence is explaining his first. Challenging (難 *nan*) Confucius is not injurious to moral appropriateness (義 *yi*), *because* attacking Confucius' words in order to clear things up does not violate the correct moral principles that make certain acts appropriate or inappropriate. This is also argued in another passage in the *wen kong* chapter,[42] in which Wang criticizes Confucius for violating *li* by picking on the weaknesses of Meng Yizi and thus acting "contrary to the will of the Duke of Zhou" (違周公之志).

If we take these uses of *li* to be the same as that in the above passage from the *dui zuo* chapter, then it looks like the passage gives us two separate goals of the *Lunheng*—a moral goal, uncovering true moral principles, and a non-moral goal, of determining what is the case and what is not the case. Now, the question becomes, why distinguish the two? Wouldn't simply "discovering the truth" take care of both of these? Why didn't Wang simply say that the purpose of the *Lunheng* is to *uncover the truth*, to help us distinguish between *shi* 實 and *xu* 虛, which seems his main purpose as he describes it in other passages? If he is after *truth*, after all, then it looks like facts about moral principles and what is the case will just fall out of this pursuit. If we know what is true, then by definition we will know which moral principles, if any, are right, because we will know whether normative statements, such as "one should never pick on the weaknesses of another," are *true*.

There seems to be some connection between *fou-ran* and *shi-fei* in *Lunheng* 84.363.3-5 above, where Wang talks about Mencius' ability and action. According to this passage, those who have the ability to discriminate between what is the case and what is not the case (*ran* and *fou*) are able to use language to point out what is right (是 *shi*) and what is wrong (非 *fei*). So knowledge of moral principle does seem to follow from the ability to discriminate between what is and what is not the case. Does this, however, show us that there is a single property of truth, such as *ran* (what is the case) that is operative in all contexts? A consideration of *shi* (實) shows us that it is the wise person's grasp of *shi* (實) that enables him to both distinguish between what is and what is not the case *and* to distinguish between right and wrong moral principles. It is not the ability to distinguish between *ran* and *fou* that makes one able to distinguish between *shi* and *fei*, but rather the ability to distinguish between *shi* (實) and *xu* (虛) that makes one able to make both of the other types of discrimination. The fact that Mencius had the ability to distinguish between *ran* and *fou* showed that he had the ability on which the ability to distinguish between *shi* (是) and *fei* (非) rests.

The ability to distinguish between 實 *shi* and 虛 *xu* then presumes the ability to make a number of other useful discriminations involving teachings, statements, and other entities. *Shi* and *xu*, that is, seem like *higher-order* concepts, unlike *ran* and *fou* or *shi* and *fei*. I believe that the best way to make sense of this is to take 是 *shi* and 然 *ran* as ways in which something can be 實 *shi* ("actual," "true"), while 非 *fei* and 否 *fou* are ways in which something can be 虛 *xu* ("empty," "false," "only apparently true"). That is, Wang is offering a view of 實 *shi* in which what makes a statement (言 *yan*) 實 *shi* is *either* being 是 *shi*, or being 然 *ran*.

A moral principle, such as mentioned in the above case: "Don't attack people's weaknesses" can be 是 *shi* or 非 *fei*, but we can clearly see (we would share Wang's intuition) that phrased in this way, it cannot be "the case" or "not the case," because it is not an assertion about a state-of-affairs. We could reformulate this so it would look like an assertion about a state-of-affairs, and render it this way: "one should not attack people's weaknesses." This formulation seems "is the case"-apt, as it is formulated in such a way as to suggest the possibility of a state-of-affairs that makes it the case that one should (or should not) attack people's weaknesses, whether we understand this state-of-affairs to involve moral facts (whatever these are), teleological features of humans, or anything else that could belong to a state-of-affairs of the world and also explain the normativity involved in this principle.

Wang, however, does not evaluate moral principles in this way, in terms of states-of-affairs. He considers statements like "don't attack people's weaknesses" and their acceptability in terms of 是 *shi* and 非 *fei*, "right" and "wrong." If normativity in moral cases is not based on facts about "what is the case," we can explain easily why Wang distinguished 實 *shi*-making properties for moral statements from 實 *shi*-making properties for nonmoral statements. There are simply *different* properties which make these different kinds of statements or teachings 實 *shi* (true, actual). And if this is the case, then Wang can be seen as a pluralists 實 *shi*, in a way similar to contemporary alethic pluralist theorists about "truth."

Which properties then are expressed by 實 *shi*? Moral acceptability (是 *shi*) is one property expressed by 實 *shi*, in the moral domain. This property of acceptability would *not*, however, make nonmoral statements about physical objects true. This property can only be a *shi*-making property in the appropriate domain. Nonmoral statements cannot be 是 *shi*, just as moral principles cannot be 然 *ran*.[43]

At least one difficult problem remains, however. One key feature of the concept of truth, or the concept of 實 *shi*, is that it should be a *univocal* concept. Even though there might be different properties in different linguistic contexts that make a statement true, it cannot be the case that "truth" (or 實 *shi*) *means* different things in different contexts. It should mean the same thing to say that a moral statement is true as it does to say that a nonmoral statement is true. As I've shown in the previous section, one way of capturing this is to define the concept of truth by way of a number of platitudes that any property in any relevant domain must meet in order to be a truth property. Thus, the meaning of "truth" can be understood in terms of the platitudes, while the properties that the concept expresses are variable in different contexts. Wang Chong, however, does not seem aware of either this problem of univocality or the conception of fixing the meaning of truth via platitudes. Shouldn't this lead us to question whether Wang actually did have a pluralist view of truth?

I think that the question of how to account for the univocality of *shi* did not arise for Wang due to his conception of what the property of 實 *shi* is, and how it relates to the "truth-making" properties 是 *shi* and 然 *ran*. On Wang's view of 實 *shi*, there is no difficulty in accounting for univocality, because the concept of *shi* is of a unified second-order property linked to particular truth-making properties that differ by context.

We find passages in the *Lunheng* that show us that Wang did think of *shi* as univocal. The following passage from the *dui zuo* chapter is informative here:

人君遭弊，改教於上；　君臣（愚）惑，作論於下。［下］實得，則上教
從矣。冀悟迷惑之心，使知虛實之分。實虛之分定，而華僞之文滅；華
僞之文滅，則純誠之化日以孳矣。

When the ruler does badly, instruction to change conduct is directed toward the person on high. When the ruler's subjects are doltish, engaging in discussions is directed toward the people below. When the people below obtain the truth (實 shi), then instruction of the person on high follows. I hope to stir some of these minds, to help them distinguish between truth (實 shi) and falsity (虛 xu). Once the distinction between truth and falsity is established, then flowery and artificial writings can be eliminated. When flowery and artificial writings are eliminated, pure and sincere transformations will grow more abundant day by day.[44]

In this passage, we see that the ability to distinguish between *shi* and *xu* leads to transformation of conduct as well as the elimination of error in writings. Since much of Wang's criticism in the *Lunheng* is directed at physical and metaphysical as well as moral writings, we can see this second ability as reaching both moral and nonmoral domains or contexts. Wang also asserts a connection between elimination of false (虛 *xu*) writings and moral transformation (we have to assume this is what he means here by 化 *hua*, as the passage began by speaking of conduct and this should be taken to point back to that). We see again that the ability to discriminate between 實 *shi* and 虛 *xu* allows us to both distinguish between 然 *ran* and 否 *fou* and to distinguish between 是 *shi* and 非 *fei*. In order for this to be the case, there must be some univocal concept of 實 *shi* that captures the similarities between the various properties that count as *shi*-properties.

Although it is difficult to completely demonstrate the case based on what Wang says in the *Lunheng*, I suggest that the view that I outline below on the univocality of *shi* is most like the one Wang held. It explains why he didn't see a problem with maintaining its univocality while maintaining pluralism. In addition, the view that I attribute to Wang here can, I think, offer us an alternative way to solve some of the problems raised for pluralist theories.

The univocality of *shi* is based on its second-order status. *Shi*, for Wang, is the property of having properties that we actually do and should seek when we appraise statements. There are a number of parts of his analysis of *shi*. First, it is a second-order property, but a second-order *pluralistic* property. It is not "the property of having some (one) property such that [the truth-making description is met]," (as both Lynch and Wright specify the second-order view[45]), but rather it is "the property of having *properties* such that [the truth-making description is met]." This move actually has a great deal of philosophical payoff, in that it removes the force of objections to pluralism based on the problem of mixed conjunctions, as I explain below.

Shi, for Wang, can be thought of as expressing a second-order property—the property of having a property or properties that we should and do seek when appraising statements. This makes truth rest on normativity. The normativity involved here, however, is basic, in a sense that what we *should* do is linked with what we *in fact do*, but is not explained by the fact that we do these things. That is, the descriptive element is not meant to explain the normative, but to be a further basic fact beside it. Here, both concepts are in the employ of the truth function, as an explanation for what makes a particular statement *shi*. If we consider the properties of 然 *ran* and 是 *shi* that can belong to statements in the nonmoral and moral domains, respectively, we can begin to see what is meant. The properties of *ran* and *shi* are properties that humans naturally seek when they appraise sentences, according to Wang. No one accepts as true a statement that they believe to be 不然 *bu ran* or 非 *fei*. Rather, the reason a statement is accepted by anyone is because one believes (sometimes mistakenly) that this statement is either 然 *ran*, 是 *shi*, or has some other 實 *shi*-making property. It is a brute fact about humans that we do seek properties such as 是 *shi* and 然 *ran* when we appraise sentences and accept or believe statements based on whether or not we have reason to think they are *ran* or *shi*. Thus the key question to be answered when we consider whether or not something is 實 *shi* is whether the statement *actually* has the properties we naturally seek. In addition to this description of what humans actually do, however, there is an added normative element. Not only *do* we seek properties like 然 *ran* and 是 *shi*, but we *ought* to seek such properties. Why ought we? That is, what explains the normativity? I believe (though it would take much more space than I have here to argue) that Wang takes this normativity as explanatorily *basic*. Although this certainly would strike most of us in the contemporary Western-based philosophical tradition as strange or implausible, this view (if Wang's own) would not, by any means, have been unprecedented in ancient China. The Mohists give us the best example of a group of thinkers who may have had a similar view of certain normative statements as basic.

Wang's view of the univocality of *shi* has a couple of interesting features, relevant to the contemporary debate surrounding pluralism and truth in general. It is sometimes objected that pluralism cannot account for the truth of statements or propositions that are conjunctions of propositions belonging to different linguistic domains. The reason for this, in general, is that on most pluralist theories, there are particular properties in particular domains that play the truth role. For example, say that in nonmoral contexts, correspondence plays the truth role, while in moral and aesthetic contexts something like coherence plays the truth role. There then comes a problem in giving an account of what plays the truth role for propositions containing both nonmoral and moral or aesthetic conjuncts.

Wang's theory of *shi* has an easy solution to this problem. In fact, we might think that one of the reasons that the problem never occurred to Wang is that it could never have gained traction given his particular view of *shi*. Because a statement is *shi* just in case it has the properties we do and should seek when appraising sentences, it is not necessary for there to be only *one* particular property playing the truth role for a given statement. The necessity of there being one truth-making property for any given statement or proposition, I contend, is what gets the pluralist into the problem. However, if "is true" expresses a unique truth property that is linked (in virtue of being a second-order property) to the lower-level "truth properties," there is no need to rely on only one property to play the truth-making role. Lynch's theory *does* require a single property to play the truth role for any given proposition, because of his functionalist theory, and Wright appears to need it as well, because he specifies the higher-order property as being linked to the (single) property that meets the platitudes in a given domain. The truth property can be defined differently, however, so as not to link it to a single truth-making property that must belong to a statement for it to be true. If a statement is true when it has properties that we do and should seek, it is not necessary for a mixed conjunction to have a single lower-level property that makes it true. It is enough that both conjuncts are true by virtue of having properties we do and should seek.

Consider the following mixed conjunction: "Mars is the fourth closest planet to the sun and murder is wrong."

Wang can account for the truth (實 *shi*) of this statement by analysis of the properties of the logical parts, here the conjuncts. If each of the conjuncts has lower-level properties we do and should seek and on the basis of which we do and should accept statements, then the conjunction is 實 *shi*. And there is no difficulty here, because the two conjuncts are true in exactly the same way—that is, they both possess properties we do and should seek, and thus the entire statement possesses these properties. Note that the entire statement does *not* possess both *ran* and *shi* (the moral conjunct does not possess the property of *ran*, for example), but the entire statement *does* possess the second-order property of 實 *shi* in virtue of the possession of each conjunct of properties that we do and should seek. We can explain this ultimately in terms of the properties at the lowest level, in this case 然 *ran* and 是 *shi*, but we can construct higher levels in the theory of 實 *shi*. Thus, the above statement is 實 *shi* in virtue of having *shi*-making properties (然 *ran* and 是 *shi*), and the conjuncts considered separately are 實 *shi* in virtue of having 然 *ran* (in the first conjunct) and 是 *shi* (in the second). We can see here that refraining from tying the truth property to a single truth-making lower-level property has enormous advantages over the properties defined by Wright and Lynch.

So what of another objection made to the view of the truth property as a second-order property, which Lynch raises against Wright's second-order view of truth? If the second-order property obtains in virtue of a proposition's meeting the various platitudes for truth, then it looks like the truth property itself *doesn't* meet the platitudes for truth. Thus, the second-order property does not itself qualify as a truth property under the definition of truth properties on Wright's account.[46] Wang Chong's account of *shi* does not have this problem. Although it is a second-order property, unlike Wright's truth property it *does* itself qualify as a truth property under the conceptual description of truth (*shi*).

The property expressed by *shi* is the property of (actually) having properties that we do and should seek when appraising statements. Does this property itself meet the criteria for being *shi*? That is, is *this* property something that we do and should seek when appraising statements? It is. But notice that we will only be concerned about whether or not *shi* obtains when there is semantic ascent, or some question as to whether a certain statement does actually or does not have the lower-level properties we seek when appraising statements. Consider the statement: "One should imitate the actions of the Zhou kings."

This statement may be 實 *shi* by virtue of having the property of 是 *shi* (right). So there are two relevant properties here—實 *shi* (true) and 是 *shi* (right). 實 *Shi* is the second-order property. So, are we looking for *that* when we appraise this sentence? In a sense we are—we are looking for both. The second-order property is especially relevant when we engage in semantic ascent. Consider the statement: "The statement 'you should imitate the actions of the Zhou kings' is true (實 *shi*)."

What property or properties do we and should we seek when appraising this sentence? Now that we have semantically ascended, the lowest-level properties such as 然 *ran* and 是 *shi* will be out of the immediate picture, and the sentence must be appraised to see if it has the property of 實 *shi*. What we ought to and will seek here is the *second-order property* itself, because the possession of this will tell us whether the relevant statement is true. Thus, the relevant properties of this statement are the original property of 是 *shi* (right), the second-order property of 實 *shi*, and a third-order 實 *shi* property along side of that.

So the question of whether the second- (and higher-) order property of *shi* can be something itself that counts as a truth property under the given definition of truth can be answered in the affirmative.[47] The definition of truth given here does not bar higher-order properties constructed in this way from serving as truth-making properties.

So we have seen that Wang can offer us a way of understanding how the predicate "is true" can express a unique, second-order property, while avoiding some problems for such views. Of course, accepting something like Wang's view depends on how far we're willing to go with him on the explanatory basic quality of descriptive and normative facts about human behavior. We might part ways with Wang at a number of different points—whether it has to do with our objection to holding truth to be that closely linked with human behavior (is this a radical antirealism?), whether it has to do with our resistance to accepting as basic the kinds of facts Wang does, or whether it has to do with issues of possible vicious circularity in the definition of 實 *shi*. All of these issues, of course, remain to be worked out.

XU GAN

By the time we arrive at the work of Xu Gan in the late second century CE, the terminology of truth is well entrenched. Xu uses *ran* 然, *shi* 實, and related terms in ways that clearly suggest truth in any recognizable form by us or anyone else.

While Xu Gan's main concern with the concept of *shi* is in its connection with proper naming (*ming*), issues of truth enter deeply into the picture, given his position on what *shi* is and how it makes names proper. Makeham argues for what he calls a "correlative theory of naming" in the work of Xu Gan, which builds on earlier theories of naming. While I do not dispute much of Makeham's reading of Xu's theory of naming, I think there is much more that needs to be said about the theory of *truth* that grounds Xu's entire project, which is based in the concept of *shi*.[48]

Makeham describes Xu's understanding of *shi* as "a state of development peculiar to an entity or state-of-affairs by virtue of which that entity or state-of-affairs is what it is."[49] The relationship between naming and *shi*, according to Xu, is a kind of correspondence relation, which Makeham understands in terms of "correlativity." Just as in the *Zhuangzi* and *Huainanzi*, proper statements are those that correspond somehow to *dao*, in Xu's *Zhonglun*, properly used names are those corresponding with actualities.

Xu Gan's concept of *shi* gives us something very close to the correspondence theorist's understanding of "states-of-affairs." The concept of *shi* is not itself that of truth (as in the case of Wang Chong, for example), but rather of *truthmaker*.[50] Xu is at pains in *Zhonglun* to make it clear that *shi* is conceptually prior to *ming*, and that a name gets its acceptability or applicability based on its somehow deriving from (corresponding with) *shi*. On this view, *shi* is identified with objects themselves, and although it is not *identical* to objects, it is that on the basis of which the objects are correctly called as they are (and presumably *statements* about objects are also justified in being so based in *shi*).

One thing we can take from Xu Gan's discussion of the connection of names to *shi* is that names (*ming*) are doing much more semantic work here than claimed in the interpretation of earlier Chinese material by scholars like Chad Hansen.[51] Xu Gan is concerned with names as ways of referring to every type of thing and category,[52] and as constituting our *ways of talking about* these things. Names, that is, for Xu Gan have much more than a merely referential purpose. Hansen, Hall and Ames, and others argue that for early Chinese thinkers, language should be thought of as "strings of names," but for Xu Gan these names have assertoric content. Such content is one of the only ways in which we could sensibly posit a *shi* or inner reality with which a name properly corresponds. Unless a name has some descriptive and thus assertoric content, it will not do the work Xu Gan intends it to do, which is to correspond to the *shi* of an object or event. The *shi* of a human makes the name "human" a correct one because what we mean by "human" corresponds to this *shi*—that is, the description inherent in the name is an accurate one. Thus, while we see that Xu Gan's concern is on the surface distinct from that of Wang Chong (Wang is not so concerned with *names*), it quickly becomes apparent that at bottom it is the same concern—what justifies descriptions of the world is the nature of things and states-of-affairs in the world, that is, *shi*. Xu Gan, however, uses *shi* solely to refer to the states-of-affairs themselves, and not the truth property granted to statements (or rather *names*) that correspond to these states-of-affairs (unlike Wang).

Makeham mentions two positions close to Xu's on the connection between *ming* and *shi*:

> Genuine names—that is, names that are inherently appropriate to given actualities—just like actualities themselves, are "discovered" but man by not determined by man. As a corollary, the names made by man are false names. Another view is that while there are names which, having been created by "Heaven" (*tian*), are inherently appropriate to given actualities, nevertheless sages are endowed with the ability to apprehend an entity's actuality and on that basis select or coin the name appropriate to that actuality.[53]

Given what we have seen of the concept of *shi* to this point, it should be clear that Xu's conception of *shi* is some kind of mind-independent state of a thing in the world. It is unclear how the various *shi* of objects and events relate to one another, although it does seem clear that there are *shi* of events as well as objects, and that *shi* can be understood as constructive. That is, the particular components of an event or object can have their own *shi*, and the *shi* of these would seem to play a role in the *shi* of the event or object of which they are part, or vice versa. This picture begins to look like "states-of-affairs" or "facts."[54] What justifies a name is its correspondence with a *shi*, and this correspondence can only be made sense of in terms of the descriptive content of the name. Xu Gan and other early Chinese thinkers are certainly aware of the existence of numerous languages and dialects. What is called *ju* or *che* 車 (carriage) in one language may be called something completely distinct in a different language. Indeed, Indian Buddhist texts were available in China by this time, so thinkers during the period would have known of the existence of radically different languages such as Sanskrit. Xu is not concerned here with proper names—in this way the particular language would make a huge difference. "King" could not be translated into "王 *Wang*" and still have its same reference as a proper name. "Don King" does not mean the same thing as "Don Wang." Rather, Xu is concerned with descriptions—such that the Sanskrit term "*raja*," the Chinese "*wang*," and English "king" (forget for a moment that English of course did not yet exist when Xu Gan lived and wrote) would all count as acceptable *ming* for a king, because they match the *shi* (actuality) of a king. That is, the descriptive content of a name is the way in which we determine its acceptability. How else could we determine whether a name matches an actuality? Actualities do not contain Chinese sounds. According to Xu, it is possible to inquire into *shi* to determine the acceptability of given names.

名有同而實異者矣。名有異而實同者矣。故君子於是倫也，務於其實，
而無譏其名

There are cases where the name is the same but the actuality is different, and there are cases where the name is different but the actuality is the same. Thus, in regard to the principle we have been discussing, the gentleman concerns himself with the actuality rather than criticize the name.[55]

If this is the case, there must be some way for a person to assess the name on the basis of actuality, and if the name does not have relatively rich descriptive content, it is unclear how one could do this without having some kind of mystical intuitive power of unclear developmental origin.[56] Thus, it appears that we have something like a correspondence theory here—if not correspondence, then "correlation," or some other relatively correspondence-like relation. The connection between *ming* and *shi* on Xu Gan's picture is the connection between statements and states-of-affairs, and this connection either justifies or fails to justify statements.

Xu Gan's conception of the connection between *ming* and *shi*, as well as what he means by these terms, is somewhat unique in early Chinese thought. The earliest discussion of the *ming-shi* distinction is found in the work of the Later Mohists, who use the terms in a different sense from both Wang Chong and Xu Gan (though perhaps a related one), and thus understand the *ming-shi* connection in a fundamentally different way. This usage and understanding of the concepts seems to be echoed in the *Xunzi* as well. It is not until the late Warring States and early Han syncretist material, according to Makeham, that we see theories of *ming* and *shi* that begin to resemble that of Xu Gan.[57] Makeham argues that in the *Chunqiu Fanlu* we see a theory akin to that of Xu Gan on *ming* and *shi*. Although perhaps this position is closer to what we find in *Zhonglun* than earlier views, *shi* does not yet have the sense of "reality" or "actuality" that it takes in later Han works.[58]

Other terms associated with a truth concept found in earlier work also occur in the *Zhonglun*, such as *ran, dang, shi*, etc. We do not, however, find discussions of these terms, and we can do little better here than illuminate the kind of folk or assumed truth concept Xu Gan was likely working with. Though we do see theory of truth in Xu's work, he is concerned primarily with one *aspect* of truth, and leaves others merely implicit. We see similar things, of course, in previous work such as that of nearly all the thinkers covered so far. What makes Xu Gan's theory of truth so interesting is that he concentrates on an aspect of truth, as it applies to satisfaction of descriptions and application of names, which we do not see in earlier texts. Even in the most developed theories of truth in early China, such as that of Wang Chong, we do not see much consideration of name and naming. Wang Chong's considerations of *shi* are connected to *yan* (statements) rather than names. On his view, *shi* clearly plays the role of a *property* belonging to statements based in their adequacy for truth, rather than that of one of the fundamental ground of truth or one of the relata in the correspondence relationship between language and world.[59]

NOTES

1. Including that which culminated in the "Yellow Turbans" or "Yellow Scarves" rebellion at the twilight of the Eastern Han in 184 CE. Popular religious movements that started from the "ground up" in China naturally tended to become rebellions,

because the masses adopted (sometimes radically) different religious structures naturally at odds with the ideologies of rulers and governing classes.

2. Hou han shu—Xiang Kai, in a memorial to Emperor Huan mentions the Buddha (Futu) and Laozi as enjoining reduction of desire. He suggests that the ruler is an
adherent of the two, referring to the altars and statues that he has dedicated to them.
This adherence entails that the ruler should follow their teachings. Xiang clearly
sees Laozi and the Buddha as advocating the same message. Many later Chinese
thinkers would recognize the similarity between Daoist and Buddhist ideas, and
this would culminate in the use of Daoist terminology to translate Buddhist sutras
and other texts in later centuries, after the difficult and awkward beginning years
of attempted transliteration of Sanskrit Buddhist terms using Chinese characters.
We see no mentions in Hou Han shu of the acceptance of Buddhism or keeping of
Buddhist objects by lower classes. The Memorial is translated and included in Csikszentmihalyi 2006.

3. Some, such as Michael Nylan (Nylan 1997) have attributed whole systems of
thought in the Eastern Han to these political factors.

4. In general, I think we should resist the kind of reductionist materialism behind
such moves. Many are more comfortable attributing political motivations to a scholar
rather than philosophical motivations, in part because of the view that ideology ultimately reduces to economic or political considerations. While I do not get into the
debate here, this kind of reductionism seems to me demonstrably false. There are no
political or economic reasons to adopt a realist versus an antirealist view of metaeth-
ics, for example, yet this is a real debate among philosophers in the field today. Also,
presumably, one's stance on what is contained in human nature and the conventional-
ity of language make no difference in one's economic or political life or prospects.
We cannot say that these debates were not meaningful, however.

5. See McLeod 2015 for a general overview of Eastern Han philosophy.

6. And likely a compilation of his works, rather than a single text—see Forke
1962, introduction.

7. Lunheng 84.364.10–11.

8. As in Western thought, there are multiple concepts and terms associated with
truth and which different thinkers identify with the truth concept. In contemporary
analytic philosophy, for example, we have the concepts of warranted assertability,
coherence, and others, all of which are "truth-like" (or "truthy" if you will), and which
some take to be definitive of the concept of truth. Early Chinese thought has its own
cluster of concepts associated with the concept of truth, and *shi* is a relatively late
addition, but the seeds of its development can be seen in early texts.

9. Shuowen 4564. It may help to mention that this is the same guan used in the
famous (or infamous, depending on one's view of its true importance) "one strand"
passage of the Analects, 4.15.

10. It is harder to see how we get from the Shuowen's definition of *shi* to the sense
of *shi* as "particular object" or the literal sense of "fruit" (we might wonder whether
the literal sense of "fruit" could have been derived from seeing the fruit of a tree as
the "fullness" or result of the full growth of the tree.

11. Makeham 1994: 8, Shuowen 4535, *shi*.

12. Shuowen 4828.

13. Makeham 1994: 8.

14. An interesting passage of Biaoji of the Liji also expresses a sense of *shi* as "fullness": 口惠而實不至.

15. Xunzi 21.5.

16. There are uses of the term in the *Analects*, as "fullness" or "fruit," but the earliest philosophical use of the term in the Confucian texts is in the *Mengzi*. *Mengzi* 4B45, for example, reads 言無實不祥。不祥之實, 蔽賢者當之. ("Words without *shi* are not auspicious. Inauspicious *shi* conceal what the sages undertake.") Other examples of this use of *shi* occur at *Mengzi* 4A27 and 7A37, and there is a consideration of *ming-shi* at 6B26.

17. In much of the early literature, *shi* is used with the sense of "fruit," as it is mostly in the Analects, or as "solid particular object." Both these uses, along with the philosophical use outlined here, can be found in the Mencius.

18. We must keep in mind, however, that *ming* and *yan* can play the same or similar roles in a theory—as I have argued above, *ming* themselves are descriptive. And as Jane Geaney argues in Geaney 2010, *ming* and *yan* were often used interchangeably in early texts. Wang's choice of yan then is not fundamentally different than Xunzi's consideration of *ming*.

19. The distinction between *yan* and *ming* in the Lunheng in particular is clear, a distinction not always made in earlier texts. *Yan* refers to a linguistic string rather than to an individual word, unless the individual word serves as a statement—for example, the word ke 可 ("acceptable") used as a response in the Gongsunlongzi, can be an example of *yan*.

20. Makeham 1994: chapter 5.

21. specifically the 天意 tian yi, or "notions or intentions of heaven." Dong does use *shi* in connection with names in the Chunqiufanlu, (in the Chuzhuangwang chapter, for example, he says 此聞其名而不知其實者也 ["this is to be one who hears its name but does not know its *shi*"]),but his understanding of what *shi* represents seems to be based on its mirroring of *tian*.

22. One feature, and some may think as weakness, of Wang's account, is that he did not consider there to be a single underlying structure of sentences, teachings, and beliefs which make these things truth apt. One of the features of contemporary analytic philosophy of language is that it has generally made a distinction between beliefs and teachings and what makes these things truth evaluable—most often sentences or propositions (depending on one's semantic theory). Beliefs and teachings then are truth-apt insofar as they express propositions or sentences, which can be truth-apt. My belief itself cannot be true, but the sentence or proposition that I accept in the act of belief can be true or false, and it is in this sense that the belief is said to be true or false, connected to the contents of belief. There are a couple of reasons we generally think this needs to be done: (a) teachings and beliefs, we think, are not linguistic entities, and thus cannot themselves be semantically evaluated; (b) in desiring or requiring truth to be unitary, insofar as we think there ought to be a single property of truth, we cannot make sense of two different types of entity, propositions, or sentences as linguistic entities, and beliefs as mental entities or something like this, as having

the same property (of truth), because we cannot explain how a single property could belong to things of seemingly vastly different types. If one is a certain kind of pluralist about truth, however (note that not all pluralists will find this acceptable), one can make sense of these different types of entities being truth-evaluable.

23. The Buddhist "two truths" view is a kind of pluralist theory of truth—roughly the position that there are two levels of truth, relative truth and ultimate truth, and that some propositions or statements might be true in one sense but not the other, but that it is justified to call a statement meeting the normative objectives of one or other of these levels "true" (sat). For a good philosophical exposition of the "two truths" theory, see Mark Siderits 2003: chapter 8. The theory is also discussed further in conclusion below.

24. There has been debate over what kinds of entities are "truth-apt," which goes beyond the scope of this paper, and this debate connects closely to that over truth itself, as some views of truth-apt linguistic entities (such as propositions) are highly implausible as linguistic objects to certain philosophers and may constitute reasons against holding certain theories of truth (for example, correspondence theories) insofar as these theories commit one to acceptance of these linguistic entities.

25. This is described in chapter 1 above. These are all fairly loosely defined, of course, and theories within certain categories may radically differ from each other, while sharing some family resemblance to other theories of its kind. Perhaps the least well defined of the categories of theory mentioned here is that of pragmatic theories of truth, which includes antirealist theories of a variety of kinds.

26. I pass over for the moment deflationary (sometimes also called disquotational) theories of truth, which deny that there is a robust property of truth at all, and take truth as simply a semantic tool for sentence evaluation that works in the way specified by Tarski's T-schema—for any sentence x, "x" is true iff x—where the single quoted use of x is an occurrence in the object language and everything else is in the metalanguage. That is, according to the deflationist, there is nothing more to truth than the semantic rules for its use described by the T-schema, and looking for a robust property of truth belonging to linguistic entities is fruitless.

27. Wright 2001: 760. Wright offers seven platitudes here, and concedes after this "the list might be enlarged, and some of these principles may anyway seem controversial." He's not committed, that is, to exactly this list. Also see Wright 1992.

28. Mou 2009: 3. He has interestingly connected this to the concern with dao in early Chinese thought. In much of early Chinese philosophy, Mou claims, the basic truth thesis is understood in terms of capturing the dao, and different elaboration perspectives do this differently.

29. Mou calls this basic thesis of truth the "axiomatic thesis of the nature of truth" (ATNT), and formulates it thus: "The nature of truth (of the truth bearer) consists in (the truth bearer's) capturing the way things are." Mou 2009: 3. Interestingly, one of the things that Mou attempts to capture in his truth pluralism is not only the connection between truth in different linguistic contexts but also not the connection between linguistic and nonlinguistic truth. Wang Chong, like other early Chinese philosophers, had a view of truth as a property of linguistic as well as nonlinguistic entities. The issue of nonlinguistic truth has been neglected, I believe, in much contemporary work

on truth, and one of the advantages of looking to the early Chinese philosophers, as Mou does, is to understand how we might think of different types of truth.

30. Wang's xu is a much more complicated concept than even this jumble of translations suggests, and is perhaps more different from our concept of "falsehood" than *shi* is from "truth." I will discuss xu in more detail below.

31. There were a number of different views on the value of creation zuo in the pre-Qin and Han periods. Wang here is reacting against a particularly conservative strain of Confucianism in the Han which took the claim of the Analects quite literally (in Analects 7.1 Confucius says "transmit, and don't create" 述而不作), that what scholars should be engaged in is transmitting (shu 述) rather than creating, and that even the sages did not create new things. An alternative view held by some is that only the sages can and are justified in creating (zuo), and that lesser persons, mere worthies such as Wang Chong cannot and should not attempt to create. Michael Puett explores the different attitudes on zuo before Wang's time in Puett 2002.

32. A view advanced by a number of pre-Qin and Han authors, according to Puett.

33. Lunheng 84.362.15–16.

34. Lunheng 84.364.22.

35. Or "simple people" (俗人 *su ren*).

36. Lunheng 84.362.26–363.1.

37. What I mention here is similar to some forms of cognitive bias, such as wishful thinking and confirmation bias. There are many other forms of cognitive bias as well, which show how prone humans are in general to accept false statements as true even in the face of overwhelming evidence of their falsity. This is very much Wang's worry. In fact, many of the problems with the beliefs of *su ren* that he mentions in the Lunheng line up with a number of cognitive biases that contemporary behavioral psychologists discuss. He most vehemently heaps scorn upon wishful thinking, which he isolates as a particularly pressing problem among common people in his time.

38. Lunheng 84.363.3–5. It is useful here to consider Forke's translation as well, which, like my own, uses "right" and "wrong" for 是 *shi* and 非 fei: "He who knows how to discriminate between truth (ran) and falsehood (fou), must feel a pang at it; why should he not speak? . . . [Mengzi] used plain and straightforward language to recommend what was right, and to reject what was wrong."

39. Lunheng 84.364.10–11. Forke reads the *shi* in the final part of this passage as causally connected to bringing light to the right and wrong principle—he translates: "intended to explain the right and wrong principles so that future generations can clearly see the difference between truth and falsehood" (Forke 1962: 88).

40. This is somewhat contentious. Michael Nylan argues in Nylan 1997 that Wang's purpose in the Wenkong chapter was to show Confucius as an ultimately unsuccessful teacher. I argue in McLeod 2007 that Wang's purpose in Wenkong was primarily methodological rather than critical.

41. Lunheng 28.122.7.

42. Lunheng 28.123.1.

43. This seems to mesh with our own intuitions if we consider sentences like "don't attack people's weaknesses." It seems to make no sense to say that this can be

the case or not be the case, whether or not a reformulation as described above will give us a sentence that can be the case or not be the case.

44. Lunheng 84.363.12–14.

45. Although Lynch rejects a second-order property view of truth, in part due to the difficulties discussed below.

46   Lynch 2009: 64–65 "Wright is barred from identifying even this wafer-thin property—*the property of having a property that satisfies the platitudes or falls under the concept of truth*—with the, or even 'a' property of truth. For the property of having a property that falls under the descriptive concept of truth, doesn't itself fall under that description. Again, that description consists, essentially, in a list of the platitudes that a property must satisfy. But is the property of having a property that, e.g., is distinct from warrant, possessed by asserted propositions, is objective, and so on a property with all those features? No. It is the property of having a property with those features. Hence a view like Wright's which identifies truth with whatever property satisfies the platitudes in a particular domain must hold that the second-order property of having a property that plays that role is *distinct* from truth: call it truth*. And this in turn makes it hard to see how reductive pluralism solves the problem of mixed inferences and associated problems. For while she can say that there is a property preserved by valid mixed inferences, that property is truth*, not truth."

47. There may be some worry here that the property of 實 *shi* belonging to mixed conjunctions (pre-ascent) will be third-order properties rather than second-order properties. If we take the *shi*-ness of the full conjunction as a function of the *shi*-ness of the conjuncts, this will necessarily be the case. However, I do not believe this is the right way to see *shi* in cases of conjunctions, or any statement. What I propose here goes beyond anything that Wang says, of course, and is meant as simply a way of making sense of how *shi* is a second-order property even in cases of mixed conjunctions. Since *shi* is an appraisal term—it is a property that belongs to a statement if and only if that statement has the properties we do and should seek in appraising statements—it need only apply to appraised statements. That is, *shi* might be understood as a tag telling us whether a statement has the desired properties or not. It need not be the case, if we are appraising a conjunction, that the conjunction is *shi* based on each of the conjuncts being *shi*, even if those conjuncts would be *shi* if appraised individually. The reason *shi* can work like this is that it is based on human goals—what we do and ought to seek. Thus, independently of our appraisal of a particular statement, there do not have to be *shi*-facts about it. Thus, a mixed conjunction can have the second-order property of *shi* based on having the property of ran and *shi* in its conjuncts, without being based on having the individual property *shi* of each conjunct. However, if we appraise the conjuncts separately as individual statements, we can also take them as having the property of *shi*, based on the lower-level properties that each possesses. As I say above, this explanation goes well beyond anything we can find in Wang Chong, but I believe this addition keeps with Wang's general view of *shi*, and gives us a way to better understand how a *shi* property like Wang's can work.

48. Makeham translates *shi* in the context of Xu Gan's work as "actuality."

49. Makeham 1994: 7.

50. Makeham does not use the terminology of truth or truth-makers to explain Xu Gan's understanding of *shi*, but it becomes clear to one familiar with such contemporary theories that Xu's position is similar. Makeham describes the position thus: *shi* should not be taken to mean some particular 'long shape' (*chang xing* 長形), but rather that by virtue of which a long shape is 'long'. This understanding is based on an implicit conceptual distinction being made between an entity (wu) and its actuality. I stress that the distinction is conceptual rather than real because Xu Gan did not conceive of actualities existing independent of objects nor as substrata in which various qualities inhere. Rather, an object and its actuality are one; the object is the vessel in and through which its inherent actuality becomes manifest." (Makeham 1994: 7).

51. Hansen does not cover any Han thinkers in his works, an era he dismissively refers to as the "philosophical dark age." He refers to the period following Xunzi as the "death of philosophy," and makes the (odd and false) claim that Huang-Lao thought dominated China until the rise of Buddhism in the Wei-Jin period. A more accurate description of Han philosophical thought is given by John Makeham: "By the late third century BCE [beginning of the Han period], Chinese philosophy had already entered its richest period of cross-fertilization, producing new, hybrid schools of thought."

52. Zhonglun (Makeham 2003: 15) "Affairs name themselves, sounds call themselves, appearances express themselves, things place themselves, and men determine their own office."

53. Makeham 1994: 15

54. Xu Gan discusses the *shi* of disputation (*bian*), which is an activity involving numerous events and individuals. Whether something has the actuality of being a disputation will rely on the purposes of individuals (persuasion rather than simply "victory" according to Xu) and the methods by which they argue (Makeham 1994).

55. Zhonglun 12.2, trans. Makeham 2003: 159–161.

56. Of course, a common criticism of correspondence theories of truth is that it is unclear what kind of prelinguistic insight would give us access to mysterious "states-of-affairs" that could justify statements. But even this criticism is not as severe and difficult as that which would obtain if names do not have robust descriptive content. These "states-of-affairs" would have to somehow determine specific kinds of sound.

57. Makeham 1994: 85.

58. Makeham 1994: 83.

59. Makeham (1994: xvii) finds correctly that the ming-*shi* relationship does not occupy a central place in Wang's work. He looks to two chapters of the Lunheng, Zhishi and Shizhi, however, for evidence on Wang's position on the relationship. Wang Chong, however, is not using shi in these chapters (or most other places in the Lunheng) in the same way Xu Gan uses it in Zhonglun. *Shi* for Wang (as discussed above) is contrasted with xu, and is a property of statements rather than of objects or states-of-affairs.

Conclusion

Comparative Thought and Future Directions

As I have argued above, the concept of truth is not the purview of one or other culture. If the concept is truly general, basic, and foundational, then it is a concept possessed by *every* human culture. Since this is the case, learning more about the nature of truth as a property of language or operator on language (whatever the case may be) will require some exploration of the various ways in which truth is thought of around the world. We cannot hope to uncover the nature of truth from within our enclosed cultural spaces, any more than we can hope to uncover the nature of religion or culture by investigating only Christianity or only Euro-American culture. The Chinese theories of truth discussed here can advance debates concerning truth in contemporary philosophy, surely. But they are best understood in terms of the theories of truth that we see in not only the West, but also other philosophical traditions. We can understand different aspects of these theories of truth, possible motivations, and ways we can *use* these theories, when we investigate their similarities to the theories offered in other traditions, as well as how early Chinese theories might challenge or supplement these theories. In this section, I offer a few possibilities for further comparative investigation into the concept of truth using early Chinese theories.

UNIFYING A TRUTH CONCEPT

Insistence on the *univocality* of truth—that is, the consistent meaning of truth wherever it is used, regardless of the type of statement in terms of its domain (ethics, science, etc.) is something about which contemporary pluralists worry. The problem of univocality is particularly pressing for pluralists because of the fundamental pluralist claim that truth properties somehow differ over domain (though this claim is understood differently on different pluralist theories). We can, however, widen this problem of univocality beyond something that applies only to the pluralist. As discussed in chapter 1 above, "truth" has multiple senses, only one of which is the linguistic sense that contemporary analytic philosophers are interested in. However, if we are interested in understanding the nature of truth (assuming that truth does have a nature to be understood!), we cannot fail to adequately consider the wider meaning of truth beyond the "propositional" sense. We have in large part treated the senses of "true" beyond the linguistic sense as completely separate, in much the same way that we treat the distinct concepts referred to using homonyms, such as the *bank* of a river and the *bank* as a financial institution. The different senses of truth, however, do not represent different concepts. Rather, truth as a broader concept surely can be understood to have a single and unified meaning, as any user of the English language could attest. We recognize the use of "true" in "a true friend" as *sharing meaning* with the use in "a true statement." This is not simply homophony. The true friend and the true statement share something in common. That is, they both have the *same* property. If this is the case, then we have a distinct problem concerning the univocality of truth. That is, one pressing issue becomes to understand how "true" can be understood univocally across not domains, but *truth-bearers*. How can a true statement be true in the same way that a true friend is true? Making sense of a univocality that could capture the sameness of meaning of "true" in "true friend" and "true statement" would give us a much more expansive understanding of truth. And a better understanding of what it is for something to be a "true friend" or "true person"[1] may help us to better understand what it is for a statement to be true. Part of the reason, I suspect, that we today tend to brush aside consideration of these nonlinguistic senses of truth is that they complicate our task, requiring a broader conception of truth within which linguistic functions play one particular role. What we find concerning truth in early Chinese texts, however, can help us do this, in part because the considerations concerning truth there approach the problem as one of truth in its broadest sense.

NELTILIZTLI AND "ONTOLOGICAL" TRUTH

In this way, conceptions of truth in early Chinese thought (as well as in aspects of Western thought often ignored by contemporary analytic philosophers) overlap with those of traditions such as Mesoamerican philosophical traditions, primarily represented by the Maya and Nahua (Aztec) traditions. As a step forward in attempting to understand the nonlinguistic senses of truth and how they inform the linguistic sense, the comparative project looking at

Chinese theories of truth alongside of Mesoamerican theories can be very useful.

James Maffie discusses the Aztec philosophical concept of *neltiliztli*, as a central truth concept.[2] The etymology of the term appears to be startlingly similar to that of the Chinese term *shi* 實 and it also overlaps in some senses with the *Huainanzi*'s understanding of *dao*. Maffie (following the lead of Miguel Leon-Portilla) translates the term "well-rootedness." The term is associated, like the term *dao* as understood in the *Huainanzi*, with a *root*, and with the basis of things in general—not only linguistic entities. Maffie explains that the Aztec concept of truth should be seen as primarily *ontological* rather than linguistic in nature:

> Aztec philosophy . . . conceives of truth in *ontological* terms. *Truth is a way of being and doing*; a way of living, conducting one's life, and so on. It is in such an ontological sense that we commonly speak of true north, true friend, and truing a bicycle rim. Aztec philosophy does not conceive truth in *semantic* terms, that is, in terms of correspondence, reference, signification, representation, and aboutness. Truth is not defined, for example, as a relationship between the content of a sentence or proposition, on the one hand, and some fact or state of affairs, on the other.[3]

Insofar as this is the case, the Aztec conception seems completely foreign to the conception of truth focused on in contemporary analytic philosophy. We might be inclined to reject the Aztec concept of *neltiliztli* as a concept of truth at all on this basis. When we look more deeply at Chinese theories of truth, however, as well as neglected Western conceptions of truth, we find that the Aztec conception has a clear family resemblance to other theories of truth. Chinese theories in particular can serve as a good "bridge" between Mesoamerican and contemporary analytic conceptions of truth, because many Chinese theories of truth (as we have seen) offer what Maffie calls an "ontological" conception of truth *as well as* a linguistic conception. It is likely then that through consideration of Chinese theories of truth alongside more "one-sided" theories of truth like the dominant position in Aztec philosophy and those of contemporary analytic philosophy, we can come to a better understanding of the connections between the two senses of truth, and how we might achieve a truly univocal theory of truth.

THE "TWO TRUTHS" AND DAO

Discussion of truth in the Indian tradition is perhaps more widespread and recognized than it is in the pre-Buddhist Chinese tradition. I suspect, however, that this is due more to the fact that Indian truth language and theories of truth are often more recognizable to philosophers familiar with the Western tradition than are Chinese theories of truth and Chinese language about truth. Western and Indian thought share linguistic and historical connections that neither share with pre-Buddhist Chinese thought (so far as we know at least), and so the gap is perhaps wider in the ways that the Chinese tradition speaks about truth.

J.N. Mohanty assigns a number of Indian theories of truth to categories familiar in contemporary Western philosophy, claiming that the Nyaya school formulated a kind of correspondence theory (with elements of coherentism), Mīmāmsā formulated what he calls a "self-evidence theory," and the Buddhists (which he treats a single school) formulated a pragmatic conception of truth.[4] While the comparative philosophical project in general requires thinking about the views of one "tradition" through the lenses of another, and Mohanty's analysis here is not *incorrect*, we can also gain from considering traditions through the comparative lenses of *other* traditions. One of the problems I see with much contemporary comparative philosophy is our tendency to use Western philosophical thought as the single comparative universal in our works. In some ways, I have done that in this book. This conclusion, however, is intended to show ways forward in bringing additional comparative tools to our work. Indeed, part of the purpose of this book is to make Chinese theories of truth available to those philosophers who do not specialize in early Chinese philosophy but who would use them in the ways I suggest here, to advance our understanding of truth in general.

If it is a legitimate project to categorize and understand Indian theories of truth in terms of contemporary Western theoretical categories, then it is also a legitimate project to understand them (and other non-Western theories of truth) in terms of early Chinese theoretical categories. That is, we can profitably look at theories of truth like those of Nyaya, Mimamsa, and various schools of Buddhism in comparison to early Chinese theories of truth. If Nyaya fits into a correspondence/coherence theory based on contemporary Western categories, what kind of theory would it be, given the categories of early Chinese thought? Is the Nyaya theory Xunzian? Zhuangist?

One example of an Indian theory that we can categorize in this way is the Buddhist "two truths" theory. The idea of two "levels" of truth, ultimate and conventional, originated in the early Pali texts, but remained a key position of later Buddhist schools, including Mahayana schools such as Madhyamaka, which used the distinction to its greatest potential.

The doctrine arose likely as a response to difficulties that the Buddhist conception of the self lands them in. According to the traditional view, originating in the early Pali *suttas* (discourses), the fundamental truth about the world is that *sabbe saṅkhāra aniccā, sabbe saṅkhāra dukkhā, sabbe dhammā anattā* ("all phenomena are impermanent, all phenomena are involved with suffering, and all things are without self").[5] The basic problem is that if there ultimately are no selves, then how can we make sense of the seeming fact that it is *true* that "I live in Colorado," while it is *false* that "I am six feet eleven inches tall"? If there is no self, it seems that we should deem *both* statements false.

The general solution to this, according to the Buddhist schools, is to make a distinction between ultimate and conventional truth, based on which it is *conventionally* true that "I live in Colorado," while *ultimately* false. A statement is only ultimately true when it involves actually existent entities, and involves no conventional constructions. Since the self is ultimately a conventional construction, statements about the self can only be true, when they are true, conventionally. But not just *any* statement about the self is conventionally true. As mentioned above, it is conventionally *false* that I am six feet eleven inches tall. What makes this conventionally false? According to the early Buddhist schools such as Abhidharma and Sarvastivada (although later schools such as Yogacara and Madhyamaka differ on this point), conventions are *based on* ultimate constituents of the world. While selves do not exist (ultimately), basic atomic units called *dharmas* do. There are facts about these ultimate constituents of the world, and conventions, insofar as they are true, have to be reducible to facts about the *dharmas*. There might be *different* ways in which we formulate conventional truths, depending on different conventions, but those conventions and statements about them must reduce to facts about *dharmas* in order to be conventionally true. Thus, my claim "I live in Colorado" is conventionally true because it makes a claim about the conventional object (myself) that refers to a collection of mental and physical *dharmas*, locating for most of their time in a place conventionally delineated as "Colorado," etc. There is no corresponding reduction in terms of the ultimate truth for "I am six feet eleven inches," and so this claim is conventionally false.

This position of two truths in some ways echoes the Zhuangist conception of truth as bound to perspective. There are key differences, however. Conventional truth, according to the Buddhist schools, is something still available universally. It is based on agreement and convention, rather than individual perspective. Like the Zhuangist view of truth, it is *based in* ultimate truth (for the Zhuangist a link to *dao* fixes this ultimate truth), but these conventions are only in the end for the purpose of aiding in realization and ending suffering. The conventions have a *pragmatic* purpose, similar to what we see in the consideration of *ming* (names) in a number of the Chinese theories of truth. Conventional truth, however, is not *thoroughly* conventional—and in this sense it maps fairly closely onto the Zhuangist conception of perspective. Truth can be expressed through perspective based on the connection of a perspective and *dao*, which is ultimately inexpressible through language. The same can be said for ultimate truth in the Buddhist view. What understandings might we gain of this conception of truth and of truth in general if we investigate the Buddhist "two truths" theory as a Zhuangist theory of truth, rather than (as Mohanty characterizes it) as a pragmatist theory?

WHAT IS A PHILOSOPHICAL TRADITION?

Part of the difficulty in the comparative project in general is making sense of just what constitutes a "philosophical tradition" and makes one distinct from another. We have a better idea of how to distinguish other features of human culture such as language, though even here the boundaries are far more porous and vague than we often recognize. We often seem to accept the distinction and uniqueness of traditions such as the Chinese, Indian, and Western philosophical traditions, for example. But when we delve deeper into these traditions, it turns out to be more difficult to maintain these divisions than we think.

Take the issue of language. These three "traditions" are not neatly divided by language. Perhaps the Chinese tradition, if we define it in terms of the textual tradition beginning with the Zhou classics, is linguistically unified in a way the other two are not. A person who understands contemporary Mandarin, Cantonese, or another Chinese language, or even Japanese or Korean, has the tools to read the classical Chinese texts. The characters in classical Chinese have the same meanings as those in contemporary East Asian languages that use the script, even though the words are pronounced differently in different languages, and will be combined in grammatically different ways. The character 仁, for example, has the same meaning in Mandarin, where it is pronounced *rén*; Korean, where it is pronounced *in*; and Japanese, where it has numerous pronunciations, including *jin*. We might say that the Chinese tradition can be linguistically defined as that in which philosophy is done in the classical Chinese characters. Of course, if we define the Chinese tradition thus, then much of the philosophical tradition of East Asia collapses into the Chinese tradition. The Korean and Japanese philosophical traditions before the modern period must then be considered part of the Chinese tradition, for example, and these traditions only diverge in very recent history when philosophy is done in native regional scripts, such as Korean *Hangeul*.

The case is even more difficult to make for the Indian and Western traditions. Much of classical Indian philosophy was done in Sanskrit, which was a kind of philosophical *lingua franca* for the subcontinent, much like Latin was for Europe. But not *all* philosophy in the region was Sanskrit philosophy. The early Buddhist literature was in Pali, a relative of Sanskrit, and philosophy was written in numerous regional languages throughout the subcontinent, including languages unrelated to Sanskrit such as the Dravidian languages Tamil and Telugu, spoken in the southern part of the subcontinent (today southern India). Much of this philosophical material is heavily influenced by Sanskrit philosophy, but it is not *identical* to Sanskrit philosophy.[6] We cannot then limit the Indian philosophical tradition to philosophy done in Sanskrit, or we eliminate important schools and thinkers, such as all of Pali Buddhism and all of Dravidian philosophy.

But then, if we include these schools, we open up another difficult issue. How closely related should a language or school be to others considered part of the same tradition? If Pali Buddhism counts as part of the Indian tradition on the basis of the close relationship of Pali to Sanskrit and the shared philosophical ancestry of Buddhism and Sanskrit schools, why should we not then also include Stoicism in the Indian tradition? The Stoic school of the Hellenistic West is clearly similar to Pali Buddhism in many of its features. It is closer to Pali Buddhism in its views than most schools of Sanskrit philosophy are. And there is linguistic and cultural relationship between Pali Buddhism and Stoicism as well! Pali, Greek, and Latin (along with Sanskrit) are all Indo-European languages, derived from their common ancestor Proto-Indo-European. Hellenistic and Pali Buddhist culture are likewise linked through this common ancestor. Such ubiquitous cultural features as the horse, the chariot, and the pantheon of gods in these cultures likely derive from the culture of the Proto-Indo-Europeans of the central Asian steppe that was the ancestor of both of these cultures (and others).[7] In addition, schools of Sanskrit philosophy and Greek philosophy were likely also connected and influenced one another even during their heyday, and may have been connected through the intermediary of Persia.[8] We know that Hellenistic thought and Pali Buddhist thought were historically connected, as we have texts such as the *Milindapañha*, which tells the story of a philosophical debate between a Buddhist monk and a Greco-Bactrian king[9] in the region of Gandhara (modern-day Afghanistan). It is as likely that there was Indian influence in Greek and Hellenistic philosophy. The "gymnosophists" discussed by Plutarch and later Diogenes Laertius were Indian ascetics, likely associated with some philosophical school (though we cannot be certain which).[10] Diogenes Laertius associates the gymnosophists with the Pyrrhonian school, claiming that Pyrrho of Elis encountered the gymnosophists as he accompanied the philosopher Anaxarhus on his travels to India with the army of Alexander.[11]

The boundaries between the Indian and Western traditions begin to appear insufficient when we subject them to scrutiny. The philosophy of the Hellenistic schools and of the Sanskrit and Pali schools are much more closely related than either is to the thought of Descartes or logical positivism, for example. Yet the Hellenistic schools are included in a "Western" tradition with the latter, while the Sanskrit and Pali schools are pushed into a different category of "Indian" thought. Our categories of "philosophical tradition" appear even more artificial than categories such as race, culture, and language, and it is far from clear what standards are used to draw these boundaries, other than historical familiarity. Western scholars include Plato, Aristotle, the Hellenistic schools, Aquinas, Descartes, and the logical positivists in the "Western" tradition perhaps in part because of a traditional notion of a Western "canon," one that was created on the basis of the desire to construct a Western European identity, which was then adopted in America as well as by Euro-Americans. This idea of a "Western" canon and tradition is neither completely honest nor accurate. The founders of this tradition desired to adopt the thought of the ancient Greeks, for example, but Greek thought after the classical period is conspicuously absent. The Greeks did not cease thinking and writing in philosophical ways, nor did others in Eastern Europe. Nonetheless, later Greeks and Eastern Europeans are left out of the "Western tradition" as it is seen in contemporary America and western Europe. The "Western tradition" thus appears to be a carefully selected and artificial category, having more to do with perceived and desired identity than with philosophical interaction, natural similarity, and intellectual lineage.

Similar issues face Chinese and Indian philosophy. In the period after the Han dynasty, Buddhism became a major (perhaps *the* major) philosophical influence in China, and many ideas from the Sanskrit schools were adopted in Chinese language philosophy. This puts pressure on a boundary between Chinese and Indian philosophical traditions. Again, our selection of what counts as part of a tradition and what does not most often comes down to extra-philosophical considerations, and not always the most noble or rational ones at that.

If this is ultimately the way to make sense of "traditions," then the idea of philosophical traditions may be more harmful than helpful in the study of the wider history of philosophy. I propose that when we speak of differing philosophical traditions, we do it with the same caution and recognition of its ultimate arbitrariness that we do when we more reflectively use the category of "race" applied to human beings—a classification that, as we know, has no basis in human biology. Likewise, the notion of the philosophical tradition has no basis in history, but rather in the ways we choose to think about ourselves and the philosophical movements and schools we choose to identify with, for whatever reason. With this in mind, we can consider the link between "different" traditions of philosophical thought, in the positions concerning the concept of truth we find in them. In examining thought about truth across various traditions, we come to a better understanding of this universal and foundational concept. While the focus in this book has been on early Chinese philosophy, we find that in numerous other traditions there are shared views of truth, as well as unique ways in which the concept is understood. If truth truly is a universal, abstract, and foundational concept, we should expect to find patterns of understanding of the concept across traditions. It turns out that we do find shared features of thinking about truth concepts in the early Chinese tradition and other traditions, including the Indian and Mesoamerican traditions. A wider comparison, which hopefully will be undertaken in the future, will look at a number of additional traditions as well, including a variety of additional American, Asian, and African traditions. Truth is a concept that has always been with us, and, like much in philosophy, regardless of what we think we know about it, there is always more to discover, and more to learn.

NOTES

1. The Chinese term *zhen* 真 often serves in this capacity in the early texts, especially in the *Zhuangzi* and *Huainanzi*.
2. Maffie 2014: 100–113.
3. Maffie 2014: 102.
4. Mohanty 1980: 439.
5. This formula appears numerous times in the Pali Canon. One well-known appearance is in *Dhammapada* 277–279.
6. Surendranath Dasgupta was surely wrong when he claimed, in Dasgupta 1922, that there is no philosophical literature in Dravidian languages. When we look at the reasoning behind this claim, he seems to have fallen victim to the same kind of thinking that led western philosophers to dismiss non-Western traditions like those of India, China, Africa, and Mesoamerica. Dasgupta admits his own ignorance of Dravidian literature, then proceeds to claim that while there is poetry in these languages, there is no philosophy. Dasgupta puts forward a fallacious "argument from ignorance" similar to what we find in Western philosophers dismissive of non-western philosophy. He writes: "It appears that Tamil was particularly rich in poetry, and we have many devotional songs both in Tamil and Kanarese, but I do not know of any systematic philosophical work in either Tamil or Kanarese which is not presented in Sanskrit." He thus concludes "there is hardly anything of value from the philosophical point of view in Dravidian literature which is unobtainable through Sanskrit" (Dasgupta 1922: 149). It is unfortunate that Dasgupta would employ this clearly fallacious argument against Dravidian thought that was used so widely by western thinkers to disparage and dismiss all of Indian thought, including Sanskrit thought. Compare, for example, the infamous words of Thomas Macaulay on the Indian tradition, startlingly like those of Dasgupta (even down to dismissing the rejected tradition as mere "poetry"):

> It will hardly be disputed, I suppose, that the department of literature in which the Eastern writers stand highest is poetry. And I certainly never met with any orientalist who ventured to maintain that the Arabic and Sanscrit poetry could be compared to that of the great

European nations. But when we pass from works of imagination to works in which facts are recorded and general principles investigated, the superiority of the Europeans becomes absolutely immeasurable. It is, I believe, no exaggeration to say that all the historical information which has been collected from all the books written in the Sanscrit language is less valuable than what may be found in the most paltry abridgments used at preparatory schools in England. In every branch of physical or moral philosophy, the relative position of the two nations is nearly the same. (Macaulay, note on education, 2 February 1835. In Sharp 1965: 107–111)

Or, in other words, there is nothing of value in Sanskrit philosophical literature that cannot be found in western philosophical literature.

7. David Anthony discusses the identity and origin of the Proto-Indo-Europeans in Anthony 2010.

8. Thomas McEvilly focuses on the striking similarities between Indian and Greek philosophies, their shared ancestry, and the role of Persia in McEvilly 2002.

9. In the lineage of Alexander the Great, who conquered the region.

10. Vassiliades 2000: 49.

11. Diogenes Laertius *Lives of Eminent Philosophers* IX.11. in Hicks 1925.

Bibliography

Alston, William, 1996. *A Realist Conception of Truth*. Ithaca, NY: Cornell University Press.

Anthony, David, 2010. *The Horse, the Wheel, and Language: How Bronze-Age Riders from the Eurasian Steppes Shaped the Modern World*. Princeton: Princeton University Press.

Asay, Jamin, 2013. *The Primitivist Theory of Truth*. Cambridge: Cambridge University Press.

Bilgrami, Akeel, 2010. "The Wider Significance of Naturalism: A Geneological Essay." In De Caro and Macarthur, eds. *Naturalism and Normativity*. New York: Columbia University Press. pp. 23–54.

Bonnett, Alastair, 2004. *The Idea of the West: Culture, Politics, and History*. New York: Palgrave Macmillan.

Brandom, Robert, ed. 1997. *Empiricism and the Philosophy of Mind* (Wilfrid Sellars). Cambridge, MA: Harvard University Press.

Brons, Lajos, 2015. "Wang Chong, Truth, and Quasi-Pluralism." *Comparative Philosophy* 6 (1). pp. 129–148.

Brooks, E. Bruce, and A. Taeko Brooks, 1997. *The Original Anaelcts: Sayings of Confucius and His Successors*. New York: Columbia University Press.

Chen, Bo, 2009. "Xunzi's Politicized and Moralized Philosophy of Language." *Journal of Chinese Philosophy* 36: 107–39.

Chen, Daqi, 1954. *Xunzi Xueshuo*. Taipei: Chinese Culture Publication Committee.

Cheng, Chung-ying, 2008. "Xunzi as a Systematic Philosopher: Toward and Organic Unity of Nature, Mind, and Reason." *Journal of Chinese Philosophy* 35 (1): 9–31.

Csikszentmihalyi, Mark, 2006. *Readings in Han Chinese Thought*. Indianapolis: Hackett.

Dasgupta, Surendranath, 1991 (reprint of 1922). *A History of Indian Philosophy: Volume 5*. Delhi: Motilal Banarsidass.

Defoort, Carine, and Nicholas Standaert, 2013. *The Mozi as an Evolving Text: Different Voices in Early Chinese Thought*. Leiden: Brill.

Devitt, Michael, 1984. *Realism and Truth*. Cambridge, MA: Blackwell.

Elder, Crawford, 2004. *Real Natures and Familiar Objects.* Cambridge, MA: MIT Press.

Elstein, David, 2004. "Xunzi." *Internet Encyclopedia of Philosophy.* ISSN 2161-0002, http://www.iep.utm.edu/xunzi, May 18, 2015.

Eno, Robert, 1990. *The Confucian Creation of Heaven.* Albany: SUNY Press.

Fischer, Paul, trans. 2012. *Shizi: China's First Syncretist.* New York: Columbia University Press.

Forke, Alfred, 1962. *Lun Heng: Philosophical Essays of Wang Ch'ung, Vol. 1.* New York: Paragon Book Gallery (reprint of 1907).

Fraser, Chris, 1997. "Review of *Classifying the Zhuangzi Chapters,* by Liu Xiaogan." *Asian Philosophy* 7 (2): 155–59.

Fraser, Chris, 2009. "School of Names." *Stanford Encyclopedia of Philosophy.* http://plato.stanford.edu/entries/school-names/

Fraser, Chris, 2011. "Major Rival Schools: Mohism and Legalism." In J. Edelglass and W. Garfield, eds. *The Oxford Handbook of World Philosophy.* Oxford: Oxford University Press.

Fraser, Chris, 2012. "Truth in Moist Dialectics." *Journal of Chinese Philosophy* 39 (4). pp. 351–368.

Fraser, Chris, 2013. "Mohist Canons." *Stanford Encyclopedia of Philosophy.* http://plato.stanford.edu/entries/mohist-canons/

Fraser, Chris, 2014. "Mohism." *The Stanford Encyclopedia of Philosophy* (Summer 2014 Edition), Edward N. Zalta (ed.), http://plato.stanford.edu/archives/sum2014/entries/mohism/.

Fung, Yiu-ming, 2012. "Two Senses of *Wei*: A New Interpretation of Xunzi's Theory of Human Nature." *Dao: A Journal of Chinese Philosophy* 11 (2). pp. 187–200.

Geaney, Jane, 2010. "Grounding 'Language' in the Senses: What the Eyes and Ears Reveal About *Ming* (Names) in Early Chinese Texts." *Philosophy East and West* 60 (2): 251–93.

Goldin, Paul, 1999. "Insidious Syncretism in the Political Philosophy of *Huai-nan-tzu.*" *Asian Philosophy* 9 (3): 165–91.

Goldin, Paul, 2000. *Rituals of the Way: The Philosophy of Xunzi.* Chicago: Open Court.

Graham, Angus C., 1978. *Later Mohist Logic, Ethics, and Science.* London: School of Oriental and African Studies and Hong Kong: Chinese University Press.

Graham, Angus C., 1986. "How Much of *Chuang-tzu* Did Chuang-tzu Write?" In Angus C. Graham, *Studies in Chinese Philosophy and Philosophical Literature.* Albany: SUNY Press. pp. 283–321.

Graham, Angus C., 1989. *Disputers of the Tao: Philosophical Argument in Ancient China.* Chicago: Open Court.

Graham, Angus C., 1895. Divisions in Early Mohism Reflected in the Core Chapters of Mo-tzu. Singapore: National University of Singapore, Institute of East Asian Philosophies. Graham, Angus C., 2001. *Chuang-tzu: The Inner Chapters.* Indianapolis: Hackett.

Hagen, Kurtis, 2002. "Xunzi's Use of *Zhengming*: Naming as a Constructive Project." *Asian Philosophy* 12 (1): 35–51.

Hagen, Kurtis, 2003. "Xunzi and the Nature of Confucian Ritual." *Journal of the American Academy of Religion* 71 (2): 371–403.

Hall, David, and Roger Ames, 1997. *Thinking From the Han: Self, Truth, and Transcendence in Chinese and Western Culture.* Albany: SUNY Press.

Hall, David, 1997. "The Way and the Truth." In Eliot Deutsch and Ron Bontekoe, eds. *A Companion to World Philosophies.* Oxford: Blackwell. pp. 214–224.

Hall, David, 2001. "The Import of Analysis in Classical China—A Pragmatic Appraisal." In Bo Mou, ed. *Two Roads to Wisdom? Chinese and Analytic Philosophical Traditions.* Chicago: Open Court. pp. 153–168.

Hansen, Chad, 2003. "The Metaphysics of Dao". in Bo Mou, ed. Comparative Approaches to Chinese Philosophy. Berlington, VT: Ashgate. p. 205.

Hansen, Chad, 1985. "Chinese Language, Chinese Philosophy, and 'Truth'." *The Journal of Asian Studies,* 44 (3): 491–518.

Hansen, Chad, 1992. *A Daoist Theory of Chinese Thought: A Philosophical Intepretation.* Oxford: Oxford University Press.

Hansen, Chad, 2003. "Guru or Skeptic? Relativistic Skepticism in the *Zhuangzi*." In Scott Cook, ed. *Hiding the World in the World: Uneven Discourses on the Zhuangzi.* Albany: SUNY Press. pp. 128–162.

Hick, John, 1993. *The Metaphor of God Incarnate.* Louisville: Westminster/John Knox.

Hicks, W. D., 1925. *Diogenes Laertius: Lives of Eminent Philosophers, Volume 2, Books 6-10.* Cambridge, MA: Harvard University Press.

Horwich, Paul, 2010. *Truth, Meaning, Reality.* Oxford: Oxford University Press.

Houser, Nathan, and Christian Kloesel, 1992. *The Essential Peirce: Selected Philosophical Writings, Volume I (1867–1893).* Bloomington: Indiana University Press.

Hunter, Michael, 2012. *Sayings of Confucius, Deselected.* PhD Dissertation, Princeton University.

Hutton, Eric, trans. 2014. *Xunzi: The Complete Text.* Princeton: Princeton University Press.

Klein, Esther, 2010. "Were there 'Inner Chapters' in the Warring States? A New Examination of Evidence about the Zhuangzi." *T'oung Pao* 96 (4–5): 299–369.

Kline, T. C., 2000. "Moral Agency and Motivation in the *Xunzi*." In T. C. Kline and P. J. Ivanhoe, eds. *Virtue, Nature, and Moral Agency in the Xunzi.* Indianapolis: Hackett. pp. 155–175.

Knoblock, John, and Jeffrey Riegel, trans. 2001. *The Annals of Lu Buwei.* New York: Columbia University Press.

Kripke, Saul, 1980. *Naming and Necessity.* Cambridge, MA: Harvard University Press.

Lai, Karyn, 2006. "Philosophy and Philosophical Reasoning in the Zhuangzi: Dealing With Plurality." *Journal of Chinese Philosophy* 33 (3): 365–74.

Lin, Chung-I, 2011. "Xunzi as a Semantic Inferentialist: Zhengming, Bian-Shuo, and Dao-Li." *Dao: A Journal of Comparative Philosophy* 10 (3): 311–340.

Liu, Jeeloo, 2003. "The Daoist Conception of Truth: Lao Zi's Metaphysical Realism vs. Zhuang Zi's Internal Realism." In Bo Mou, ed. *Comparative Approaches to Chinese Philosophy.* Farnham: Ashgate. pp. 278–293.

Liu, Xiaogan, 1994. *Classifying the Zhuangzi Chapters.* Ann Arbor: Center for Chinese Studies, University of Michigan.

Loy, David, 1996. "Zhuangzi and Nagarjuna on the Truth of No Truth." In P. Kjellberg and P. J. Ivanhoe, eds. *Essays on Skepticism, Relativism, and Ethics in the Zhuangzi*. Albany: SUNY Press.

Loy, Hui-chieh, 2003. "Analects 13.3 and the Doctrine of 'Correcting Names'." *Monumenta Serica* 51: 19–36.

Loy, Hui-chieh, 2011. "The Word and the Way in *Mozi*." *Philosophy Compass* 6 (10): 652–62.

Lynch, Michael, 2004. "Truth and Multiple Realizability." *Australasian Journal of Philosophy* 82 (3): 384–408.

Lynch, Michael, ed. 2001. *The Nature of Truth: Classic and Contemporary Perspectives*. Cambridge, MA: MIT Press.

Lynch, Michael, 2005. *True to Life: Why Truth Matters*. Cambridge, MA: MIT Press.

Lynch, Michael, 2009. *Truth as One and Many*. Oxford: Oxford University Press.

Machery, E., R. Mallon, S. Nichols, and S. Stich, 2004. "Semantics, Cross-Cultural Style." *Cognition* 92 (3): B1–B12.

MacIntyre, Alasdair, 1981. *After Virtue*. Notre Dame: University of Notre Dame Press.

MacIntyre, Alasdair, 1988. *Whose Justice? Which Rationality?* Notre Dame: University of Notre Dame Press.

Maffie, James, 2014. *Aztec Philosophy: Understanding a World in Motion*. Boulder: University Press of Colorado.

Major, John, 2014. "Tool Metaphors in the *Huainanzi* and Other Early Texts." In Sarah A. Queen and Michael Puett, eds. *The Huainanzi and Textual Production in Early China*. Leiden: Brill. pp. 153–198.

Major, John, Sarah Queen, Andrew Meyer, and Harold Roth, 2010. *The Huainanzi: A Guide to the Theory and Practice of Government in Early Han China*. New York: Columbia University Press.

Makeham, John, 1994. *Name and Actuality in Early Chinese Thought*. Albany: SUNY Press.

Makeham, John, trans. 2003. *Balanced Discourses (Xu Gan)*. New Haven: Yale University Press.

McCraw, David, 2010. *Stratifying Zhuangzi: Rhyme and Other Qualitative Evidence*. Taipei: Institute of Linguistics, Academia Sinica.

McLeod, Alexus, 2007. "A Reappraisal of Wang Chong's Critical Method Through the *Wenkong* Chapter of *Lunheng*." *Journal of Chinese Philosophy* 34 (4): 581–596.

McLeod, Alexus, 2012. "In the World of Persons: The Personhood Debate in the *Analects* and *Zhuangzi*." *Dao: A Journal of Comparative Philosophy* 11 (4): 437–57.

McLeod, Alexus, 2015. "Philosophy in Eastern Han Dynasty China." *Philosophy Compass* 10 (6): 355–68.

McLeod, Alexus, 2015. "Replies to Brons and Mou on Wang Chong and Pluralism." *Comparative Philosophy* 6 (1): 169–84.

McLeod, Alexus, 2016 (forthcoming). *Astronomy in the Ancient World: Early and Modern Views of Celestial Events*. New York: Springer.

Michael, Thomas, 2005. *The Pristine Dao: Metaphyics in Early Daoist Discourse*. Albany: SUNY Press.

Mohanty, J. N., 1980. "Indian Theories of Truth: Thoughts on Their Common Framework." *Philosophy East and West* 30 (4): 439–51.

Mou, Bo, 2006. "Truth Pursuit and Dao Pursuit: From Davidson's Approach to Classical Daoist Approach in View of the Thesis of Truth as Strategic Normative Goal." In Bo Mou. *Davidson's Philosophy and Chinese Philosophy: Constructive Engagement.* Leiden: Brill. pp. 309–349.

Mou, Bo, 2009. *Substantive Perspectivism: An Essay on Philosophical Concern with Truth.* New York: Springer.

Mou, Bo, 2015. "Rooted and Rootless Pluralist Approaches to Truth: Two Distinct Interpretations of Wang Chong's Account." *Comparative Philosophy* 6 (1). pp. 149–168.

Neville, Robert, 2008. *Ritual and Deference: Extending Chinese Philosophy in a Comparative Context.* Albany: SUNY Press.

Norton, David and Norton, Mary, eds. 2000. *David Hume: A Treatise of Human Nature.* Oxford: Oxford University Press.

Nylan, Michael, 1997. "Han Classicists Writing in Dialogue about Their Own Tradition." *Philosophy East and West* 47 (2): 138–88.

Olberding, Amy, 2012. *Moral Exemplars in the Analects: The Good Person Is That.* New York: Routledge.

Puett, Michael, 2002. *The Ambivalence of Creation: Debates Concerning Innovation and Artifice in Early China.* Redwood City: Stanford University Press.

Putnam, Hilary, 1973. "Meaning and Reference." *The Journal of Philosophy* 70 (19): 699–711.

Putnam, Hilary, 1975. "The Meaning of 'Meaning'." *Minnesota Studies in the Philosophy of Science* 7: 131–193.

Robins, Dan, 2012. "Names, Cranes, and the Later Moists." *Journal of Chinese Philosophy* 39 (3): 369–85.

Roth, Harold, 1991. "Who Compiled the *Chuang Tzu?*" In Henry Rosemont, ed. *Chinese Texts and Philosophical Contexts: Essays in Honor of Angus Graham.* Chicago: Open Court. pp. 79–128.

Saunders, Frank, 2014. "Semantics without Truth in Later Mohist Philosophy of Language." *Dao: A Journal of Comparative Philosophy* 13 (2): 215–29.

Shakespeare, W., Bate, J., Rasmussen, E., & Sénéchal, H., 2007. *Complete Works.* New York: Modern Library.

Shang, Geling, 2006. *Liberation as Affirmation: The Religiosity of Zhuangzi and Nietzsche.* Albany: SUNY Press.

Sharp, H., ed. 1965 (reprint of 1920). *Selection from Educational Records, Part I (1781–1839).* Delhi: National Archives of India.

Sher, Gila, 1999. "What is Tarski's Theory of Truth?" *Topoi* 18: 149–66.

Shun, Kwong-loi, 1997. *Mencius and Early Chinese Thought.* Redwood City: Stanford University Press.

Siderits, Mark, 2003. *Personal Identity and Buddhist Philosophy.* Farnham: Ashgate.

Smid, Robert, 2010. *Methodologies of Comparative Philosophy.* Albany: SUNY Press.

Soles, Deborah, and David Soles, 1998. "Fish Traps and Rabbit Snares: Zhuangzi on Judgment, Truth, and Knowledge." *Asian Philosophy* 8 (3): 149–64.

Stalnker, Aaron, 2007. *Overcoming Our Evil: Human Nature and Spiritual Exercises in Xunzi and Augustine.* Washington, DC: Georgetown University Press.

Sun, Zhenbin, 2015. *Language, Discourse, and Praxis in Ancient China*. New York: Springer.

Tan, Sor-hoon, 2012. "*Li* and *Tian* in the *Xunzi*: Does Confucian *li* need metaphysics?" *Sophia* 51 (2): 155–75.

Van Norden, Bryan, 1993. "Hansen on Hsun-tzu." *Journal of Chinese Philosophy* 20 (3): 365–382.

Van Norden, Bryan, 1996. "Competing Interpretations of the Inner Chapters of the 'Zhuangzi'." *Philosophy East and West* 46 (2): 247–68.

Van Norden, Bryan, 2007. *Virtue Ethics and Consequentialism in Early Chinese Thought*. Cambridge: Cambridge University Press.

Vassiliades, Demetrios T., 2000. *The Greeks in India: A Survey in Philosophical Understanding*. Delhi: Munshiram Manoharlal.

Waley, Arthur, 1938. *The Analects of Confucius*. London: George Allen & Unwin.

Williams, Bernard, 1985. *Ethics and the Limits of Philosophy*. London: Fontana.

Wright, Crispin, 1992. *Truth and Objectivity*. Cambridge, MA: Harvard University Press.

Wright, Crispin, 2001. "Minimalism, Deflationism, Pragmatism, Pluralism." In M. Lynch, ed. *The Nature of Truth: Classic and Contemporary Perspectives*. Cambridge, MA: MIT Press. pp. 751–787.

Xu, Keqian, 2010. "Chinese 'Dao' and Western 'Truth': A Comparative and Dynamic Perspective." *Asian Social Science* 6 (12): 42–49.

Zhang, Yunyi, 2007. "Philosophy's Predicament and Hegel's Ghost: Reflection on the View That 'There Is No Philosophy in China'." *Frontiers of Philosophy in China* 2 (2): 230–246.

Zheng, Jiadong, 2005. "The Issue of the 'Legitimacy' of Chinese Philosophy." *Contemporary Chinese Thought* 37 (1): 11–23.

CHINESE SOURCES

Lau, D.C., ed. 1996. *Lunheng zhuzi suoyin (A Concordance to the Lunheng)*. Chinese University of Hong Kong Insitute of Chinese Studies, Ancient Text Concordance Series, No. 22. Hong Kong: The Commercial Press.

Lau, D. C., ed. 2006. *Mengzi zhuzi suoyin (A Concordance to Mengzi)*. Hong Kong: Shang wu yin shuguan.

Xunzi Yinde, Harvard-Yenching Institute Sinological Index Series, Supplement no. 22.

D. C. Lau, Ho Che Wah and Chen Fong Ching, eds., 1995. *Lunyu zhuzi suoyin (A Concordance to the Lunyu)*. Chinese University of Hong Kong Institute of Chinese Studies series. Hong Kong: Commercial Press.

Ding, Fubao. 1959. *Shuowen Jiezi Gulin (Glosses on the Shuowen Jiezi)*. Taipei: Commercial Press

Zhuangzi Yinde, Harvard-Yenching Institute Sinological Index Series, Supplement no. 20. Cambridge: Harvard University Press, 1956.

Index

About the Author

Alexus McLeod is Assistant Professor of Philosophy at Colorado State University. He is author of *Understanding Asian Philosophy: Ethics in the Analects, Zhuangzi, Dhammapada, and Bhagavad Gita* and *Astronomy in the Ancient World: Early and Modern Views on Celestial Events*. He has written numerous articles on a variety of issues in Chinese, Indian, and Mesoamerican Philosophy, including agency, moral responsibility, truth, methodology, and knowledge. He also works in Comparative Philosophy more generally.